BEST PRACTICE IN
PERFORMANCE COACHING

BEST PRACTICE IN
PERFORMANCE
COACHING

A Handbook for Leaders, Coaches, HR Professionals and Organizations

Carol Wilson

KOGAN
PAGE

London and Philadelphia

First published in Great Britain and the United States in 2007 by Kogan Page Limited
Reprinted in 2008

120 Pentonville Road
London N1 9JN
United Kingdom
www.kogan-page.co.uk

525 South 4th Street, #241
Philadelphia PA 19147
USA

© Carol Wilson, 2007

The right of Carol Wilson to be identified as the author of this work has been asserted by her in accordance with the Copyright, Designs and Patents Act 1988.

ISBN   978 0 7494 5082 3

British Library Cataloguing-in-Publication Data

A CIP record for this book is available from the British Library.

Library of Congress Cataloging-in-Publication Data

Wilson, Carol.
    Best practice in performance coaching : a handbook for leaders, coaches, HR professionals, and organizations / Carol Wilson.
        p. cm.
    Includes index.
    ISBN-13: 978-0-7494-5082-3
    ISBN-10: 0-7494-5082-7
1. Employees--Coaching of. 2. Performance. 3. Mentoring in business. I. Title.
    HF5549.5.C53W55 2007
    658.3'124--dc22   2007022193

Typeset by Saxon Graphics Ltd, Derby
Printed and bound in Great Britain by MPG Books Ltd, Bodmin, Cornwall

*For my parents who believed I could do anything,
and my sister who saw only the best in everyone.
With loving thanks for the support of my husband
Paul Tabley.*

Contents

USA: career coaching an environmental scientist 170; From Australia: management development at Orica 173; From Abu Dhabi: corporate coaching in the United Arab Emirates 177; From Australia: leading for performance; building a values-driven organization in IT services 182; From Japan: management styles and succession planning 185; Moral dilemmas and coaching challenges 190; Coaching for Performance ROI 202

Foreword by
Sir John Whitmore

I must begin by acknowledging my bias. I know Carol well, have experienced her delivery of coaching, and I admire her track record with Richard Branson at Virgin, with the Association for Coaching, and elsewhere. Furthermore it is largely because of all this that she now works with me at Performance Consultants International. It is therefore fairly obvious that I am going to be upbeat about her contribution to the growing coaching library. However, those that know me are aware that I am not inclined to hold back if I don't like something. To make that more credible I have been looking for something to criticize about this book, but after several readings I have failed.

Starting to read another book is always a bit of a struggle because I am goal oriented and the beginning is always too far from the end. The first few pages are always accompanied by the thought, 'Do I really need to read this?' coursing round another part of my brain, before I get into it. This did not occur this time and I found myself in Chapter 3 before I knew it.

Ah! here is the error. In that chapter, she attributes the GROW model coaching sequence to me. However I was just the first person to publish it, in my book *Coaching for Performance*. It originally emerged in a discussion between several coaches with whom I was working at the time, including Graham Alexander, in the McKinsey office in London, and it has been in the public domain ever since. This is worth mentioning because unlike so many coaches who get fixated by GROW, Carol rightly places awareness, responsibility and self-belief at the top of her seven principles of coaching. GROW is no more or less than an easy to remember and useful sequence for a coaching conversation to follow.

Carol gives us another such model, EXACT, which she prefers, as do I, to the overused and incomplete SMART for goal setting. She goes on to explore the structure of a coaching relationship, the training of coaches and the pleasures and pitfalls of setting up a coaching practice. She ends the main text with a chapter on coaching in organizations. All of this essential information to a new or practising coach, or to a potential client, is very easy to absorb largely because she provides numerous coaching dialogue examples, plenty of headings and quotations to break it up visually, some exercises at the end of each chapter, and it ends with 15 pages of seriously useful appendices.

This is the best coaching starter kit I have come across to date, but it goes beyond mere starting to provide a real understanding of the depth of coaching in a very practical readable way. Thank you, Carol. I am glad to have you on board, and I hope this book will attract more to join us, as well as enriching existing fellow travellers on the coaching express that is charging through the world of work.

Sir John Whitmore

Sir John Whitmore is executive chairman of Performance Consultants International Ltd. A pre-eminent thinker in leadership and organizational change, John has personally trained some of the leading organizations in the world, such as McKinsey, Deloitte, Pricewaterhouse Coopers, Barclays, Lloyds, Rolls-Royce, British Airways, Novo Nordisk and Roche. He has produced and directed a feature film, and performed in many guises on radio and television and on conference platforms.

One of John's greatest achievements is to have founded the groundbreaking 'Be The Change' conferences that are held in London each May, to bring together the top minds in the world to discuss sustainability, environmental and social issues, and geo-political change.

John has written five books on sports, leadership and coaching, of which Coaching for Performance *is the best known, having been translated into 19 languages.*

Sir John Whitmore
Executive Chairman
Performance Consultants International
Tel: +44 (0)20 7373 6431
Email: johnwhitmore@performanceconsultants.com

Foreword by Sir Richard Branson

When I started Virgin, none of us had worked anywhere else so we didn't know how managers were 'supposed' to behave. We approached it like everything in our lives at the time; it had to be lots of fun and we chose our staff the way we chose our friends – on gut instinct. It was like a family and we partied and went on holiday together all the time.

Not much has changed in that respect – it has just got bigger, and the great thing about owning an airline is that you can ship 300 people across the world to a party. In Carol's day, it was more like eight of us in a ski chalet where the hot water ran out before everyone had showered. But the main thing was that work had to be fun.

Carol fitted in because her approach was quite similar to mine in a lot of ways; she would always 'come up to the plate' and do whatever needed to be done, whether it meant staying in a studio half the night and attending an 8 am meeting the next morning, or flying to Los Angeles and back on the same day for a breakfast meeting. She was not afraid of trying new things or taking risks. One of the reasons her divisions worked well was because she built strong teams and looked after them. She made a great role model because she was completely passionate about everything she did and I think that, to this day, no other woman in the world has matched her achievement of founding a successful record company.

The way we hired people in the early days was that if their faces fitted, we would find them something to do; qualifications and experience were pretty irrelevant. I think I gave Carol the publishing company to run because she said she didn't want to be a secretary, which was what most women were doing in 1974, and because it was the only job going in Virgin at the time. As far as we knew, it mainly involved filling out copyright forms, but before long she was signing chart-topping acts like Sting and the company was showing up as Top Three in the *Music Week* trade press chart, alongside Warners and CBS. So I suggested we start a record label together and within six months the acts she signed to that were topping the charts as well. That record label pioneered the 'small label within a big label' format that proliferates throughout the record industry today.

Carol shared my view on mistakes being part of the learning curve. Whenever I experience any kind of setbacks, I always pick myself up and try again. I prepare myself to have another stab at things with the knowledge I've gained from the previous failure. My mother always taught me never to look back in regret, but to move on to the next thing. The amount of time that people waste on failures, rather than putting that energy into another project, always amazes me. At Virgin, we allow people freedom to be themselves and we trust them to make the right decisions, and the odd mistake is tolerated. Our people know we value them.

When I see Carol now, writing books and at the top of another profession altogether, it doesn't surprise me at all and I sometimes wonder what we might have achieved if she had stayed at Virgin instead of wanting to spread her wings all those years ago; I used to call her a 'golden girl' because of the people, business and opportunities she attracted to Virgin, and it seems she has not changed at all.

Sir Richard Branson

Acknowledgements

For his Foreword I thank Sir John Whitmore, who lit the first beacon at the start of my own journey into coaching, and who, I was delighted to discover as I got to know him, remains an original and maverick thinker. I followed from a distance in the early days, and as I moved closer, the trail led me along some fascinating, powerful and moving pathways, like the series of 'Be The Change' conferences which John instigated in 2002. Earlier than either of us remembers, or cares to, we were born in Essex villages a stone's throw from each other, albeit he to the Lord of the Manor and me in the shadow of the castle walls, but we have somehow come, in certain ways, to the same place in the global village of shared values, interests and hopes for ourselves and the world.

I am grateful to Sir Richard Branson, without whom I would almost certainly never have run a record company at a time when most working women were chained to typewriters, and whose management skills have been the blueprint for my own and the foundation for this book.

And I thank the elusive David Brown, who provided a bridge for me to John and many other people, experiences and opportunities; indeed without him I might not have entered the coaching profession at all.

Thanks to James Wright for skill and fun, Wendy Oliver for wisdom and wit, and both for their infinite support and true friendship, plus all the coaches who have taught me through teaching them and all the coachees who have coached me through coaching them.

Thanks to Jacqui Rolfe, who was always there when I needed her, and to Chris Tilley for proofreading.

Thanks also to the generous and expert coaches who have contributed to this book:

Steve Breibart (01628 627677; slbreibart@tsocommunication.com), consultant, coach, coach trainer and co-founder of the Coaching Foundation, for painstaking and perceptive editing.

John Whitmore and Hetty Einzig for their contributions to 'Transpersonal coaching'.

Gladeana McMahon for co-writing 'Contrast between coaching and its related fields'.

Jonathan Passmore for help with the Harvard-referenced book list.

For case histories (in alphabetical order): Katrina Burrus, Mike Daly, Alex Feher, Niran Jiang, Gillian Jones, Viktor Kunovski, Liz Macann, Bill McDermott, Jo Miller, Wendy Oliver, Philippe Rosinski, Anne Stanley, Paula Sugawara and James Wright.

Thanks to Viki Williams, Charlotte Atyeo, Martha Fumagalli, Helen Kogan, Joanne Glover, Kerrisue Morrey, Peter Gill and everyone at Kogan Page for their encouragement and hard work, to Susan Curran of Curran Publishing Services for her copy editing, and to Caroline Carr for her proofreading.

Special thanks go to Katherine Tulpa and Alex Szabo, two extraordinary women who somehow decided they could set up an Association for Coaching, an organization which has since become a driving force in the industry.

Introduction

This book is a compendium of all the things I wish I had known when I started coaching, plus some of the pointers that I have learnt since then, and then some tips and tools I have developed myself along the way. The learning journey has by no means ended, and I am happy to say that I am sure it never will.

I have attempted to make the first half of the book a good read, as well as being a practical guide to the 'what' and 'how' of performance coaching, in reaction to the many books I have come across which seem to float across the theories of disciplines, techniques and methodologies at a great height, while leaving us with more questions at the end than when we started.

I have seen John Whitmore, with his associate Hetty Einzig, write on a flipchart 'THIS IS NOT THE TRUTH' at the start of a workshop; then, when at some point they receive the inevitable question from a participant who has a different view, they can indulgently refer to the quote. Our field of coaching is constantly evolving, changing and developing; people may agree or disagree with different parts of the text in this book, and my guess is the variations will be countless. So I urge the reader to bear in mind that this is not necessarily the truth, and to take what is useful, leave what offends you and, if you find anything I have said objectionable, then please do write your own book and contribute to the fund of knowledge that is growing in the coaching world every day!

The second part of the book digs down into detail and specifics, about coaching models, actual case histories, paperwork and all such stuff. This is because I share the common malady of our times, of having shelves groaning with books which are all carefully marked at the place where I gave up reading them and set them aside to finish 'when I have more time'. I hope to have spared my readers the drudgery of ploughing through irrelevant detail to find the nuggets that are golden for them.

This book is intended as an introduction for anyone thinking of becoming or hiring a coach, whether private or corporate, and as a reference guide to experienced coaches. There are exercises at the end of each chapter for those who wish to practise the skills, and, if you are going this route, I recommend you enrol at least one partner to travel with; the learning will be more deeply embedded if you have peer support for practice and feedback. The exercises will work equally well by phone as face to face.

All the topics in this book are considered from the personal and the executive coaching angle. Rather than having separate sections, the distinctions are made within each chapter. There is an additional chapter on coaching in organizations which deals with information that is specific to that field.

Coaching may be used in formal sessions, or where appropriate informally with colleagues, family, friends, direct reports and bosses. For convenience I refer to the person coaching as the 'coach' and the one being coached as the 'coachee'.

Coaching is not the answer to every situation. There are times when instruction and direction are required. For instance, if someone shouts 'Fire', you would not be wise to hang around asking, 'And how do you feel about the fire?' would you?

I have given my own definition of coaching at the beginning of Chapter 1, and quote also the one provided by the Association for Coaching, a non-profit making coaching body of which I am Head of Accreditation, which defines coaching as:

> A profession which helps individuals or organizations to achieve optimal performance, overcome obstacles and barriers to growth, and reach specific goals and challenges as a means to fulfilment, personal & professional development, work–life balance and prevention.
> www.associationforcoaching.com

For many years I worked closely with someone regarded as a 'natural' coach: Sir Richard Branson, who founded his Virgin Empire on the core principles of performance coaching, although no such definition existed at the time, and who has kindly contributed a Foreword to this book. I ran some of the early Virgin companies, and although it seemed like anarchy there at the time (as well as a delightful place for a bunch of 20-something hippy rebels), it is evident that Richard's personal style of management unknowingly adhered to all the principles currently recognized as 'performance coaching'.

As Branson's managers, we made our own decisions, received plenty of positive feedback and could count on his unconditional support. Mistakes were treated as learning experiences and Branson himself was the first port of call in a crisis, unlike the traditional manager who is usually the last to know.

Richard conducted his business as if he stood at the beginning of a maze through which he had to pass to achieve his goal (which we know now was world domination!). Every path we took which led nowhere was regarded as a step closer to finding our way through the maze – an opportune piece of new knowledge to point us in the right direction. One of Richard's great strengths as a leader was his unshakeable conviction that there would *always* be a path through the maze, however unlikely it seemed. Nothing was considered impossible.

The coaching principles of openness, building self-belief, ownership and a blame-free culture were core, although inherent and unstated, values at Virgin. There was nothing soft or 'touchy feely' about that environment: its people were ambitious, outspoken and competitive, and Branson himself has always been a shrewd and tough businessman. Although coaches tend to be amiable people, coaching is not about being 'nice': it challenges coachees to muster all their inherent resources to work for them in achieving whatever it is that they want.

The principles exhibited at Virgin tied in well with my own background, which is one of the reasons I enjoyed success there: my mother, who had been raised by a cold and highly critical father, read a book about positive psychology in the 1950s. From then on she made a point of highlighting every achievement or quality in her children which could possibly be worthy of praise; blame simply did not exist in our house.

My father shared Branson's philosophy that nothing was impossible; had he been born 30 years later I am sure he would have become a very rich man. He had a phrase he repeated often which used to irritate us in the extreme at the time: 'There's no such word as can't.' However, it must have taken root, because I have found it runs through my own attitude to the core. While no stranger to fear, I have never struggled with the 'do it anyway' part (as in *Feel the Fear and Do It Anyway* by Susan Jeffers). Wholly thanks to the combined philosophies of my remarkable parents, terror may have stalked me but it never stood in my way.

Coaching is a growing profession in many countries of the world today, and the discipline is on its way to becoming a universal means of communication which, I am convinced, will one day rise above differences in language and culture to unite the world.

Part I

Fundamentals

The how, who, when and where of coaching for performance and good leadership

1

What is coaching?

Performance coaching is a process which enables people to find and act on the solutions which are the most congruent and appropriate for them personally. This is achieved through a dialogue which assists coachees to see new perspectives and achieve greater clarity about their own thoughts, emotions and actions, and about the people and situations around them. In this chapter, we start by exploring where coaching came from, its fundamental principles, where it is positioned in other related fields and, finally, I share some of my personal experiences of working in the model coaching culture at Virgin Records during its first decade.

THE HISTORY OF COACHING

A sea of confusion surrounds the term 'coaching'. The expression has not even made its way into dictionaries yet, where 'coach' is defined simply as 'tutor' and yet there is nothing new about the practice other than its name. Socrates seems to have been a prime exponent:

> I cannot teach anybody anything – I can only make them think.

This quote is a good description of the principles of performance coaching, which will be explored throughout this book.

One reason for the current confusion is the use of the term 'life coaching', which came into use in the United States in **Tim Gallwey** the 1980s and has since been adopted by a variety of practitioners, from crystal healers to prime ministerial wife advisors. Rarely has a methodology been so inaptly named: to this day, the uninitiated assume that life coaches, like sports coaches, tell their coachees what to do, bully them into shape and point out where they are doing it wrong. Nothing could be further from the truth: the types of coaches described in this book are not advisors, instructors or gurus with answers. We are facilitators who enable coachees to develop their knowledge about themselves and thereby improve performance in their personal and their working lives.

To confuse the issue further, many coaches tack on adjectives to their titles in order to distinguish their field of work. Hence we now have 'executive', 'career', 'fitness' and numerous other types of coaches. In this book, the term 'coaching' will cover all aspects of the profession, as the underlying tenets are the same, and the generic term we will use is 'performance coaching', which was developed in the following way.

Prior to the spread of the term 'life coaching', in the 1970s the Captain of the Harvard tennis team Tim Gallwey discovered that his coachees enjoyed greater success when taught how to learn, than when given techniques for hitting balls over nets. He realized that the most challenging opponent is the one inside the player, rather than the adversary on the other side of the net. Tim put these principles into a best-seller called *The Inner Game of Tennis* (1974) and later focused on applying them to life and work.

Sir John Whitmore Soon after Gallwey's work became well known, an English ex-racing driver and baronet discovered it and made coaching his life's work: Sir John Whitmore (now my colleague and the author of a Foreword to this book) with his associates at Performance Consultants, introduced the 'Inner Game' to Britain, developed the techniques in sport and business, and coined the term 'performance coaching'. John has since done more than any other proponent of coaching to promote the techniques and benefits of the profession, including his seminal book, *Coaching for Performance*, which has been translated into nineteen languages.

These events coincided with the development of practices arising from cognitive therapy, brief solution focused therapy, psychosynthesis and positive psychology. All of these elements, and others, have contributed to the type of coaching that we explore in this book.

Self-directed learning The core principle of performance coaching is 'self-directed learning': what Tim Gallwey described as, 'teaching people how to learn'. Coaches do this by asking questions that are not closed or leading, but open – turning the coachee's focus inside. It is amazing how many answers lie undiscovered, in the quiet spaces of the mind – answers which have become obscured by the pace of living, or past events, or by twists and turns of life, which may have happened yesterday or 50 years ago.

In Bulgaria a nod means 'no' and a shake of the head means 'yes'. This is a result of cultural background, and big misunderstandings can result if we visit such a country without this knowledge. People have different customs too, arising from their individual cultural backgrounds, upbringing and experiences in life. It would take a lifetime for a coach to map all of these elements in enough detail to understand where the coachee has come from and where he or she should best go next. However, in the space of an hour, an effective coach may reveal sufficient significant points on this map to the coachee, who in the heart of hearts has access to all of them, allowing coachees to uncover whatever self-knowledge they need to see the way forward.

It is only since the turn of the millennium that coaching has begun to reach a wider audience. Rumour has it that famous names such as Andre Agassi, Nelson Mandela, Mikhail Gorbachev, Margaret Thatcher, François Mitterrand and Bill Clinton have all availed themselves of the services of coaches. In addition, the majority of corporate and public organizations in the United States and United Kingdom are either employing coaches or training them internally, followed closely by the rest of Europe and Asia. Coaching is flourishing in education and through organizations such as Youth at Risk, where the sessions help deeply troubled youngsters in a way that no other intervention has managed before.

How then can such a powerful skill be learnt on a relatively short training course? The answer is twofold. First, coaching is a process, not a knowledge base. Like an accountant, the coach can adapt the process to suit any person or organization. However, whereas accountancy requires several years of training in order to accumulate the knowledge required to give advice to clients, the coach needs nothing more than fluency in coaching skills. The coach is not there to give advice but to facilitate the coachee's self-learning.

This premise does not exclude the desirability of the coach acquiring a knowledge base: additional training in the tools and methods mentioned in Chapter 8 (which is by no means an exhaustive list) and applications from the coaching profession and other areas, such as psychology, business and leadership, will undoubtedly increase a coach's effectiveness. However, this comes about through the integration of elements which are separate from, even if complementary to or parallel with coaching; the process required for the coaching itself remains simple.

Second, coaching is 100 per cent coachee-led. Coaches are trained not to force their own judgement or opinions on the coachee, or to decide on a solution and lead their coachees towards it. As long as this principle is adhered to, it is not possible for a coach to do the type of psychological damage which an inexperienced therapist might inadvertently inflict. In coaching, the coachee is always in control. (This does not mean to say that a coach never gives advice or makes a suggestion, but that these are delivered in a coaching style, as described in Chapter 2 under 'Clarifying, reflecting and intuition').

Coaches open up a space inside the coachee in which there is room to look around, see what is no longer required, what might be rearranged, and where there are gaps that could be filled. A good coach will support, listen and direct the coachee's focus forward to the future. The result for coachees is that they make decisions with conviction and are more likely to stick to plans which they have come up with themselves.

In the following chapters we shall examine the techniques, principles, structure and models of coaching, which combine to make coaching effective, and the results that these different elements can achieve. In Chapter 8 (page 136) there is a diagram called 'The relationship between the component parts of coaching', which sets out all these different components and shows how they work together. This diagram is intended as a foundation to refer back to during the course of reading the book, and the reader new to coaching would be well advised not to attempt to make sense of it before having read the relevant section.

THE SEVEN PRINCIPLES OF COACHING

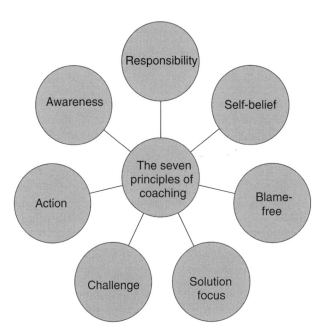

Figure 1.1   The seven principles of coaching

1 Awareness

Awareness is the most common outcome that coaching delivers, and many of the benefits the coachee receives from it arise from this. There is a misconception that coaching is about pushing people, or bullying them, or leading them to solutions. The opposite is the case, and yet the result is that through coaching people do move forward, identify their goals and make changes. This is because everything the coach says and does is focused on raising the coachee's own awareness and self-knowledge. How the coach brings this about will become clear in later chapters.

2 Responsibility

The core principle of coaching is self-responsibility, or taking ownership of our decisions: we learn better when we discover things for ourselves than when others tell us. We like to create our own solutions rather than be told what to do. Think of a child learning to walk; she takes her first few steps and falls over. Would you explain to the child why she fell, or tell her where to put her feet next time? Of course not. The child already has all the knowledge she requires; all she needs now is support and encouragement. This is one of the roles that coaches take with their coachees.

Whatever we do, we always have an agenda, whether conscious or otherwise, but the agenda is not necessarily our own. Our parents may hold ambitions for us that are sometimes more to do with their own aspirations than ours; teachers want us to achieve good grades; friends have multiple agendas, positive and otherwise; then again we have our own agenda for ourselves, which might not coincide with any of the others.

Coaches have only one agenda: their coachee's. Coaches learn to set aside the judgements and opinions triggered by their individual cultural history, which we talked about earlier, by using the tools of their profession. The coach is in charge of the process and the coachee is in charge of the content. If the coach gets sucked into the content, he or she is no longer of any use to the coachee. Sometimes, as coaches, we become interested in the story, and then we have to step back and ask ourselves: is this useful or interesting? Good coaching should be useful to the coachee rather than interesting to the coach.

3 Self-belief

Confidence that we can do something is a key factor in achieving it. People develop self-belief by being given the space to learn, both through making mistakes and achieving goals. When employees are learning a new task, what helps them is to be left alone to work things out for themselves, supported by encouragement and role modelling from others.

Giving people praise when they deserve it builds their confidence, their belief that they can achieve more and the energy to do it. Returning to the analogy of the child learning to walk, instead of explaining why she went wrong, parents praise the child for every new attempt. Half the incentive for getting up and trying again is to get that heady mixture of attention and praise. You don't need to tell the child how to walk because she will eventually find out for herself; however, your encouragement may speed up the process. If you take the fun out of the experience by shouting or scolding, you will slow everything down. Exactly the same principle works in adult relationships, whether in the office or elsewhere.

4 Blame-free

Children cannot learn to walk without falling over. In a coaching culture, mistakes are viewed as learning experiences, not reasons to look for a scapegoat. Coachees are likely to learn as much from the actions they have not completed as those that they have, and the coach is there neither to form an opinion on what is right or wrong for the coachee, nor to measure the coachee's life against the coach's own yardstick. The coach is a stranger in the strange land of the coachee's interior cultural world, created by the unique experiences and influences of the coachee's life. The only person who is a native here is the coachee, and he or she alone can identify the signposts and find the right pathways. The coach adds value by clearing whatever mists may be in the air, so that those signposts are legible.

It is inevitable that judgements arise when we are listening to someone talk about their lives. For instance, for the person who has taken on so much that they are not doing anything properly, the obvious solution is to prioritize what they most want and shelve the rest. However, at this point in the coachee's life it may be that such exciting opportunities have arisen that the coachee prefers to do everything by halves rather than one thing perfectly. It is neither the coach's decision nor the coach's place to have an opinion. The coach is there to help bring about clarity of purpose: once coachees can see clearly enough to understand which decision is congruent with their inner world, they can stop feeling guilty about it and move forward.

5 Solution focus

When we dwell on a problem, it gets bigger. When we focus on the solution, the problem becomes manageable and we find more energy to deal with it. Try it out; think about a problem you have – it could be small, like losing your pencil sharpener, or something more serious, perhaps involving your bank manager, boss or ex-partner. Now think on for a minute – about the problem, not the solution. After one minute, ask yourself, 'And what would I like to have happen?'

Notice the changes in your mind and in your body. You are immediately thrown forward towards solutions, and even if no obvious answer presents itself, you feel more optimistic and you find your energy levels have risen. As you think about the solution, the problem shrinks. Net result: you have a smaller problem and more energy to deal with it.

6 Challenge

Most of us like to be challenged and stretched within a supportive and encouraging environment. If we aim higher than is absolutely necessary, it is easier to hit the mark we wanted to in the first place, and quite likely even higher than that. A coach helps the coachee to step back and see the wood for the trees, encouraging the coachee to look for new perspectives. Coaching is sometimes described as 'holding up a mirror' to the coachee. Seeing their lives reflected back enables coachees to see their lives in proportion, often for the first time.

7 Action

Coaching uncovers new perspectives and awareness. In this way, coachees gain new insight, which leads to more options, which in turn lead to a desire to take action and change. Coaches ensure that this energy is channelled into action and a change of habits.

THE CONTRAST BETWEEN COACHING AND RELATED FIELDS

I am grateful to Gladeana McMahon (www.gladeanamcmahon.com) for co-authoring this section.

Coaching draws its influences from and stands on the shoulders of a wide range of disciplines, including counselling, management consultancy, personal development and psychology. However, there are a number of core differences which distinguish coaching from its related fields, and below are definitions of the purpose and practice of each field:

Performance coach

Performance coaching is a process that enables people to find and act on the solutions that are most congruent and appropriate for them personally. This is achieved through a dialogue which assists coachees to see new perspectives and achieve greater clarity about their own thoughts, emotions and actions, and about the people and situations around them. Performance coaching can be practised with individuals and groups, not by telling, but by questioning to facilitate awareness and self-directed learning.

There are a growing number of categories in coaching, such as life, executive, team, group and career coaching, but the process is largely the same and all can be generically defined as performance coaching. Just as the more successful an athlete is, the more likely he or she is to work with a coach, performance coaching is not necessarily about fixing problems and is often used to help successful individuals and teams to become more so.

Occasionally, some emotional baggage may surface during coaching and the coach may need to refer the coachee to a counsellor or therapist. However, sometimes the process of coaching dissolves deep-seated blocks and traumas which have been holding the coachee back, simply by its solution-focused approach, without the necessity of deeper exploration. Coaching has also produced results in physical healing, sometimes combined with related fields such as neuro linguistic programming and Grovian clean language.

Psychiatrist

A psychiatrist is a medical doctor with further specialized training in the field of psychiatry but, surprisingly, not necessarily any training in psychological therapies. Psychiatrists are concerned with diagnosing mental illness and prescribing drugs to treat it. A psychiatrist may have undertaken training in psychology and therapy, or may refer a patient on to a therapist. The UK professional body for psychiatrists is the Royal College of Psychiatrists, and there are comparable bodies in most other countries.

Psychologist

A psychologist will normally have an academic degree in psychology plus additional training in a specialist field to become, for example, a clinical psychologist, or an educational psychologist. The specialist UK body for psychologists is the British Psychological Society, and again there are comparable bodies in other countries.

Counsellor

Counselling is focused on helping people suffering from emotional distress which stops them from being able to function as well as they would like. It is generally concerned with getting people who are functioning below normal back to a normal level. The types of problems that are suitable for counselling are bereavement, relationship difficulties, parenting problems, work-related issues such as bullying and stress, a general unhappiness with life and family challenges.

A counsellor practises one or more different types of therapeutic intervention. The training extends from a part-time diploma up to higher-level degrees. The British Association for Counselling and Psychotherapy (BACP) is the main professional body for counselling and psychotherapy in the United Kingdom.

Psychotherapist

Psychotherapy relates to therapeutic interventions that are geared towards people whose personality is damaged in some way. Perhaps the person has been given a label such as 'personality disorder', which is a way of describing the variety of ways an individual may not be able to function. For example, a dependent personality disorder means that a person is unable to function independently and is always looking to another person to look after him or her, even if it means staying in a highly destructive relationship. Alternatively, someone may develop a condition such as obsessive compulsive disorder, where the person cannot leave the house or continue to work because the fear of contamination is so great, leading the person to wash his or her hands obsessively many times, even to the extent of making them bleed from washing. This would not be considered a personality disorder but is a condition serious enough to warrant more specialist help. Psychotherapy is usually long-term, of up to four or five years, and, if the psychotherapist is of an analytical persuasion, visits may be twice instead of once a week during this time.

A psychotherapist will have received training to work with deep-seated emotional difficulties. There are a number of bodies that represent psychotherapy in the United Kingdom, the two lead bodies being the BACP and the United Kingdom Council for Psychotherapy (UKCP).

Mentor

A great deal of confusion is caused by different uses of the term 'mentor'. In some organizations, the word is used to describe performance coaches as defined in this book. I would define mentors as people who impart their own experience, learning and advice to those who have less experience in the particular field. Like coaches, they may empower and motivate their mentees, but it is not their primary role to do so. In modern business, the practice of delivering mentoring in a coaching style is on the increase.

Consultancy

Consultancy performs several different roles for organizations, such as filling gaps in knowledge, experience or staff availability, and advising on direction and strategy. A consultant may bring in services from all the other coaching-related disciplines as well as areas such as finance, logistics and marketing.

Now we have looked at the various types of practitioner, let us examine the differences between the disciplines themselves:

Coaching is solution focused

Coaching always focuses on moving the coachee forward. Counselling and therapy may sometimes do this, but not all the time. Psychotherapy is a broad field, and is usually sought in order to fix a particular problem arising from past trauma. While therapy and counselling are usually about dealing with damage and distress, coaching is about identifying and achieving desire.

Coaching is coachee-led

Psychotherapists sometimes use techniques which lead and influence the patient and which could cause damage to the psyche if applied by an insufficiently experienced practitioner. However, coaches are trained not to lead, judge, advise (except occasionally and with permission) or influence their coachees. Their role is to respond to the desires and expressed needs of their coachees, and to operate with the belief that the coachee has all the required knowledge to solve his or her own problem. The role of the coach is thus limited to one of a facilitator and supporter, unleashing the coachee's potential. There are some models of coaching, such as the cognitive-behavioural coaching approach, that have a psycho-educative element, where the coach may facilitate coachees in uncovering information which they are unlikely to find out or understand on their own.

Coaching is about improving performance

The focus of coaching is to enhance performance. Although this may be the result with therapy and counselling, it is not a driver. Mentoring is usually aimed at improving performance; however, coaching sometimes deals with psychological issues in order to achieve this, whereas mentoring is about imparting facts and experience.

Coaching is about facilitating self-directed learning

Mentoring, while having similarities to coaching, is fundamentally different. A mentor has experience in a particular field and imparts specific knowledge, acting as advisor, counsellor, guide, tutor or teacher. In contrast, the coach's role is not to advise but to assist coachees in uncovering their own knowledge and skills and to facilitate coachees in becoming their own advisors.

A simple analogy with driving a car helps to define the differences (see Figure 1.2).

> ❖ A therapist will explore what is stopping you from driving.
> ❖ A counsellor will listen to your anxieties about the car.
> ❖ A mentor will share tips from the experience of driving cars.
> ❖ A consultant will advise you on how to drive the car.
> ❖ A coach will encourage and support you in driving the car.

Figure 1.2 Differences between coaching and other disciplines

A COACHING CULTURE AT WORK: THE VIRGIN EMPIRE

I experienced a coaching culture at first hand while working at board level with Richard Branson in the **The culture at Virgin** formative years of Virgin Records. This was back in the authoritarian days of the 1970s when we went to school and did as our teachers told us, then found a job and did as our bosses told us.

Joining Virgin was a pleasant culture shock, mostly because instead of being told what to do, everyone did exactly as they pleased. And what seemed to please them the most was to work harder than I had ever seen anyone work before. This group of 20 or so people, with virtually no music business experience and all under the age of 25, were stealing the market from under the noses of global corporate giants like EMI and CBS.

It was only in retrospect, after later years spent working in corporations, that I was able to identify the values that made Virgin one of the most successful and fastest-growing companies of its era. They were the values underlying the principles described earlier in this chapter, and are set out below in relation to organizational culture: in this instance, the Virgin coaching culture.

Self-belief

Richard Branson constantly, and sincerely, let his staff know how good they were. He started in business as a dyslexic 17-year-old magazine publisher who knew nothing about publishing, progressed into a record company boss who knew nothing about music, probably knows nothing about trains or planes, and certainly knows zero about spaceships. However, he has a gift for empowering those who work for him, is always genuinely impressed by their talent and knows how to show it. Through his encouragement, our confidence rocketed, and having been told by Richard that we could achieve anything, we found that we could. Significantly, Branson never allowed himself to be drawn into the detail of learning the nuts and bolts of the businesses he was involved with; he trusted his staff to be his knowledge base. Hence the second value of:

Responsibility

In the early days of Virgin few of us had any executive experience elsewhere. I do not recall an MBA among us, and quite a few were school or university dropouts. As there was no one to tell us what to do, we had to work out our own strategies to make our divisions successful. If we succeeded, all the credit would be ours, but if we failed, we shouldered the responsibility of that too. Having put exceptional effort into devising our schemes, and been assured by Branson that they would work, we strived above and beyond the call of duty to succeed. In short, Branson told us we could do it and therefore we did. Confidence is one of the greatest gifts one person can give to another.

Blame-free

Research shows that the only way children learn language is through their mistakes. The same applies to the infant learning to walk and the novice learning to ski; both learn through falling over. At Virgin, we were encouraged to take risks, and mistakes were almost welcomed as part of the learning process. Compare this with conventional company cultures where staff go to any lengths to hide mistakes from the boss, and end up with a situation where whole teams of people are putting all their time and energy into concealing an error, which would be simple to rectify if only it could be admitted to. Without a blame-free culture an organization can stagnate.

CREATING A COACHING CULTURE

Virgin was a unique situation and I would not suggest that anyone tries to change a company's culture overnight; Branson had the luxury of choosing all his people from the start and took all the financial risk. In my own case, the result was that my division – Virgin Music Publishers – became one of the top three music publishing companies in the United Kingdom within five years, followed by my own successful record company which I launched in partnership with Virgin.

There is no need to rush the process of building such a culture, because the beauty of coaching is that it can start from small beginnings, with just one person, and spread like a happy virus. It spreads simply because coaching feels good: when people experience giving or receiving coaching, they want more because it makes both parties feel better.

Of the three principles above, the key to creating a coaching culture is *self-belief*. You may not be working in a creative culture where you can encourage staff to come up with their own ideas and take risks; you may be in payroll, compliance or the legal profession, where there is only one correct answer and it is whatever the law dictates; you may be responsible for checking the work of other staff and ensuring that mistakes are corrected. However, if for every time you have to correct people (perhaps 10 per cent of the time), you also tell them when they are getting it right (correspondingly 90 per cent of the time), you will start creating a culture where people are enthusiastic. Your workforce will be satisfied at the end of the day by more than the money they have earned; they will be part of a culture where people will go the extra mile and turn down offers of higher-paid jobs elsewhere; you will have started to create a coaching culture.

The principles above and the techniques described later in this book can be used to coach upward as well; praising people when they do something the way you like it encourages them to do it that way again, like giving dogs a biscuit when they get the trick right. Complimenting the boss when he or she treats you the way you want to be treated will encourage more of the same in the future.

There is more information on creating a coaching culture in Chapter 7, 'How to create a coaching culture in organizations'.

Exercise

Ask your practice partner (or a friend) to talk for two minutes about something he or she wants to achieve. The only response you are allowed to make is to ask, 'And what would you like to have happen?' and you are only allowed to ask this question when your partner is stuck or becoming negative about the issue. So you must remain absolutely silent except for that question, and only that question, which you are permitted to ask a maximum of three times.

Then swap over so your partner can do the same for you.

After each session, the partner playing the coach asks the coachee the following questions:

- What did you learn about yourself?
- What new insights did you obtain?
- What were the advantages of being listened to?
- What were the disadvantages?
- What do you know now about your issue that you did not know before?
- Is there any action you would like to take?
- When?

Both write your actions down. And do them!

2

Coaching techniques

Now we move on to the nuts and bolts of coaching: the specific skills required for transforming people and organizations. Starting with an activity that most people think they have been doing all their lives, but some may never have done, we look how to listen in a way that helps others to hear themselves. Then we move on to the precision tools of the coach's toolkit, and explore the questions that can unlock new insights and clear the way forward. Clarifying and reflecting are the means by which coaches prompt their coachees and keep things moving, and I cannot place too much emphasis on how important it is for coaches to use their intuition at all times. The section on asking permission highlights something we take for granted and often see no necessity for, yet it is the key to creating rapport and trust between people. Finally, all these skills are brought together in an example of how to give constructive feedback the coaching way.

LISTENING

It is not hard to guess that to be a good coach is going to require a lot of listening. However, it is not as tedious as you might think: the coach is not there as a sponge to absorb the coachee's misery or self-obsession. We call the type of listening coaches practise 'active' listening.

The five levels of listening

Figure 2.1 shows the categories into which most of our listening falls. In normal conversation we mostly tune in somewhere between Levels 1 and 3. Coaches, however, learn to pay attention at a much higher level, and the value of being properly listened to is one of the reasons that coachees are prepared to pay for the experience.

5   Intuitive listening

- I really want to write my book but there's never any time.
- Is this about not having the time or is something else getting in the way?
- I'm afraid my book won't be good enough.

4   Listening and asking for more

- I want to get the very best out of my team.
- Tell me more about that.

3   Giving advice

- My manager is a bully.
- What you should do is complain to HR.

2   Giving our own experience

- I went on the Leadership course last week.
- I went on it last year. I learned a lot.

1   Waiting for our turn to speak

- I think we should arrange a meeting with the stakeholders first.
- Did you see the football last night?

Figure 2.1   The five levels of listening

Level 1 is probably the most irritating level of all. Have you ever been in a meeting with someone and known that they are not listening but just waiting for you to finish so they can have their say? At this level, the conversation is entirely on the listener's own agenda and not the speaker's. *Level 2* is still on the listener's agenda, though at least on the same subject. *Level 3* gives advice without exploring whether it is appropriate to the listener. At *Level 4* some real listening starts and the speaker experiences the luxury of being asked to tell more. At *Level 5* the speaker is using intuition and exploring whether there might be more behind the speaker's words than is actually being said.

Levels 2 and 3 have their place, particularly in terms of good management; however it is only at Levels 4 and 5 that coaching takes place.

I once trained a coach who was a very entertaining talker and always in demand at social events precisely because people liked to listen to him. During the training he realized that he had never really listened to another person in his life before. Listening at the lower levels in everyday life is not necessarily a bad thing, but on the whole it is not coaching.

Coaches listen at Levels Four and Five, ideally throughout every session. It sounds like hard work, but is in fact quite stimulating and energizing, rather like being in a game of chess where you are enthralled by calculating the next move.

QUESTIONING

Another activity at which coaches spend a large proportion of their time is asking questions, but not the type of questions we ask in everyday life. In conventional conversation, we ask questions in order to find out information, either because we want to know something for ourselves, or, even if it is for the other person's benefit, because we think we require the information to give advice.

There is only one reason coaches ever ask questions of their coachees: so that the coachees can find out information *about or for themselves*. Asking the right question enables coachees to access knowledge they did not know they had.

★ *A coach asks a question to enable the coachee to acquire information.*

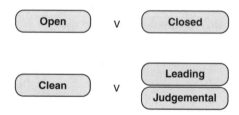

Figure 2.2   The five types of questions

Open, closed and clean questions all have a place in coaching. However, although coaches may occasionally make suggestions to their coachees about a way forward, coaches never ask leading questions. Neither do we ask judgemental questions.

Open questions

Open questions encourage people to dig deeper and explore further:

■ What could you do?
■ What will you do?
■ What impact is that having on you?
■ Who will you contact?
■ When will you call her?
■ Where will you go?
■ How will you do that?
■ How do you feel about that?
■ Where do you want to take it from here?

- Who would you choose as a role model?
- What's stopping you from doing that?
- What impact will that have?
- How important is that to you?

Closed questions

Some questions elicit a short answer: *yes* or *no*. These are known as 'closed' questions:

- Is there anything else about that?
- Will you commit to doing that?

The majority of the questions used in coaching are open because most of the time is spent encouraging the coachee to explore new possibilities, ideas and self-knowledge. Closed questions come into play when a new insight arises, in order to tie it down to an action or a goal. The way to recognize open and closed questions is that a closed question always starts with a verb whereas an open question never does.

Clean questions

Clean questions are those that least influence the coachee's judgement:

- Is there anything else?
- Is there anything you would like to do about that?
- Would you like to talk to someone else about that?
- Is it OK if I ask you more about that?

Although these are technically closed questions, in the appropriate setting they become the most open questions of all. This is because they give the choice to the coachee completely. For example, in certain situations an open question such as 'What will you do?' becomes a leading question, because it implies that the coachee must take action at this point. Who is the coach to decide that it is a time for action rather than thinking and absorbing new insights for the next week? Good coaching is not about pushing people into action. It is about raising insight and awareness, out of which action will arise naturally at the best time for the coachee.

Leading questions

Solutions that occur to the coach may not be appropriate for the coachee, because of the difference in their cultural maps, described in Chapter 1.

A common pitfall for new coaches is to think of a solution for a coachee and then ask questions that will lead the coachee towards that solution. The danger here is that coachees sometimes go along with this because it seems expected of them. However, if no new insight arises through this process, no coaching has occurred and no change will take place.

Judgemental questions

Some questions make people feel comfortable and help them to open up; others tend to put people on the spot and make them defensive.

Questions beginning 'Why' are rarely used in coaching because they invite us to judge ourselves.

Questions beginning 'What', 'Where', 'How', 'Who' and 'When' enable us to gain new insight and awareness about ourselves, our situations and each other. Sometimes a 'Why' question masquerades as an awareness question. Tacking the word 'What' or 'How' in front of a 'Why' question does not turn it into an awareness question.

'Why' questions in disguise include:

■ What did you do that for?
■ What's your excuse for not going to the gym?
■ How did that happen?

A rule of thumb is that your questions must never invite coachees to defend their position.

Although it is important to understand the distinctions between types of questions, and the reasons behind them, it is not advisable to remember consciously these differences while coaching. Good coaches follow their intuition in the moment, and identify better practice in retrospect or through practice with experienced peers who will give them accurate feedback.

To sum up:

■ Never use questions starting with 'why' (clean v judgemental).
■ When in doubt, start the question with 'what' (open v closed).
■ Take care not to push the coachee into action before the coachee is ready (clean v leading).

Questions are the precision tools in the coach's toolbox. By choosing the right type of question, the coach can shape the process – challenging, supporting and encouraging the coachee, without ever getting in the way of the content. There is a comprehensive list of useful coaching questions in Appendix A on page 205.

CLARIFYING, REFLECTING AND USING INTUITION

Clarifying

Clarifying means repeating people's words back in a different form. We do this all the time in normal conversation, to confirm that we have heard correctly and understood. Many an argument has arisen because two people firmly believe that they are right about two conflicting versions of what was said. In a domestic situation this can be explosive; imagine the consequences when it happens between two world leaders who do not even speak the same language.

In addition to checking the meaning, the benefits of clarifying are:

- To create rapport with other people. Clarifying shows we are making every effort to listen to what they are saying.
- To help us understand what we ourselves have said. Speaking our thoughts aloud can help us organize them and clarifying supports this process.
- To move people forward politely when they get into too much detail. For example, a long ramble about traffic on the journey to the coaching session can be curtailed by some neat summing up. This enables people to feel that the matter has been dealt with – they have been understood and can now move on.

These benefits hold true whether in a coaching session or everyday conversation:

Coachee: Sorry I'm late. Everything conspired against me this morning. The phone rang twice as I was leaving and I knew I shouldn't have answered it. Both times it was people trying to sell me something. Then the postman came and on the way out my neighbour grabbed me to talk about the bin situation...

Coach: Sounds like you've had a stressful morning. Well done for getting here at all.

Coachee: Thanks. What's on the agenda?

In this case, the clarifying has been combined with some positive feedback to make the coachee feel better about being late, allowing the coachee to stop making excuses and start looking forward.

Reflecting

Reflecting means repeating someone's words back exactly as they were spoken, including tone and body language, although it must not appear mechanical or the effect will be noticeable and irritating.

When we hear our own words reflected back, it has the effect of validating what we have said, reassuring us that we have been heard and that the listener is interested in what we are saying. It can also help us to hear and reassess what we have said. Reflecting is a great rapport builder, and as useful as clarifying when you want to move someone forward:

Coachee: I like the company I work for but the work's tedious. I'd like something more challenging.

Coach: More challenging.

Coachee: Yes, something where I feel I'm stretching myself, with a bit of risk.

When in doubt about what question to ask next, a good tactic is to reflect coachees' words back to them. This often has a more powerful effect than any question could.

★ *When in doubt, reflect back the coachee's words.*

Intuition

Intuition is the sharpest tool in the coach's box. However, it is essential to follow the maxim of being on the coachee's agenda and non-judgemental to make sure that your intuition does not turn into unwelcome advice.

If a coachee's words flag up an idea in your mind, one of two things is happening: either your own cultural background is getting in the way or you have sensed something that the coachee is not telling you and may not even be aware of. The simple answer is to ask the coachee. If your intuition leads to a new insight, then you can pat yourself on the back. If the coachee does not seem to relate to your hunch, then you must let it go without a backward glance.

The coach should not be afraid to challenge the coachee in order to uncover new insight:

Coachee: Money's tight, but I don't want to raise my fees. I like helping people.

Coach: Can I share with you what's coming into my mind?

Coachee: Yes please.

Coach: Are you able to give yourself permission to want to make money?

I actually held this conversation a number of years ago, and whe
last question, the coachee began to cry with relief as he agreed th
wanted more than anything was to make money, but he had never all
himself to admit that before. There was some uncomfortable feeling attached to
commercial thinking which, he then realized, arose from his relationship with
his father.

These skills of listening, questioning, clarifying, reflecting and using your
intuition are the cornerstones of good coaching.

Linguistics

Coaching is not just about a conversational exchange **Tone and pace**
between people; it involves non-verbal signals, such as
body language (see Chapter 8), plus the tone and pace with which the words are
delivered. The coach will usually follow the coachee's tone and pace, which
creates rapport and allows the coachee to feel in control of the exchange; this is
important if the coachee is going to be relaxed enough to look inside and
discover new insights. Sometimes a coach may quicken the exchange, or inject
more energy, to move the coachee forward, or to invoke a situation where the
coachee will deliver spontaneous reactions which might be hampered by having
too much time to think. These changes usually take place intuitively and neither
coach nor coachee will be aware that they are happening, although an observer
might notice the difference easily.

Coaches also have a natural tendency to start sentences **Clean language**
with 'and' or 'so' at times; this tendency has been identified by David Grove in his 'clean language' methodology (see Chapter 8) and
incorporated as a specific technique, because it is so effective at creating rapport
and producing a good flow of thought from the coachee.

Another aspect of communication that coaches **Precise and concise**
need to be aware of is the benefit of being concise and
precise in what they say; this is good advice at all times, not just in coaching
sessions. The fewer words you use in order to get your point across, the more
people will listen and understand what you have said. The requirement to be
concise makes us stop and think before we speak, which is never a bad thing. I
often ask coaching students, or coachees, if they can put something they have
said more succinctly. The result will not just be shorter, their thoughts will have
been processed along the way. This is an excellent way of acquiring new
insights.

PERMISSION

Asking permission is something we tend to do only when it is obviously required: for instance when we knock before entering someone else's house. In coaching, we find that asking permission, whether or not it is obviously required, helps people to feel safer and in control of the process. In short, it creates rapport.

Another advantage of asking permission is that it makes people stop and listen to what we have to say, particularly in meetings. Offering the simple question, 'Can I add something to that?' can reduce a meeting room to expectant silence, as everyone pauses to hear what you have to say.

- Can I add to what you've just said?
- Would you like to brainstorm this with me?
- Is it OK if I coach you on this for a while?

It may seem unnecessary to ask the last question of someone already in a coaching session with you, because it follows that he or she must have already granted permission for you to coach him or her. Nevertheless, this is a great way of relaxing people and opening them up so that they are in a good space to get the best possible benefit out of the coaching.

In Chapter 1, we looked at an example of different customs in different countries, such as nodding meaning 'no'. We saw that although differences between international cultures may be easy to spot, it is more difficult to recognize differences in people's own personal cultures, which may have been created by their parents, teachers and life experiences. Asking permission frequently is a way of respecting any boundaries of which we may not be aware. It is particularly important if the coachee is venturing into an area that could be sensitive.

GIVING AND RECEIVING FEEDBACK

It is worth bearing in mind that feedback is usually offered as a well-meaning gift. However inappropriate, it is likely to arise from generosity and a desire to help rather than malice. Whether positive or negative, we may think it is one of the following:

- undeserved;
- of no use to us;
- of great value to us.

In all cases, the best response is a simple 'thank you'. Giving feedback on feedback to justify one's own position can make both parties feel uncomfortable. It is of course acceptable to ask for more detail if you feel it will be useful to you.

Feedback is most effective when it is:

Specific

These statements are too vague to mean much to the recipient:

> That was great.
> That didn't really work for me.

These statements give the recipient useful pointers:

> You were effective during the meeting when you made the analogy between our team and a pride of lions.
> Your report is informative and I think it would benefit from being more succinct.

Personal

Present the feedback as coming from you personally, not as a judgement from the world in general. You are entitled to your own opinion but presenting yourself as an authority may be resented. In these statements the speaker is taking ownership of the opinions:

> I think you did that well.
> What would have worked better for me is…

Accentuating the positive

We tend to exaggerate the negative feedback we receive and sometimes do not take positive feedback on board at all. Make sure that some of the feedback you give is positive and that it has landed. Remember that people may go away having heard only the negative feedback and beating themselves up all the way. As we highlighted in Chapter 1, building people's self-belief is the essence of good coaching, and gives them energy and confidence to change:

> What I liked was…
> Can I suggest something you might do differently?
> You are always so good at…

Invited

People will be more receptive to your feedback if they have asked for it. When you are asked, you must tell the truth, while always remembering to accentuate the positive.

Self-directed

The coaching way of giving feedback is to ask people to come up with their feedback themselves. Use reflecting and clarifying to affirm what they have said. Ask specific questions if you think they have left anything out, and be sure to congratulate them where they feel they have succeeded. If they focus too much on the negatives, ask them directly what they liked about what they did. After they have answered, they are likely to ask for your own opinion, which gives you an opportunity to give your feedback at a point when they are ready to listen to it.

These two statements, asked consecutively, encourage people to be kind to themselves. Looking at the positive first will build their confidence as they recognize their strengths. This in turn will help them to be honest about what they need to work on:

> What did you like about what you did?
> If you could do it again, what would you do differently?

Appropriate

Negative feedback is best given in private to the person concerned. There are times and places for giving positive feedback. These are the parameters:

- as often as you can;
- only when it is deserved;
- immediately;
- in public if the recipient is not too shy;
- direct to the recipient;
- to the recipient's boss.

Surveys show that people value satisfaction in their work even more than money. One of the best ways of raising employees' satisfaction is to tell them specifically the difference they have made and where they are good at their jobs, every day and as often as is appropriate. The same principles apply to parenting, marriage, schooling and every other area of life. Giving your coachees positive feedback as a coach will help them find the energy and motivation to face up to the challenges they have set themselves.

As Ken Blanchard said in his classic *The One Minute Manager* (Blanchard and Johnson, 1996):

> Catch people doing something right!

Exercise

1. Practise with your partner asking alternate open and closed questions. Then ask your partner to do the same for you.

2. Afterwards, ask each other to describe how it felt to be asked the various questions.

3. Try asking three questions starting 'Why', then get your partner to do the same for you. Afterwards, ask each other how it felt to be asked 'Why'.

4. Now ask your partner to talk about something he or she wants to achieve, as you did at the end of Chapter 1. Restrict yourself to listening, clarifying and reflecting. Do not ask questions. Then, have your partner do the same to you.

5. Afterwards, both make a note of what you noticed during this experience by asking these questions:
   - What did you learn about yourself?
   - What do you know now about your issue that you did not know before?
   - Is there an action or actions you would like to take about the issue?
   - When?

6. Finally, do some coaching. Ask your partner six open questions about his or her issue. You can intersperse some clarifying and reflecting where it seems appropriate – use your intuition! After the six open questions, ask one or more closed questions to tie your partner down to action.

7. Ask your partner to give you feedback on the whole practice session according to the guidelines given earlier in this chapter, and then swap over.

8. Write the actions down. And do them!

3

Coaching models

Coaching models are frameworks which support our intuitive powers and our coaching skills. I have included in this section the increasingly well-known theory of emotional intelligence, or EQ, as best-selling author Daniel Goleman put it. Emotional intelligence runs through coaching and leadership like the writing through the proverbial stick of rock; it is both the foundation stone and the result, employed in the techniques and delivered by them.

The second model, GROW, is regarded as the DNA of coaching and was first developed by Sir John Whitmore (although in his Foreword to this book he modestly demurs) and his colleagues at the dawn of performance coaching some 25 years ago. A number of similar models have sprung up which add to the value, but they are all based on the robust and enduring GROW.

I developed the third model, EXACT, to improve on SMART which, although efficient for some uses, is not entirely aligned with coaching values and aims.

Some further models are included in Chapter 8 on 'Coaching tools' (page 109). They are outside the main body of the book because they are not essential to the coach; however, most coaches go on to further training and research and pick up several useful techniques, including but not limited to those outlined in Chapter 8, through training, working with coachees, reading, internet surfing and meeting other coaches.

Rest assured that you can get excellent results as a coach once you have acquired the basic skills and learned the first three models, EQ, GROW and EXACT. Most coaches incorporate perhaps one to three of the other models, and the ones listed are only a small sample of the various models developed from sport, psychology, leadership development and other fields which are out there waiting for you to discover them.

EQ and GROW are essential, and EXACT useful for goal setting, as soon as you start coaching. If that is where you are in your coaching practice, then it is suggested you study these three, become fluent and experienced in them, and then embark on your own journey of discovery with the rest.

EQ

Emotional intelligence is an extensive field, developed by many psychologists and other practitioners over the last 30 years, of which the most well known is Daniel Goleman. Goleman hypothesizes that to become successful at work tends to require one-third of IQ (intellectual intelligence) to two-thirds of EQ. This rises to a whopping 85 per cent of EQ in the case of directors and CEOs.

It can be useful to show clients the quadrant shown as Figure 3.1 when they are in a situation of conflict with one or more other members of staff. It will help them to reach an understanding of why they are feeling this way and work out what they can do to alleviate the tension.

The following description of EQ is based on notes I took during a talk given by Sir John Whitmore.

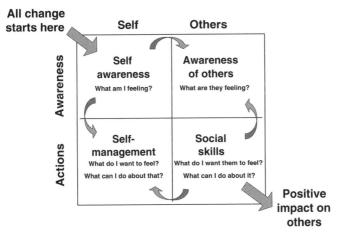

Figure 3.1   The quadrants of EQ

In Goleman's model, self-awareness is what leads to the other qualities. This involves being aware of what is happening here and now with you, not in the past or the future. In our lives and upbringing, we are generally not encouraged to become more self-aware. For example, if I meet you in the morning in the office and we have an altercation, I will go back to my mate and say 'A is a bit grumpy this morning,' and A will say to his mate, 'B was aggressive this morning.' We both have the same problem – we are asking 'What's the matter with him?' instead of asking what is happening in ourselves. We do not take responsibility.

We see the world through the coloured glasses of our childhood experience. For instance, if you are a small child with a violent, alcoholic father, and you were hit for no reason occasionally, how will that affect you as an adult? One result might be that you start to see the world as a threatening place. Various programmes come into being inside you which are survival mechanisms, and they continue to crank into action indefinitely, although they may no longer be required because the situation that created them has changed.

For example, life has moved on and you are learning to drive. Because of your violent father, you have an idea that the world is a dangerous place. How does that affect your driving? You are likely to be an aggressive driver. Those habit patterns are recurring, and however much you hate the behaviour, you are likely to repeat it.

Through processes of self-examination, such as coaching or therapy, you do not eliminate these hindrances but it is possible to become aware of your tendencies and to manage them. So if I become aware of the fact that I am grumpy in the morning, I will be careful to monitor myself, perhaps noticing that if I have a coffee first I won't be grumpy. Once I become aware of something about myself, I can start to manage it.

It does not work if somebody else tells you to do this; the only thing you can change is yourself – even if it is only by 10 per cent – and you must ask yourself, 'What do I need to do?' As a result, all you can do for other people is to give them feedback (such as, 'When you do this, I feel like this') and it is up to them to decide whether they want to change. It is very important that such feedback is non-judgemental.

Our culture conditions us to think that when our education ends we stop learning. But the whole of life is a continuing education – you are in the University of Life until you die!

The combination of the quadrants in Figure 3.1 illustrates our social skills. Some of us are fortunate enough not to have been too damaged in childhood, so we have more EQ, and others have more work to do. That gives you what we call your 'ground of being'. We each have our 'ground of being', and then the behaviour we put on top of it.

An important part of self-development is the capacity to self-observe, because that gives you the opportunity to change. Once you have noticed your thoughts you can be selective about them: you can choose whether they are positive or negative. This is the foundation stone for self-awareness. Once you have the capacity to notice your thoughts, and then your feelings and body sensations, all the other things will grow out of that.

Where there is a show of anger or resentment, what is underlying is often sadness. When you are angry at me, if I say to you, 'What are you sad about? What's upsetting you right now?' the relationship will change instantly. 'Someone understands me!' you will think.

We all have an act. As we are aware, we become more authentic. It does not matter what your personality type is as long as you are authentic. The whole point of self-development is being able to slough off your act and become who you really are. That is the essence of leadership.

GROW

EQ is a broad model underlying everything in coaching; GROW is a very specific model showing the steps that a coach needs to go through in order to be effective. It gives us a structure and a framework to support the coaching.

Good coaching is 80 per cent the coach and 20 per cent the coaching model. However, that 20 per cent is vital – without the human body underneath it, the clothes you have designed will not have any shape. There are a growing number of coaching models, and they are all broadly similar. They encompass the forward movement of coaching and highlight the stages that the coaching must pass through – whatever the personal style of delivery – if it is to be effective.

GROW is the original coaching model, developed (with others) by the pioneer of coaching in the United Kingdom, Sir John Whitmore:

Goal
Reality
Options
Will

This sequence emphasizes the solution focus of coaching, and breaks down like this.

Goal

Identifying what we want to achieve puts us on the path to achieving it and focuses on the solution rather than the problem. The Goal section of GROW is addressed at the beginning of each session, and referred to again from time to time to keep the focus moving forward, especially if the coachee becomes stuck.

Some Goal questions are:

What would you like to achieve out of this session?
What would you like to have happen?
What elements would you like to see in place in xx months' time?
What do you really want?
How would you like it to be?
Can you say what you want in one sentence?
How would you like it to be in an ideal world?
How will you know when you have arrived there?

Reality

This is an exploration of where the coachee is right now. It is essential to spend time here so that the coachee can find out what needs to be brought out and looked at. Once the coachee has everything in view, he or she will perceive greater clarity and different perspectives, so that ideas will occur naturally on how to move forward.

Some useful questions here are:

How important is this to you?
If an ideal situation is 10, what number are you at now?
Where in your body do you experience the anxiety?
How do you feel about this?
What impact is this having on you?
What's on your shoulders?
What are you doing that's working towards your goal?
What are you doing that is getting in the way of your goal?

One of the key discoveries made by Tim Gallwey (who, through his sports coaching, developed the techniques upon which performance coaching was founded, as described in Chapter 1) was that if he asked coachees to 'watch the ball' they tended to miss it. This is because such a question brings with it all the baggage of fear of failure, memory of having failed before and the uncomfortable subject of whether the player is good enough.

Gallwey found, however, that if he rephrased the question by asking the player to count how many times the ball spun as it went over the net, or how many centimetres it cleared the net by, the hit rate improved significantly. Neither of these measurements matters in terms of technique, but this type of question is simply a request for information and does not carry the 'baggage' mentioned above. This compelled the whole of the player's concentration to be on the ball, which resulted in it being far more likely to be hit. In addition, Gallwey theorized that the second process taps into a player's non-rational mind and harnesses his or her intuition.

Our coaching Reality questions listed above are the equivalent of Gallwey's questions about the trajectory of the ball, but applied to someone's life or work. It does not make a great deal of difference which Reality questions you choose; by asking a number of them you are inviting coachees to look at their current situations from different angles and perspectives, and it is this that will bring them new insight and awareness, which will in turn deliver clarity on how to move forward.

Thoroughly exploring the coachee's Reality is one of the keys to good coaching, and it is the part that is usually missing from everyday conversation. We tend to start by describing what was happening in the past (which you will notice does not even feature in our GROW model) and go straight from there to what we shall do. For example, we go from 'He said this, so I said that,' to 'I'm going to resign.' Notice that the speaker has taken all the anger inherent in the first statement through to the future. Asking Reality questions enables people to step back from their emotions, see the situation clearly, and decide how to move on from a new place of clarity instead.

It feels awkward at first to explore Reality, and new coaches tend to fall back on questions about the past, asking for options or, unfortunately, offering solutions instead. Until the Reality questions become automatic, which they will in time, it pays to keep a list close to you while coaching to ensure you have asked enough before moving on to Options.

When do you know it is time to move on? The coachee will often do it for you, as new awareness starts to arise. Reality questions help people dig deeper into their own awareness, until they reach a bedrock of understanding and gain an insight they have not had before. They will show signs of energy: for instance, lightness in the voice, brighter eyes, a smile and more upright posture. That is the time to ask them about options, if they have not started offering some already.

Note that we are exploring the present, not what has happened in the past, and that we are focusing on what the situation means to the coachee more than on the facts. We are asking questions not to find out what has happened, but to find out what impact it is having on the coachee. When the coachee reaches a new insight or level of understanding, it pays to explore the new Reality, with the same types of questions, to embed new insights, and to revisit the Goal. Possibly a new Goal or direction will emerge. Then the 'Options' and 'Will' sequence starts again.

When the coachee reaches a new insight, these Reality questions are useful:

What does that tell you about yourself?
What do you know now that you did not know before?
What is your insight about that?
What have you learned about yourself from that?
Where else could you use this in your life?

Options

When the coachee is ready, as described above, you can ask some Options questions:

What are your options?
What else?
What has worked in the past?
If there were something else, what would it be?
Is there anything else?

Notice that these questions are almost all open. Keep asking open questions until the coachee runs out of options. Once it seems that the list is complete, ask the closed question 'Is there anything else?' to finalize the process.

If the coachee gets stuck, simply go back to the Reality or Goal questions. Repeating back to coachees the key words they came up with during the Reality questions almost always opens up some new clarity, which will in turn enable some Options to surface.

It helps also to keep throwing coachees' focus forward by referring to the Goal statements they have made. Asking Options questions when the coachee is stuck is the least helpful thing you can do. It is the mental equivalent of Tim Gallwey asking people to 'watch the ball'; they would dearly love to hit it, but they can't see any way of improving their shot. This is because the question goes straight to the conscious mind, whereas exploring the Reality and the Goal addresses the issue obliquely and allows the subconscious mind to come into play.

There is also a left brain/right brain communication going on here; by asking coachees what they want to achieve, and what their dreams are, you are engaging the right side of the brain which deals with imagination and creativity. Throwing in a left-brain question like 'What can you do about it?' engages both sides of the brain in giving the answer, double the normal resources that we have when sitting around getting stumped by the question, 'What on earth do I do now?'

However, I cannot stress enough how important it is to spend time in the Reality set of questions, and to return to them throughout the session. The dreams and the solutions delivered by the Goal and Options questions are often blocked by fear, anxiety and confusion which the coachee has not faced. The Reality section is where monsters are brought out from the shadows. Then they can be dealt with – that is, if they have not simply dissolved merely through having been identified.

Will

'Will' covers what action coachees will take. The first three sections of GROW create awareness; once everything is in view, coachees obtain more clarity and they are naturally motivated to take responsibility for changing what they can see:

Some Will questions might be:

What do you want to do about that?
Is that an action you can commit to?
What could you do to become more committed?
Could you do more?
Is that a stretch for you?

When will you do that?
How many?
How much?
How often?
Who will you talk to?
What else could you do?
Can you do more?

Many coachees come to coaching precisely because they do not know what it is they want to achieve. Modern life offers abundant options in terms of career, investment, where to live, who with and how to spend one's leisure time. It also carries with it some limitations, such as holding down a job, paying the mortgage, getting the children into a decent school and surviving divorce or bereavement. The awareness delivered by the initial 'Reality' questions helps coachees to focus their energy where it will be most beneficial during the Options and Will stages.

Note that the components of GROW do not necessarily follow that order; an effective coaching conversation moves about between the elements as required. In the example of a coaching conversation given in Table 3.1, the shape of the conversation is shown by the headings. In the right-hand column, the types of questions are shown by G = Goal, R = Reality, O = Options and W = Will (what the coachee Will do).

Note:

- how great a proportion of the time the coach spends in Reality and how the coach hops about with questions from all four sections within the conversation;
- that the coach goes back to check the Reality when the coachee names an action where the coach senses some doubt: it is by exploring Reality that fear evaporates and new insight, awareness and energy come to the coachee;
- that the coach keeps the focus forward and positive by asking occasional 'Goal' questions throughout;
- that the question 'And can you commit to doing that this time?' is marked R and W because it is about an action (W) but is also exploring how committed the coachee is to doing the action (R) (some questions can apply to different parts of GROW depending on where they are used).

This example is provided to illustrate the flexibility of the GROW model and the power of returning to Reality when there is any confusion. Do not try to plan or be aware of which category your questions are in while you are asking them – all of your focus should be on what will benefit the coachee and move

Table 3.1   A sample GROW coaching conversation

G	**Setting a direction for the session**	
Coach	What would you like to achieve in this session?	**G**
Coachee	I would like to start feeling on top of everything.	
Coach	You would like to start feeling on top of everything.	**G**
Coachee	Exactly.	
R	**Investigating where the coachee is now**	
Coachee	I said I would finish my report this week but haven't done it.	**R**
Coach	You haven't finished your report. And how do you feel about not having done it?	**R**
Coachee	Terrible. I'm always late with reports.	
Coach	So you're always late with reports. Is it OK if we talk about that for a few minutes?	**R**
Coachee	Good idea.	
Coach	Can I ask what is happening for you around 'always late with reports'?	**R**
Coachee	I just don't have time. I have too many things going on.	
Coach	And is there anything else about not having time and too many things going on?	**R**
Coachee	I find it hard to say 'No' when people ask me to do things.	
Coach	And what's hard about saying no?	**R**
Coachee	I want to please everyone.	
Coach	You want to please everyone. And is there anything else about it being hard to say no?	**R**
Coachee	I'm anxious that they won't think I'm good enough.	
Coach	So you want to please everyone and you're anxious they won't think you're good enough. Anything else?	**R**
Coachee	That's about it.	
Coach	Can I ask you if anything else gets in the way of doing reports apart from not having enough time?	**R**
Coachee	Actually, it's the same thing - I'm afraid the report won't be good enough so it's hard to get started.	
Coach	Can I tell you what I'm hearing?	**R**
Coachee	Yes, please do.	
Coach	It sounds like this is all about anxiety over whether people think you are good enough.	**R**
Coachee	Yes. I never realized that before.	
Coach	On a scale of 10, how high would you rate your anxiety about this?	**R**
Coachee	A 7.	
Coach	So you would rate your anxiety at a 7. Do *you* think you're good enough?	**R**
Coachee	Yes – I feel I have all the right qualities and talents for this job. I get great feedback too. And my six-monthly reviews are always good.	

Table 3.1 *continued*

Coach	You sound confident that you are good enough.	R
Coachee	Yes, I am.	
Coach	Are there any grounds for believing that other people don't think you're good enough?	R
Coachee	No, I suppose there aren't.	
Coach	What would it be like if you knew that everyone regarded you highly?	G
Coachee	Fabulous. I could get so much done.	
Coach	What is the impact of feeling that people think you aren't good enough?	R
Coachee	It's taking up a lot of energy.	
Coach	How does that feel in your body?	R
Coachee	Tightness around the shoulders. A pit in my stomach.	
Coach	Imagine for a moment that you are in an ideal world and all obstacles have been removed. You know you are good enough and so does everyone around you. How does that feel in your body?	G
Coachee	Lighter. My shoulders are lifting. I feel much more energetic. I can do anything! Next time I feel bad I will try this.	
O and W	**Investigating the coachee's options for change and tying down to action**	
Coach	And what could you do to stop the 'not good enough' feeling getting in the way?	O
Coachee	I could write some of my positive feedback on a Post-it and stick it where I can see it next time I start dithering.	
Coach	Excellent. When will you do that?	W
Coachee	Straight after this session.	
Coach	And what else could you do?	O
Coachee	I could ask my colleagues for some feedback. I have a feeling it would be better than I thought.	
Coach	And how do you feel about doing that?	R
Coachee	A bit nervous.	
Coach	Whereabouts in your body do you feel the nervousness?	R
Coachee	In my solar plexus.	
Coach	In your solar plexus. And how nervous are you out of 10?	R
Coachee	A 4. It's OK. I will be able to do it.	
Coach	Are you absolutely committed to doing it?	R
Coachee	Yes. Absolutely.	
Coach	So when will you do that?	W
Coachee	On Tuesday after the staff meeting.	
Coach	And what else do you want to do?	O
W	**Coachee commits to action and recognizes new insight**	
Coachee	I could finish the report!	
Coach	So you could finish the report. And can you commit to doing that this time?	R/W

Table 3.1 *continued*

Coachee	Yes. Definitely!	
Coach	And when will you do that?	**W**
Coachee	Over the weekend. I'll have it done by Monday.	
Coach	And where would you say you are now on a scale of 10, regarding your anxiety about being good enough?	**R**
Coachee	That's gone down to a 3.	
Coach	Well done.	

the coachee forward. Dissect what you have done after the conversation, and in time you will find that you choose the most appropriate part of GROW quite naturally.

EXACT

One of the key principles of coaching is 'solution focus'. In order to get somewhere it is essential to know where you are going, as Lewis Carroll identified in *Alice in Wonderland*:

> Alice: Would you tell me, please, which way I ought to go from here?
> Cat: That depends a good deal on where you want to get to.
> Alice: I don't much care where.
> Cat: Then it doesn't matter which way you go.

It is essential for the coachee to have a clear understanding of what it is he or she wants to achieve. Many of our goals are determined by the agenda of others, or by pressures upon us to be something we are not. The EXACT model takes coachees through a process which helps them identify objectives that are congruent with their own values. The aim can be termed 'goal', 'outcome', 'objective', 'mission statement', or any other expression that suits the coachee and coach.

EXciting   ⇨ Positive, inspiring

Assessable   ⇨ Measurable

Challenging ⇨ Stretching

Time-framed ⇨ Within a deadline

Figure 3.2 EXACT

There are two more criteria to bear in mind:

- **Of one focus**: more than one focus dilutes the goal.
- **Succinct**: a few words that are easy to remember so that the goal works for the coachee all the time without having to look it up.

These parameters give the goal energy and focus, keeping us motivated to achieve what we may not have thought possible.

EXciting

A positive goal will inspire the coachee, exerting a magnetic pull and triggering the reticular activating system, a function of the brain described on page 48 of this chapter to bring seemingly amazing coincidences into the path of the coachee.

Positive

Assessable

When asked to do so, coachees are usually able to come up with an exciting goal. It is sometimes more difficult to identify the specific point when the goal will have been reached. It is quite common to experience a period of 10 minutes or more where the coach is asking questions from different perspectives and the coachee seems to be unable to come up with anything that could act as a measure. It is essential to persevere during these moments, as I have found that the more identifiable the measure, the more inspiring the goal will be. I would go so far as to say that a goal is not truly and deeply motivating until there is a measure in it.

Getting the measure

A common pitfall is for the coachee to set a goal about the journey, not the destination. For instance:

Find out about implementing a new sales drive

instead of

Double our sales

Speak up more at staff meetings

instead of

Have my proposal accepted

Ask the coachee what will be different when these things are achieved:

- What will be the result of speaking up more at staff meetings?
- What tangible differences will there be in your life/work?
- What do you want to achieve by this?

A good rule of thumb is that both the coach and the coachee must be able to identify clearly when the goal has been achieved.

It is hard to attach a measure to some types of goal. A goal popular with coachees is something about being their best – they have an inner sense of what great shape they could be in, physically, mentally and emotionally, and when asked for a measure, they insist that they will 'just know'. These questions can help:

- How will I, your coach know when you get there?
- Imagine having achieved this goal: what will you see/hear/feel around you?
- What elements will be in place that were not there before?
- What will you be able to do that you could not do before?
- What tangible changes will there be in your life/work?

Listen for a measure as they reply – they may not recognize it themselves, but you can latch onto it and reflect it back to them. Usually, there is one element that will cover all the others. For instance, although a crucial part of the goal might be to lose weight, a coachee may not feel that this is where her real focus lies. So although an obvious measure could be 'Become a size 8', that goal will not inspire her, or engage her enthusiasm in the very difficult task of losing weight. Rather like Gallwey's rejected instruction, 'Watch the ball', this goal might carry with it the baggage that the coachee will have to go hungry, will be miserable, has failed before, and so on.

However, if the coachee, facilitated by the coach, calls the goal 'Shining in my red dress at the Christmas party', this satisfies the 'assessable' criterion (because the red dress happens to be a size 8) as well as the desire to recapture peak physical and emotional fitness.

Another solution is to ask for a comparative measure: 'Was there a time when you felt the way you would like to feel now?' Then the goal might become 'As energetic as I was at 21.' Another alternative is to identify a role model: 'As slinky as Sienna.'

If, after all this, no measure has emerged, it is acceptable to fall back on settling for a percentage:

Coach: What percentage are you at now in terms of feeling good about yourself?
Coachee: 20 per cent.
Coach: And what percentage would you like to be?
Coachee: 80 per cent.

It is amazing how accurately people are able to respond to percentage questions. They seem to have a sure inner knowledge of where they are at the moment, and rarely set 100 per cent as where they want to be, because for most people that would be impossible. A percentage-based goal exerts a strong pull on the coachee. However, it is always preferable to have a real measure. It may be tempting to settle for a goal that sounds inspiring, such as 'Floating on a cloud of my dreams,' but a goal does not become truly motivating until it has the structure of a clear measure in place.

★ *A goal without a measure is a dream, not a target.*

Challenging

Coachees tend to set goals that are limited by their own lack of self-belief and fear of failure, for instance:

Find a new coachee

instead of

Win three corporate contracts

These questions and statements can help the coachee rise above such limitations:

- If all obstacles were removed, what would the goal be?
- If you don't achieve the goal, you won't go to jail or have your head cut off.
- What do you really want?
- What can you give yourself permission to aim for?

Something else that gets in the way is when a coachee has been diverted from his or her true nature, often at an early age and usually by a parent or seminal influence. People can live out their whole lives driven by a 'mission statement' overlaid on them by someone else. I knew of one coachee who exclaimed during coaching, 'It was my mother who married him – not me!' What she meant was that all her life she had been living her mother's mission statement, not her own, even to the point of using her mother's criteria to choose a husband.

If you sense that something like this may be happening, some useful questions to ask are:

- What is your mission statement in life?
- Is your mission statement yours or someone else's?
- If not yours, whose might it be?
- What do you know now about your mission statement?

While reflecting on this, coachees may find their mission statements change. To ensure the coachee ends this exercise in the present and not the past, finish with some of these questions:

- ■ And what do you know about your mission statement now?
- ■ What else do you know about your mission statement now?
- ■ And is there anything else about your mission statement now?
- ■ And what would you like your mission statement to be?

Ensure that the coachee is left in a positive place and looking forward, not backward, by asking further open questions with a forward focus until he or she is comfortable.

Trainees often ask what will happen if coachees fail to reach their goal. Will they be depressed or worse off than before? This is never a problem, because it is the journey rather than the destination that is valuable. The new discoveries that coachees make about themselves along the way usually mean more to them than the goal did in the first place. What is crucial is that coachees set a target that is inspiring enough to engage their whole commitment, however difficult it may seem at the start.

Time-framed

We have found that the ideal time period for a goal is 12 weeks; it takes six weeks to break an old habit and six weeks to ingrain a new one. Twelve weeks is long enough to achieve a serious goal and short enough to maintain motivation. If the coachee is able to work with you only once a month, then a six-month goal will be more effective.

Of one focus

The goal-setting process often reaches a stage where a number of elements are identified, such as '£5000 a month working in the city and keeping my work–life balance with my boyfriend'. It is impossible to focus on something so broad. Work with the coachee to find one focus that will cover all the others, or divide the goal into several separate goals.

The way to decide whether goals are separate is to ask the coachee to consider roughly what the pathway would be to each goal. If the same things need to be done, then the two goals are one and the focus should be on the element that incorporates the final stage of the journey. If the actions required to reach each goal are completely different, then you know you are looking at two separate goals.

One focus

Succinct

A goal consisting of only a few words acts like a mantra which can stay in the coachee's mind, working for the coachee all the time. For example:

A six-grand speaking event

instead of

Getting my public speaking to the level where I can charge £6,000 a performance

25 per cent legacy

instead of

25 per cent of the kids who have never done sport before will feel enabled by my workshops providing a legacy for them to reach their full potential in the future

As energetic as I was 10 years ago

instead of

An energetic size 12 with my old enthusiasm back

Short, snappy goals are far more effective at engaging the reticular activating system, which is explained in the next section.

The difference between EXACT and SMART

The traditional business model for setting goals is SMART:

Specific
Measurable
Agreed (or Achievable)
Realistic
Time-framed

SMART goals

Although a SMART goal is sometimes positive, it can result in a negative goal, such as 'give up smoking' or 'lose 2 stone'. Goals like these carry all the baggage of past failure and future deprivation; they are chores instead of magnets.

SMART goals may work for corporate goal setting, where targets set by managers for their employees must be realistic and will be about quantitative measures such as profit or number of sales. It is very unlikely that such a goal would be negative.

However, for performance coaching a different approach is required, hence the inclusion of 'EXciting' and 'Challenging' in the EXACT model.

'Realistic' is not included because I have never found a coachee who set goals too high. Coachees' goals are often limited by lack of confidence, whereas a manager setting corporate goals for the staff runs the risk of setting them too high and discouraging people; hence the inclusion of Realistic in SMART.

'Agreed' is not included in EXACT because this refers to agreement with the organization, and it is essential in coaching that a coachee's goals are owned by the coachee and remain completely confidential.

The reticular activating system

There is a neurological reason why positive goals work: they trigger an area in the brain called the *reticular activating system* (RAS). Have you ever bought a new car and then noticed that everyone was driving one? Of course, the other drivers were always there, you just never noticed them before. The RAS filters out 99 per cent of our sensory input, allowing us to notice only what is relevant to us at the current time. Therefore, if you identify a goal that is powerful and attractive to you, the RAS will throw up opportunities which you might otherwise have missed. It is said that once you set a goal, the universe brings it to you; this may well be true, and I have no idea how the universe works, but if it does fulfil goals, I would not be at all surprised if it used the RAS to do so.

Neural pathways   So if we hypothesize that you are the coachee and your goal is 'Be in my dream career,' your RAS might cause you to notice an article in the paper that relates to your goal and flags up a possibility you had not thought of before. Alternatively, the pointer could be getting into a conversation about careers with a stranger at a party and discovering he has connections with precisely the company you want to join – which you will know because of the action you set with your coach to research all the types of companies offering the sort of position that would satisfy you. These 'coincidences' seem to crop up all the time when you know what you are looking for.

A common technique used by champion golfers is to imagine playing the winning shot: they picture the lead-in, the exact trajectory, hitting the target and the ovation from the spectators. The reason that this technique is successful is that the subconscious mind cannot distinguish between fact and fiction: that is why we get goosebumps while watching a scary film, or why we cry when a character in a novel dies. By imagining the winning shot, new neural pathways are created in the brain and information is stored that appears to the subconscious to be a memory. The mind is tricked into believing that the player knows how to make the shot, and it is easier to repeat behaviour than to do it for the first time.

By asking coachees to focus on the 'future reality' ('G' of the GROW model) and describe it in detail, you are helping them to forge neural pathways in their brains which will make it easier for them to achieve their dreams.

In conclusion, the purpose of delving so deeply, instead of accepting the goals coachees initially propose, is to ensure that the goal you are going to work on together for the next three or six months is absolutely congruent with the coachee's values and needs and is one which will inspire the coachee to achieve deep-seated changes in his or her life and behaviour.

For more information on setting goals within a session, see Chapter 4.

Exercise

1. Set up some time when you can practise with your partner for half an hour each.
2. Start by asking what your partner wants to achieve out of this session, then work through the GROW model for 10 minutes, using awareness questions, permission, clarifying and reflecting.
3. At the end, ask each other these questions:
   - What did you learn about yourself?
   - What new insights did you obtain?
   - What do you know now about your issue that you did not know before?
   - What action would you like to take about the issue?
   - When, where, how?

   Each write down as many actions as required.
4. End the practice session by giving each other feedback.
5. Fill in the values questionnaire in Chapter 8 (page 120).

4

Structure

Most people find that one coaching session alone will bring them new enlightenment, and it is not so very unusual to feel that one's whole life has been changed, as long as the coach follows the skills and models which I have outlined so far. However, although a single session is likely to leave a coachee highly motivated, old habits die hard, and without further support, the initial enthusiasm may fade and everything will return to the way it was before. Therefore I recommend coaching to a structure. I share the one that I use below.

THE COACHING SERIES

Working with a coachee over a period of time ensures that:

- the groundwork is laid for effective action;
- plans can be worked out and followed through;
- the coachee is supported through unexpected challenges;
- old habits are permanently replaced by new ones.

Habits I have found that it takes around six weeks to break an old habit and another six to ingrain a new one. Therefore an ideal length of time for a coaching series is three months, or possibly six if sessions are less frequent than once a week. The time between the sessions is dictated by the amount of time a coachee has available and what issues are being addressed.

Some coaches work with coachees on a session by session basis. This might result in coach and coachee working together for only one or two sessions, or in a relationship that lasts for years. Some senior executives will fix a monthly fee with a coach, during which time they are permitted to call on the services of the coach as and when coaching is required.

There are advantages to setting goals to work on over a fixed period, in that coachees will have a sense of what they can expect to achieve over that period and therefore know how much it is going to cost them. Some coachees are wary of becoming 'coach dependent', although an effective coach should ensure that this does not happen.

One pitfall is that if sessions are too far apart, the coachee can lose motivation and the coaching goes to waste. Ideally, therefore, sessions should be no more than one or two weeks apart. A great deal of the benefit occurs between sessions, when coachees are exercising their new-found knowledge and taking action in the knowledge that they will be held accountable in the next session.

I work to four basic types of session: introductory, strategic planning, intermediate and final, all of which are described more fully later in this chapter.

LENGTH OF SESSIONS

On average, the length of coaching sessions varies between half an hour and two hours. Outside of these parameters, whole teams can be coached for 15 minutes apiece, one after the other, or one coachee for an entire morning.

Fifteen minutes might not sound like very long but I have known people achieve extraordinary insights about their entire lives or careers by taking a quick spin through the GROW model. A coaching session that extends over periods of longer than two hours is likely to include some exercises, games and unstructured conversations to keep the coachee's (not to mention the coach's) attention focused.

In addition, informal coaching can take place around the water fountain or in the lift, when it is possible to offer the one key question that could change someone's entire perspective in a moment. This type of informal coaching is invaluable for managers who may not have time to give individual formal sessions to their staff.

There are only two things to take into account when setting the time period for a formal coaching session: what is best for the coach and what is best for the coachee. In the case of a personal coach who is working on the phone and wants to fit as many sessions as possible into a day, there will have to be enough time in between each session to prepare for the next one (a minimum of 10 minutes to re-read the coachee's notes), and for a comfort break. A 40-minute session is probably ideal for this, although the coachee may get more depth and progress out of an hour.

Corporate sessions are often longer, and the coach is usually paid on an hourly, half-day or day rate. A session that lasts longer than an hour tends to unwind at a more relaxed pace, which can be beneficial or otherwise, depending upon the coachee. An analogy is to compare a short, sharp workout at the gym to a session of slow, measured yoga. They both have their time and place.

Managing the time   The key points are that coach and coachee should agree the length of sessions in advance, and that once agreed, the coach must ensure that the times are adhered to. Time is part of the process of coaching and therefore under the management of the coach. If time runs short in a session, it does not mean the coach is at fault; an area loaded with content may have been discovered and the coachee will have gained great benefit from exploring it. However, in that case the coach should keep an eye on the clock and say something like, 'We have 20 minutes left. Do you want to stay with this or make time to talk about other areas?'

There must always be time at the end of the session to close comfortably, set or check the actions and arrange the next session. It is acceptable for a session to run for longer than planned provided both coachee and coach agree.

EARLY TERMINATION AND CANCELLATION

There may come a time when the relationship ends earlier than envisaged or contracted for. This could happen for a variety of reasons, including:

- A personal coachee (someone who is paying for the coaching personally) finds that his or her financial situation has changed.
- The issue for which the coachee required coaching has resolved itself.
- The coachee appears to require a different intervention, such as therapy or counselling.
- The coaching is not making a difference.
- The coachee is behaving in a way that is contrary to the coach's values.

If the coach has been contracted for a certain period of time, and it is the coachee who cancels, the decision on whether to enforce the financial commitment regardless of the fact that the sessions have stopped is up to the individual coach.

My own stand on this is, in general, to charge for the sessions that have taken place but not for the sessions that have been cancelled. I have had two personal experiences of this. In the first, I had a contract for 12 sessions with an executive who was paying for the coaching herself. Her financial situation changed dramatically and I asked her if she would like me to recommend her to a coach with lower fees or terminate the coaching altogether. I did not feel this situation warranted offering free sessions as she was a highly paid executive. We agreed she would move to a cheaper coach and I passed over my notes. I refunded the advance payment she had made for sessions that would not now take place.

In the other case, I did three sessions with a senior executive and it seemed to me that we were going round in circles, possibly because she felt she 'should' change but was not committed to it. None of my techniques appeared to be making any difference, so I gave her the option of ending the arrangement earlier than our contract permitted, which she accepted. I charged the organization only for the sessions which we had completed, although it would have been within my right to charge for the full course.

There are also times when a coachee cancels a session without notice. Again, it is up to the individual coach to decide what to do. It is recommended that a cancellation charge and time period is specified in the initial contract (see a sample in Appendix C). However, for me personally, I am always busy and it is nothing but a relief when a session is cancelled and frees up time for something else! It gives me the added advantage of being able to feel comfortable if I need to postpone a session at some point, perhaps because of an unexpected speaking engagement or similar. Then again, I would charge for a cancelled session if I felt the reasons for cancellation were not genuine and that the coachee was not treating either coach or coaching with respect. I always include a cancellation schedule in the contract.

None of the above scenarios should be taken as a recommendation; coaches have a right to run their coaching businesses in the same way as any other industry, and to charge cancellation fees for time booked or early termination of a contract.

THE INTRODUCTORY SESSION

Most personal coaches (where the individual is paying) **Free first session** offer the first session free of charge; it is difficult to explain what coaching is and more efficient to demonstrate its benefits, after which the coachee will have a clear idea of whether a programme is likely to be of benefit. If the coachee and coach decide to go ahead (and this is not just the coachee's decision – the coach must feel there is a good fit too), then the first session can be included in the billing. If the potential coachee does not go ahead, then the session has cost nothing. Coachees are usually happy with this arrangement as long as it is clearly explained to them at the start.

In a corporate setting it is not the custom to deliver free sessions; a company will always expect to be billed for the coach's time. However, the coach will probably have put in more unpaid time in marketing and nurturing the relationship than in a private coaching programme.

GOAL SETTING

The best way of demonstrating to coachees the value of coaching is to spend the first session setting a goal or goals which they might not have set by themselves, either because you have motivated them to set their sights higher than before, or because you have helped them obtain clarity and awareness about their lives and where they want to be. A good session will probably provide a combination of both.

Finding out what the coachee's most deeply desired goals are is fundamental to the success of coaching, and since coaching is about change, it is not unusual for goals to change midway through a series of coaching sessions as new insight is gained. Some coaches start a session by asking 'What is your goal?' However, a large number of coachees come to coaching precisely because they are not at all sure what it is that they want.

Modern life throws up a bewildering number of options in every area: some of our grandparents considered themselves privileged if they managed a holiday once a year and the cinema once a week. It did not take long to decide what film to see: there was only one choice and it showed for a week then moved on. If you missed the film, there was no chance of seeing it again – there were no televisions, let alone satellite movie channels.

On the job front, you considered yourself fortunate to find one and you would hang on to it until the retirement clock was presented at the age of 65. As far as relationships were concerned, many couples remained in intolerable relationships because there were no other social or financial possibilities.

Sorting the options available to us today takes up a great deal of our time and energy. We not only have hundreds of holiday destinations to choose from, there are wide variations in costs and activities. The 'portfolio' career is becoming common – like it or not – and it is quite possible to find yourself stuck in a job precisely because there are so many career options out there that it is impossible to make a decision about where to move. When it comes to the variety of marital, romantic and sexual combinations available – hetero, homo, monogamy, adultery, casual, committed, childless, parental, Platonic – well! It is amazing we have time to think about anything else at all, isn't it?

Coachees often say they have an inner sense of a 'pathway' – a 'life's purpose' perhaps, or the 'mission statement' we spoke of earlier – but that they cannot identify what it is. They are not afraid of hard work and sacrifice, but without being certain where they are going, cannot summon up the commitment to get there. To return to the analogy of Alice's *Wonderland*, such a place should be a treasure trove of experiences and opportunities – shouldn't it? Yet there is a pervading sense throughout the book of confusion, and occasionally fear, both of which surface all too often in our lives.

Modern life is not unlike Alice's domain. In the western world today, compared with the middle of the last century, we enjoy an almost universally high standard of living. A teacher once told me that in her school days in England during the 1930s some of the children were allowed to wear their school-issue gym shoes all day, because they had no shoes of their own. In 1940s America, Elvis Presley started high school in bare feet. Such situations are unthinkable in western society today, and in theory educational and career opportunities are available to all. Yet this plethora of opportunities can have a reverse effect, with choices so wide creating nothing but anxiety, disillusionment and resentment. Now that anything seems possible, where do we begin? One of the saddest effects of this is the high suicide rate among young adults, and particularly the ones who often seem to be the most talented, attractive and high-achieving of their generation.

So if you ask coachees straight off, 'What's your goal?' then spend an hour coaching them on how to reach that goal, it is possible that the wrong goal will have been set in the first place and the time wasted. It pays to spend time exploring the current reality. Get an overview of everything that is happening in the coachee's life, not just the problem areas but the good stuff too. This phase relates to the Reality section of the GROW model described in Chapter 3 and will bring a life into perspective.

Once the Reality has been explored, ask coachees to outline the Options they have for possible goals, with questions like 'And what would you like to have happen?' Sometimes it helps to focus first on five years from now, then one year, and then bring it down to what the coachee could achieve in the next three months. These time periods can be varied according to the coachee's issues, but the final goal will work best if it is set three or six months ahead. This process is described in more detail in Chapter 3.

Holistic goal setting

It is quite likely that there will be more than one area that needs sorting out in the coachee's life. Many people want to set a big career or business goal, but if other parts of their lives are holding them back, such as their fitness levels or relationships, these will act like a sea anchor throughout the whole coaching series and drag them backwards. If we set several goals holistically – covering the coachee's whole life instead of just one area – the coachee is much more likely to succeed.

Prioritize the goals

Once you have the coachee's list of goals, which will probably be somewhere between two and seven, ask the coachee to prioritize them. Some of the goals will be simple, like 'Get the study decorated' or 'Buy a new computer,' and the coachee would not need to work with a coach to achieve them. These types of goals can sit on a list which you check in on once a month during the coaching to see what progress has been made. It is satisfying for the coachee to tick them off, one by one, as they get done. Some may have been hanging around, draining energy, for years. Just highlighting what needs to be done and getting it down on paper is often enough to trigger action.

Other goals will be bigger, and coachees should be encouraged to set their sights higher than they may have done before. Try to get them to couch the goal in short sound bites like 'Be in my dream job' or 'Exchange on a new house.' Try to get some pizzazz into them, like 'Sizzling size 8 Suzie.' A short, punchy goal will stick in the coachee's mind and act like a magnet, drawing the coachee towards it.

Complex goals, which are the ones you will work on for months, should be in completely separate areas; otherwise they will start to collapse into each other as the coachee moves towards them. In a corporate setting, coachees may wish to set goals solely around their jobs or businesses. Although these goals are all in the one area, as long as you ensure that the pathway to each goal will be different it is fine to do this.

If your sessions are at least an hour long, you can probably work comfortably on two or three goals during each session. The coachee should decide which goals are complex enough to be worked on during every session, and which can go onto the simple goals list for checking on from time to time.

It is not uncommon for coachees to achieve a goal that they had thought would take months in a matter of weeks. Reaching the clarity to identify a goal is sometimes all that is needed to make it happen. If you are working to a fixed series, such as 12 weeks, you can give coachees the option of either setting another goal to be worked on over the remaining time period, or concentrating on the goal or goals that they already have.

If two or three inspiring goals have been identified by the end of the first session, the coachee will now have a sense of:

- being able to achieve the goals;
- knowing how long it will take;
- knowing how much it will cost.

Anxiety over the expense of open-ended coaching is avoided by setting a fixed time period. If the coachee wishes to continue with the coaching after the fixed time period, you could start all over again with another goal-setting session and another contract signed for a further period.

SECOND SESSION: STRATEGIC PLANNING

You have completed an inspiring introductory session, set some powerful goals, booked the next session and left a coachee brimming with enthusiasm to get started. The time for the next session comes around and you may be faced with a coachee full of doubts. How could I have set my sights so high? How will I find the time, the energy, the talent, the courage?

Because the nature of EXACT goal-setting challenges coachees to raise their sights, it is not uncommon for doubts to surface later. On the other hand, they might be so full of enthusiasm that they want to rush into the final stages of the project without adequate research or preparation.

Let us suppose you want to decorate your house; you choose a divine paint colour and can't wait to see it on the wall. So instead of stripping, drilling, filling and smoothing first, you slap on your gorgeous colour – and lose heart halfway through because of the tacky result. The outcome is that the wall remains half-painted for the next six months while you tell yourself that pressures of work, life or watching television are getting in the way.

This is not what you want to have happen with your coachees. First, you will not get the satisfaction of having made a difference, which is probably why you became a coach in the first place, and second, they will not recommend you to other potential clients. Creating a plan has a number of benefits:

- The coachee stands back and looks at the whole picture and all its component parts. If we think of the goal as a tree, you will facilitate the coachee in considering the leaves, the branches, the trunk, and the whole forest in which the tree stands. This enables the coachee to reach a new level of awareness.
- Working through the 'baby steps' of a strategic plan is less daunting than facing the challenge of the end goal every day.
- A plan gives the coach an understanding of the shape of what is to come, enabling the coach to keep the coachee on track.

The second session is spent taking the goals one at a time and brainstorming with the coachee how to reach them. Start with a simple question: 'What steps do you need to take to reach this goal?' The coachee will come up with a jumble of actions. Returning to the analogy of the tree, some actions will relate to the leaves, some to the trunk and some to the entire forest.

The coach's job is to assist the coachee in sorting these actions into categories, to form a series of strategies which will take the coachee to the goal. There will probably be between three and ten broad strategies. After you have helped the coachee to shape the action sets into strategies, ask him or her to put them into chronological order. You may find that some strategies will occur concurrently. Where possible use the coachee's words, but you are more at liberty to suggest words during this planning session than during normal coaching.

The strategic plan for a small business might look something like this:

Sample strategic plans

1. Create the vision.
2. Assess current reality.
3. Create time schedule.
4. Research.
5. Create materials.
6. Identify potential coachees.
7. Contact potential coachees.
8. Close the deal.
9. Celebrate the achievement.

For a career goal the coachee might do this:

1. Create the vision.
2. Assess current reality.
3. Create time schedule.
4. Research.
5. Create CV.
6. Identify potential companies to approach.
7. Contact companies.
8. Get the job.
9. Celebrate the achievement.

For a sports goal, this could be the plan:

1. Create a schedule.
2. Watch my diet.
3. Monitor my performance.
4. Win the event.

Although the actions within each of the above strategies might be quite different, there is a similarity in shape in all these cases. Do not take any of these plans as a blueprint: it is important to facilitate coachees in creating strategic plans that suit their own needs, not one made up of the things you might do if you were in their shoes.

A coachee will not normally come up with strategies like 'Create the vision' and 'Celebrate the achievement.' However, many coachees welcome these suggestions because they add inspiration and motivation to the journey. Coachees may couch their strategies in very different words from those above; for instance 'Create the vision' might mean writing a page about the goal, or creating a vision board where they stick relevant pictures, or writing the goal on a

Post-it and sticking it on their shaving mirror. 'Create the vision'-type strategies are about finding a way to ingrain the goal and keep it at the forefront of the coachee's mind.

'Celebrate the achievement' could be a reward at the end or a series of rewards when certain stages are reached.

If you suggest these strategies and neither appeals to the coachee, remember to let them go. It is the coachee who will have to tread the pathway, not you, the coach.

After you have created a strategic plan for a goal, ask the coachee **Actions** what actions he or she would like to take as a first step. If you set a few actions after each goal, coachees will end up with a sense of having achieved something tangible out of the planning session, and of being on their pathway to their goals.

We have explored the process for setting actions in the W section on the GROW model in Chapter 3, and I will enlarge on that only slightly here.

You will be setting actions throughout the remaining sessions; after the planning session, the time to ask the coachee for an action is when the coachee arrives at a new insight, in order to pin it down to concrete steps that will lead to change:

What action you would like to take around that?
How will you do that?
When will you do that?
Is there anything you need to do before that?

There are times when coachees set actions because they **Knee-jerk actions** feel it is expected of them. This is a subtle trap and one of the most common pitfalls for coaches. For instance, let us imagine that you are coaching a woman about her untidiness. It is clear to both of you that she needs to start tidying up; she does not need to pay a coach to find that out, so you can assume that there is something more complicated getting in the way. If you ignore that possibility and ask for an action straight off, she may well say, 'Make up a schedule to tidy one area a week,' but it is unlikely she will actually do the action. If she could, why has she not done it before now?

The key to setting actions is to understand that:

Actions must be set only when impetus drives the coachee to act.

This is the truth at the heart of coaching. If you can get this right, everything else will fall into place. In coaching, actions are not chores; when the coachee reaches a new level of awareness, action will become irresistible. This is why John Whitmore declared 'awareness' to be one of the foundations of coaching.

Two questions beg to be asked here:

Q   *How do we get a coachee's 'impetus' into 'driving' mode?*
A   Use the GROW model (Goal, Reality, Options, Will). All the work you have been doing on exploring the coachee's life, setting goals and

digging for insights will have freed the coachee from some inner 'blocks' and ignited his or her enthusiasm. Asking open questions is like peeling an onion: each question reveals another layer to the coachee until a core of inner certainty is reached. The word 'insight' means literally to 'see inside'. The new knowledge found there acts like a springboard, catapulting the coachee into action. When coachees reach a new insight, it is hard to stop them taking action even if you want to. If you have the patience not to rush these explorations, you cannot fail to awaken hidden knowledge and make a difference.

Q   *How can we be sure that coachees are not simply setting the action because it is expected of them?*

A   When a new insight occurs, the body becomes charged with energy. Coachees will suddenly sit upright, smile or change position. On the telephone, their voices become lighter, more colourful and lyrical.

An action that arises from the impetus of a genuine insight will significantly change the tone or look of the coachee. If you sense there is no energy behind setting the action, remember the maxim, 'Ask the coachee.' Check it out by asking questions like:

> How committed are you to doing that action?
> Is that what you really want to do?
> How do you feel about doing that?
> Is that the right action for you to take?
> I have a sense that you are not really committed to doing that action – is that the case?

Either the coachee will insist on doing the action, or some doubt will surface. If this happens, then go back to the GROW model and ask more Reality and Goal questions until new insight is reached.

You can expect to uncover several new insights and actions during a session. Not all of them will be life-changing. That may only happen two or three times during the whole series!

INTERMEDIATE SESSIONS

From the second session onwards, the coach is working with the coachee to move towards the goals. Additionally, at a deeper level the coachee is gaining new layers of awareness, insight and self-knowledge which will provide whatever changes are required to reach his or her goals.

A second factor in helping coachees towards their goals is accountability: having set a series of actions, coachees feel uncomfortable if they come to the next session without having completed them. If they are paying out of their own pockets for the coaching, they will have a sense of wasting their money too.

The coach spends the sessions between the first and the last in reviewing actions set in the previous session, goal by goal, looking for insights and sign-posting the way forward with new actions, which should always be set by the coachee, facilitated by the coach.

The primary tool in play here is the GROW model, **Reviewing actions** using lots of open questions, such as:

> How do you feel about that?
> What is the impact of that?
> What did you learn from that?

A long list of useful questions for creating awareness is given in Appendix A.

As well as questioning, the key to reviewing a coachee's actions effectively is to use liberal amounts of clarifying and reflecting, as described in Chapter 2. This will help the coachee's thought processes and progress towards the goals.

When the coachee has reached an insight, highlight it by asking more specific questions such as:

> How important is that insight to you?
> Is there anywhere else in your life you could apply that knowledge?

Both coach and coachee should make a note of important insights on their respective worksheets (see Appendix B for coach and coachee worksheets). They will come in useful when reviewing the coaching series in the final session.

What happens when coachees come to sessions **Actions not completed** without having done their actions? This is an excellent learning opportunity and a chance to uncover new insights. Work through the situation, asking open questions until you see signs of energy, then channel that energy into action. One of the most common reasons a coachee will give for not having completed an action is lack of time. It is worth checking this out, sensitively, to see whether procrastination is coming into play:

> Can I ask whether it was about not having the time, or might you have put other things in the way to avoid having to do this?

At the end of each session, always ensure the coachee is left in a comfortable and positive place, by using questions and comments such as:

> What do you know now about your goals?
> Is there anything else you would like to say before we close this session?
> Well done for being so honest during this session.
> I really admire the way you get things done.

The end of a session is an excellent chance to give coachees some positive feed-back which will encourage their progress during the period before the next session.

How to handle tears

First aid It is possible that some buried emotions may surface during the coaching process, bringing feelings of sadness or depression for the coachee and taking the coach into the territories of therapy and counselling. To bring the coachee back to a forward focus, you can ask questions like:

> Is there a question you would like me to ask to help you with this?
> What do you need to say to help you feel better about this?
> What needs to be in place to move you forward on this?

At times like this it is particularly important to ensure that the content is coachee-led and that you are in charge of the process, supporting the coachee in finding a more positive state of mind. If you feel out of your depth, simply ask, 'Would you prefer to work with a therapist on this?' On the whole, coaching is a positive process which people are drawn to because they are ready to move forward, and traumatic moments are rare.

Reviewing the strategic plan

Once you have formulated a strategic plan in the second session, it is useful to review it regularly during the coaching series, say once a month. Review the list of simple goals regularly too, and set actions for them if need be. It is a good idea to ask coachees how the coaching is going for them from time to time as well. There is not much point in waiting until the end of the series when there is no time to do anything about it. Ask for feedback on what they like about what you are doing and whether there is anything they would like you to do differently.

During the penultimate session, check the strategic plan, the simple goals and how far coachees have to go to get to their main goal or goals. This is their chance to make a last-ditch effort to reach the goals.

FINAL SESSION

The keynote here is for coachees to see how far they have come, to celebrate their achievements and to provide closure on the whole series. Even if they have already decided to book another series of sessions, these elements are important.

Taking the session goal by goal, start by briefly reviewing the actions set in the previous session. Then review major insights and turning points during the series. Finally, ask them how close they are to reaching the goal, expressed as a percentage. Give plenty of positive feedback whether or not they have reached the goal. Ask if they would like to record their new insights in case they are needed again further down the line.

When you have reviewed all the goals, you can ask coachees for feedback and, if they are willing, for a testimonial for your marketing literature. Make it clear that you are comfortable whether the answer is 'Yes' or 'No' and that they can choose to remain anonymous, if they prefer.

Feedback and testimonials

Some coaches offer a free follow-up session, or suggest a paid check-in session, say three months down the line. If the coachee does not want to book another series immediately, you can offer to make contact at a later date or invite the coachee to contact you.

If you feel it is appropriate, follow the coaching series up with a thank-you note or celebratory card.

STRUCTURE WITHIN A SESSION

After the first session, topping and tailing the sessions with some short, regular exercises helps to give the coaching series additional structure.

Dale Carnegie once said:

> Say what you're going to say, then say it, then say what you have said.

He was referring to the art of public speaking at the time, but the principle sits well with a coaching session, in order to focus the attention of both coach and coachee and ingrain any new learning. Set out below are some examples of how a coach might do this.

Setting the scene

Wherever you are in a session, it helps to let coachees know what is going to happen. Doing this makes people feel safe, creates rapport, and enables them to relax and concentrate better.

Do this:

- at the beginning of a session, by telling the coachee how the session will be structured;
- at the beginning of a coaching series, sharing the shape of the time ahead;
- whenever you introduce a new model or practice like the ones described below.

This process harks back to our analogy of being a stranger in a strange land: what you take for granted may not be expected now that you are a visitor in the coachee's culture.

Bouquets and baggage

Life today is complicated; at any one time, most of us are carrying around in our heads six or seven duties, obligations or anticipated pleasures and they are often in completely separate areas. No one can concentrate with that amount of clamour going on, so asking people to dump their bouquets and baggage at the start of every session helps to clear their minds so that they can concentrate on the task ahead.

'Bouquets' refer to positive distractions, like going on holiday the following week. 'Baggage' covers the anxieties and obstacles we have to deal with in everyday life.

Start each session by asking coachees what their bouquets and baggage are this week, then ask how they feel and how they can put these distractions aside. This could be by making a straightforward statement, like 'I'll put that aside,' or using a metaphor, such as 'I'm locking it all away in a filing cabinet' or 'I'm kicking it right out of the door.' Some people take a deep breath and breathe their worries away, while others use a silent process in their heads and simply tell you when they are ready and focused.

Deal with the items one at a time. Usually the baggage will surface first, and once that is gone, positive distractions appear. When this happens there is an added benefit in demonstrating to the coachee how negative aspects can hide positive ones. For example:

Coach:	What's on your mind that might distract you during this session?
Coachee:	The sale on our flat hasn't gone through yet.
Coach:	How do you feel about that?
Coachee:	Really worried. If it falls through we're in big trouble.
Coach:	Can you put that worry aside for the rest of this session? We can talk about it later, during the session, if you want to.
Coachee:	I'm putting it up on a high shelf where it can't distract me.
Coach:	And is there anything else?
Coachee:	I've been invited to speak at a conference next month.
Coach:	How do you feel about that?
Coachee:	Scared stiff and excited!
Coach:	How can you put those feelings aside?
Coachee:	I'm putting aside the 'scared stiff' – now. And I'm putting aside the 'excited' – now.

Notice that the coach is asking the coachee to put aside not the subject of the distraction, but the emotions associated with it. During this process, it is important to ensure that the coachee has dealt with each item specifically.

The process works successfully in meetings too. If **Meeting techniques** you are chairing a meeting, you can begin by asking people if they have anything to offload that might distract them during the meeting. Go first yourself, to demonstrate, and then work round the table. If someone arrived late, for instance, she or he may not be able to concentrate until an explanation has been made.

Revisit the goals

At the beginning of each session, ask coachees to tell you in a word or two how they feel about their goals right now. Their response doesn't have to be positive – they may well say 'cynical' or 'scared'. You just want a snapshot of where they are at with the goals at the moment. No coaching takes place at this point. Both coach and coachee should write down the response and move on.

The purpose of this is to refocus the coachee's attention on the goals and to flag up for both coach and coachee the shape of the work to come. This practice also reminds the coachee exactly what the goals are. Quite often, after you have both spent the previous session carefully working out exact wording which would most motivate the coachee, a coachee will repeat the goal back at the start of the second session using different words, which may not capture the inspiration or the measure as well as the original.

Sometimes the coachee will need to change the wording of a goal during the coaching series, or even the direction of the goal itself. This is all fine: coaching is about change, so it is natural that sometimes the goals change too. If this comes up during the goal revisit, let the coachee know that you will return to this later in the session when dealing with that particular goal.

Session outcome

After revisiting the goals, find out what the coachee would like to achieve during that session. After the brief review, the coachee will be well placed to do this. The session outcome could relate to all the goals, or to one specifically. It is like a mini-goal for the session.

This technique is useful not only during a coaching session but also in the context of meetings or one's personal life. For instance, you could set yourself an outcome for the day or for the week ahead. Setting an outcome for a period of time works in the same way as setting a long-term goal: it gets your unconscious mind as well as your conscious one working towards the goal.

Other benefits of setting a session outcome are:

■ ensuring that the coach and coachee/s are going in the same direction;
■ checking that everyone is happy with that direction;

■ setting a benchmark so that later the coachee can measure how far he or she has come.

The session outcome is always expressed positively, so rather than 'feel less anxious' you would say 'feel more confident'. It can be visionary, like a goal, although you would not spend more than a minute deciding upon it.

Examples

In a session:

> See a clear path towards my goals.
> Get some movement on Goal 2.

For self:

> Work as a team with my colleagues.
> Eat healthily.

In a meeting:

> Get clarity on Item 4 of the Staff Review plan.
> Reach an agreement around item 3 on the agenda.

Closure

At the end of a session, we ensure that we leave the coachee in a comfortable place. Closure is an opportunity to give coachees some recognition on what they have achieved, to refer back to the session outcome, to mark how far they have come, and to deal with any aspects that have been left hanging during the session. The coach closes before the coachee in order to model the process.

For example:

> Well done for losing two pounds this week. You said at the beginning of the session you wanted to get some clarity about the many options facing you in your career goal, and you seem to have achieved that. Is there anything you would like to say to close the session?

Closing a meeting If you use the technique of setting an outcome for a meeting, you can round it off nicely by using the closure process, referring back to the desired outcome, marking what has been achieved and giving some positive feedback to the group, as individuals and as a whole.

The same applies if you use this technique on yourself – at the end of the time period, measure how far you have come and be sure to recognize what you have achieved more than what you did not.

Exercise

1. Before coming to your practice session, ensure that you have completed the Values Questionnaire from Chapter 8 (page 120).
2. Set up a situation with your practice partner where you will be uninterrupted for an hour.
3. Spend five minutes debriefing with your partner on the Values Questionnaire by asking some or all of the following questions. You can ask other open questions if they seem appropriate. Let your partner do most of the talking and reflect your partner's words back as well as asking questions. Make a note of any new insights arising from the exercise and then swap over:
   - What have you learnt about yourself?
   - What new insights do you have?
   - What impact is this having on your life?
   - What impact on your work?
   - What is the impact of not changing?
   - How would you like it to be?
   - Is there anything you would like to do about it?
   - When/where/how?
4. Work through a goal-setting session using the GROW model, and set at least one goal which complies with the EXACT criteria.
5. Remember to use questioning, clarifying, reflecting and permission.
6. Write your goals down.
7. Give each other feedback.

5

Training as a coach

The coaching industry is as yet unregulated, so anyone can set up as a coach without training or qualifications. However, it takes more than a telephone and a pair of ears to make a good coach.

Training is essential in order to understand how to implement the core principles of coaching. Nevertheless, there exist consultants, therapists, counsellors and former executives who describe themselves as 'coaches' without any real understanding of the current meaning of the word, in order to take advantage of the growing market.

Fortunately, however, most of the people attracted to the profession are precisely the ones who are likely to make good coaches. They are people with integrity who like helping others and enjoy making a difference. Anyone without this incentive would very quickly tire of spending an hour on the phone focused entirely on the coachee's agenda, and would probably not be much help to the coachee anyway. I estimate that what makes a good coach is 80 per cent the person – empathy, focus and understanding – and 20 per cent the training.

In this chapter we look at the options available for training to become a professional coach, or an internal coach in an organization, or simply to acquire the skills required for managers to lead in a coaching style.

WHO CAN BECOME A COACH?

Natural skills People are sometimes described as being 'natural coaches'. However, no one is born with coaching skills; they are learnt at an early age from parents or other role models such as teachers or employers. It follows that anyone can be trained to be a good coach.

Coaching is like a happy virus – it spreads quickly because of the feel-good factor. If something is nice, people will want more of it. For so-called natural coaches, formal training is useful because it identifies the tools they already have and clarifies to them why these tools work so well. Others have partly developed coaching skills, and they take to the training like ducks to water – they usually find that the more fluent they become in a coaching style, the more comfortable they feel.

The third category of trainee comprises those who have no inherent coaching skills. They frequently come from backgrounds where directive management is the tradition, or they have been successful high-pressure sales people. These trainees find it harder than any others to learn coaching skills because their customary style is ingrained in the opposite direction. They are in the minority, as they are not usually attracted to learning how to coach at all. However, it is possible for them to absorb the new style of communication through intensive training, provided they make a determined effort to put old habits aside and absorb the new learning. After that, like any coach, they continue to learn and improve with every session.

The fourth category is the sector that trainers dislike working with – participants whose organizations have decided to send them on a coach training course whether they want it or not, which, human nature being what it is, immediately sets them against the programme altogether. I recall running a workshop where one senior executive, who had witnessed our first coaching demonstration of the day, exclaimed, 'This wouldn't work with my team. I'm the manager – I tell my team what to do and they do it!' While saying this, she sat bolt upright with her arms folded in front of her. Yet by lunchtime, after having tried the process out with a practice partner, she was hooked, and by the end of the training was one of the most vociferous supporters of coaching I have ever come across.

Coaching is not like other training – the effects are immediate and make communication so much easier that all trainees, however reluctant initially, soon lower their defences and join the party. Coach training is stimulating and fun – quite simply, people enjoy it.

LEVELS OF MASTERY IN COACHING

Different levels of mastery and training in coaching are called for, depending upon the outcome required. In simplistic terms there are three levels of coach:

- Line manager able to:
  - integrate coaching skills into the management style.
- Professional coach able to:

- deliver effective coaching sessions to individuals, whether corporate (the organization contracts and pays the coach) or personal (the individual contracts and pays);
- supervise/mentor other coaches.

■ Master coach able to:
- integrate models from other disciplines, such as the ones described in Chapter 8;
- deliver group and team coaching;
- supervise/mentor other coaches;
- train coaches;
- assess coaches;
- contribute to the theory of coaching by writing papers, delivering presentations etc.

The recommended standard of training required for each level is detailed below.

Line manager

A manager needs to be able to integrate the skills so that in any given situation the coaching toolbox comes to mind automatically. It may be thought that a two-day course in coaching skills can provide this. However, although all of the skills can be experienced in such a time period, it is not sufficient for them to be learnt or assimilated.

Let us take the analogy of driving a car. All of the basic skills are taught in the first lesson: accelerating, stopping, changing gear and turning corners. However, it will probably require several weeks of lessons, with practice in between, before the learner can drive competently and safely. There will also be some advanced skills to be covered, such as the emergency stop and how to reverse, and the meaning of all the signs the learner is likely to meet along the road.

For managers to successfully integrate coaching skills into their management style, it is recommended that their training takes place:

■ in a group of 6–24 trainees with a trainer ratio of 1:8;
■ over a period of at least one month:
- preferably for three sets of two-day sessions over three to six months;
- at least for one day plus one day, with a month in between;
■ with paired practice between the training sessions.

Professional coach

A minimum of four days training split over a month, followed by six months of monthly supervision/mentoring sessions which can take place individually or in a group, and face to face or by phone. Practice sessions with other trainees are essential here, along with a gradual transition to working with real coachees. It is during these sessions, both practising and with coachees, that the key learning takes place. These first six supervision/mentoring sessions should be run by a coach at master level, and will provide an arena for trainees to share their experiences, discuss challenges, obtain advice, build confidence and alleviate anxiety.

It is recommended that trainee coaches undergo some form of assessment to ensure that they are coaching competently. The various types of accreditation available are discussed in the next section.

Master coach

To achieve this level of competence, the coach is likely to have delivered at least 500 hours of coaching and undergone further training in various models which can be integrated into a coaching session. At present most coaches at this level have trained in at least two or three of the models mentioned in Chapter 8 (or others not included), but this is not to imply that a coach has to be familiar with them all.

CHOOSING A TRAINING SCHOOL

If you are an individual thinking about become a professional coach, or an individual manager wishing to join a course in order to integrate coaching skills into your management style, there are a bewildering number of options available throughout the world for public courses. Some of the criteria people use to choose their training school are:

- whether it shows up high in search engines;
- how many staff it claims to have;
- the quality of the glossy brochures and how frequently they are sent out;
- credentials awarded by a body or academic institution.

However, all that these tell you is that the organization is good at marketing or filling out forms. I am not saying that these criteria are without value, but they are not in themselves a guarantee of the quality of the training.

Training is an idiosyncratic subject, and one trainee's requirements may be quite different from another's. The sure ways to find out which training will give you what you require are:

1. Decide what it is you want out of the training. Some organizations will offer some or all of the following:

- a coaching model;
- a manual;
- a network of like-minded coaches;
- after-course support in the form of supervision/coach mentoring, and networking;
- work opportunities (but make sure these are not idle promises);
- an internal accreditation by the school.

2. Find coaches to network with (through coaching bodies like the Association for Coaching and the International Coaching Federation) and ask them about their training.
3. Ask the schools to put you in touch with people who have completed their training.
4. Make a shortlist of the schools that appeal to you, and try a session with one of their trained coaches – sample the merchandise.
5. Talk to the management and decide whether they are people you can like, respect and admire. Are they honest and ethical? Did they give you straight answers to all your questions?
6. Ask for the ratio of trainers to students on the courses and the maximum number of students allowed per course.
7. Attend any open events or workshops the organization is holding.
8. Ask for details of after-course support such as supervision/coach mentoring and continuing professional development.

And if you come across any of these, look for another coaching school:

What to avoid

- more than 25 on a course, whether by phone or face to face;
- a trainer ratio greater than one trainer to eight trainees;
- previous trainees given commission or goods in kind to recommend the course (if you get a recommendation, ask if this is the case, then wonder why the organization has to pay for recommendations: it is human nature to want to spread the word if you find something good).

Do not sign up for a course until you are absolutely certain it is the right one for you. Coach training is not cheap, and I have retrained quite a few coaches who failed to get the standard of training they were looking for first time around. The poorer the quality of the school, the less likely it is to refund your money.

The very great majority of coaching schools in the world today are honest and well-intentioned organizations delivering training to the best of their ability. However, one or two elements have crept in that regard the business as an opportunity to 'get rich quick'. Bear this in mind and they will not be hard to identify.

STYLE OF THE TRAINING

Coaching is a skill, like learning a language or how to drive a car. It is essential that the learning is expe-

Experiential learning

riential. A book like this or a correspondence course can get you on the road, but nothing will hone your skills so effectively as practical experience. If nothing else, you need to find out what it is that you don't know. The training can take place either face to face, by telephone or by listening to and interacting with CDs.

Remember when you first thought about driving a car? You were probably in the passenger seat next to a parent, enjoying the view and thinking that driving looked pretty easy. Now recall your first driving lesson. You discovered you had to put your foot on the clutch, control the gear lever and keep the car on the road – all at the same time. What? Impossible!

Yet how do you drive now? Have you ever taken the road to your gym instead of your home, because you are on such an automatic pilot you are thinking about something entirely different?

That is what it is like learning to coach. At first, talking like a coach feels awkward and you are convinced that you sound weird. With practice, it becomes more natural and your confidence grows as you see what your coaching can do for people. Finally, coaching becomes integrated into your personal style of communication and you find yourself using your skills with everyone, whenever appropriate – at work, at home and when talking to the plumber.

You will need a good source of training to understand what the techniques are and how they are used, then practise, practise and practise. Because of this, it is recommended that the training extends over a period of time – at least a few weeks – with practice in between.

I have heard managers say that they went on a three-day coaching skills course, loved what they learnt, then came back to 300 e-mails and did not think about coaching again for a week. By that time, they had forgotten most of what they had been taught. Some tried to put their new skills into action, awkwardly through insufficient practice, so crashed and burned and never risked using the skills again.

Imagine trying to drive a car after three days of lessons. Even if you have the best teacher in the

Embedding the skills

world you will have a hard time passing your driving test without some practice in between the sessions. Ideally, your coach training will incorporate formal lessons interspersed with practice with other students and eventually practice with potential coachees. Your trainers should be experienced coaches who can model the skills to a high standard.

I am indebted to Zoe Dawes of Chartwell Coaching (www.chartwellcoaching.co.uk) for the results of the survey outlined in Figure 5.1, which she carried out in 2005.

COACHING AND TRAINING FOR ORGANIZATIONS

If you are an executive in an organization looking to train staff in coaching skills, the minefield may have a few more mines in it. There are hundreds of consultancies and companies offering coaching and coach training to organizations, ranging from corporate consultancies employing large numbers of coaches and trainers to small partnerships who do all the work themselves or bring in associates. The size of an organization does not dictate the quality of its programmes.

Most decision makers in companies rely on their personal contacts and word of mouth to choose a provider. The questions to ask are the same as those listed above for public training, with a few more besides, such as:

- How are the coaches trained or qualified?
- How are they monitored?
- What previous experience do they have?
- What are their testimonials?

If you are a line manager or HR executive wanting to bring in coach training for your staff, it is recommended that you go through much the same process described above for choosing public training. Your criteria should incorporate:

- experiential training;
- training extended over a period of time with practice along the way;
- after-course support;
- experienced, formally trained coaches as trainers.

ASSESSMENT AND ACCREDITATION

At present, the coaching industry is entirely unregulated by any government anywhere in the world. A number of non-profit making organizations have been

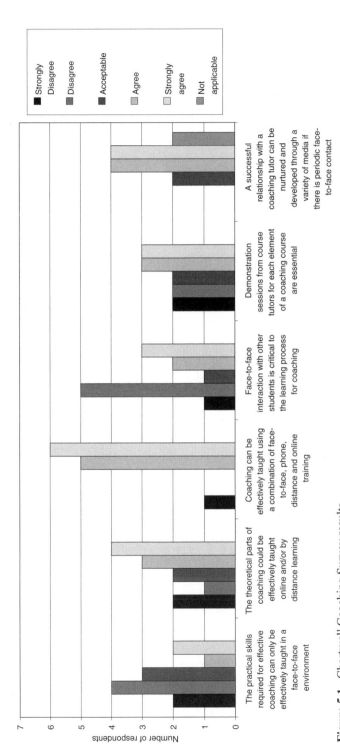

Figure 5.1 Chartwell Coaching Survey results

formed by coaches, such as the Association for Coaching (AC), the International Coach Federation (ICF) and the European Mentoring and Coaching Council (EMCC). All three maintain high standards of ethics and excellence for the industry and act as accrediting bodies. Their criteria for accreditation can be found on their websites, listed in 'Resources'.

Coaching bodies At the time of writing, these three coaching bodies are working with a commercial standards-setting organization called ENTO to define coaching industry standards in the United Kingdom.

As well as the excellent schemes run by the three international coaching bodies, AC, ICF and EMCC, some private training schools run their own assessment and accreditation programmes for students they have trained.

The types of accreditation vary from oral assessment to delivering essays or theses. Choosing the best form of assessment depends on the purpose it is required for. For example, if an organization wants to know which of the managers it has trained is actually a good coach, then oral assessment is the most efficient way of doing this. The same is true if a new coach has recently finished a training course, has practised with a few clients, and needs to know that he or she is 'doing it right'. However, if coaches are being assessed at a higher level and wish to demonstrate that they have experience in the field and a sound grasp of the principles and philosophy of coaching, then written assessment is fine provided part of the criteria is a requirement for around 250 hours of coaching delivery in the field.

Some universities provide degrees in coaching, and at present these include those listed below.

University links **UK**

University of Wolverhampton (Post Grad Dip, Post Grad Cert, MA)
University of Leeds (undergraduate)
Portsmouth Business School (MSc Coaching and Development)
University of Edinburgh (MSc in Performance Psychology)
Sheffield Hallam
Oxford Brookes (MA in Coaching and Mentoring)

Australia

University of Sydney (Master of Applied Science (Psychology of Coaching), Master of Organizational Coaching)

United States

University of Michigan (MA/MSc)
Villanova University/Newfield Network

At the time of writing I am not aware of any other degrees available anywhere in the world.

Some have formed links with coach training organizations and set up schemes whereby the coach training counts as a certain number of credits towards students' degrees. This may be the ideal option for someone who wants to start coaching quickly and to have the option of extended learning as and when it seems appropriate.

Exercise

1. Reread Chapter 4.
2. Arrange a session with your partner, by phone or face to face.
3. Take a complex goal set in your previous practice session and facilitate your partner in creating a strategic plan, as described in Chapter 4, and setting a few actions. Then swap over.
4. Write the actions down and complete them before next session.
5. Reread the guidelines for feedback in Chapter 2 and give each other coaching feedback.

6

Running a professional coaching practice

This chapter covers everything a coach setting up a professional practice might wish to do. Many of the points covered are essential for in-house coaches too, such as how to get the idea of coaching across to potential coachees and the sections on professionalism and ethics. HR directors may find the sections on what coaches charge across the industry interesting too!

MARKETING

If you want to work as a coach inside the organization you work for, you may still have to sell your services to potential coachees, although not for money. This section is about marketing the idea of coaching, and many of the techniques that professional coaches use to sell their services may also work for internal coaches.

Marketing a coaching business can be fun, although coaches are often frustrated by the amount of time they have to spend doing it. In the early stages, professional coaches spend at least as much of their time on marketing as they do on coaching. Later, a successful coach will build up word of mouth referrals and a contact list wide enough to generate leads without intervention.

One of the advantages of becoming a coach is that it requires only a small financial outlay to start building a business. Initially, the essentials are a business card, a telephone, a headset (if you plan to coach over the telephone) and an ability to create rapport. If you are going to turn your leads into coachees, you will also need some training and expertise in the various methods, techniques and tools available to coaches, and these topics are covered in other chapters of this book.

You can start a coaching business without giving up your day job, gradually building up a list of clients until you are confident enough to take the plunge. You may even be able to turn your job into a coaching position at work, by training as a coach and offering your services in-house. Many organizations are spending money on training in-house coaches, and if you can put a coaching qualification on your CV it may help you get the job in the first place. If you have not completed any formal training, ask the HR department if it will pay the cost of sending you on a course. Many of the coaches I have trained have funded their training in this way.

On the whole, we find that paid advertising does not work for coaches, although one ploy that might pay dividends is to stick up a notice at the gym, where you are likely to find a target market of self-improvement coachees.

Hiring a coach is a personal thing, and the **Networking v advertising** most common way that coaches attract personal coachees is simply by meeting people and talking to them about the profession. I have found that 20 to 30 per cent of people I meet have heard about coaching and are interested. There is no need to force your services onto those who aren't – wait until you find someone who shows interest by asking questions about what you do. Answer those questions and – bingo! – you have delivered a sales pitch without either of you noticing it.

Do not shy away from people who make cynical **Dealing with cynics** remarks about what you do. I have often found that they are precisely the ones who ring up a few days later wanting to find out more. Their cynicism often hides some denial inside, perhaps a feeling of being trapped in repeating emotional patterns, and their aggressive approach may be simply a way of asking for help. They sometimes become the most rewarding coachees of all.

If meeting people is the way to attract coachees, it **Selling without selling** follows that building a coaching practice involves plenty of networking. Many people cringe at the idea of networking for business, but you can take the stress out of it by remembering that everyone's attention is centred upon what impression they themselves are making, and quite likely whether they can sell you their own services. The key is to ask them questions about themselves until they run dry, then they will be ready to hear about you.

A conversation is like a ball-game – sooner or later, there will come a point where the ball has to be handed back. That is the time to tell people about coaching and what it can achieve; try this any earlier and you will not have their full attention. Selling without selling is a relief to everyone, taking the pressure off those who are being sold to and those who have a product or service to offer.

The conversation must be led by the other person, not you, and you should never give more information than people ask for. The amount of information you impart can expand with every question they ask. For instance, say you have spent 10 minutes asking a new contact at a networking event about her profession, and she finally says to you, 'And what do you do?'

I'm a performance coach (*or a business coach, life coach, etc*).

Describing what a coach does   Notice how short the reply is. At this point either she will show interest and ask another question, or you will see her attention shut down. If that happens, either change the subject or find someone else to talk to, unless you are interested in the services of a website builder or whatever else she might be offering. If she does ask a question, you can give more detailed information:

What does that involve then?

I help people get clarity about what they want to achieve and support them in getting there.

And how do you manage that?

I am trained in a technique of asking questions which will help people see things more clearly. For instance, if I have a complex issue to deal with and say to myself, 'I must sit down and think this plan through,' I find that five minutes later I'm thinking about something completely different. As a coach I help people focus their minds on the matter in hand, so that they can get a breakthrough and move forward.

It is important to say something that you feel comfortable delivering and which is based on your own experience. It does not matter if you are a new coach and have no success stories to tell. The truth carries its own resonance, and if you speak from the heart, you will come across as congruent and authentic. That is why people talk about 'the ring of truth'.

An important element is the rhythm of the conversation: notice how it is not until the third question in the example above that the coach goes into any detail. You must be absolutely sure that the person is ready to receive your story before you tell it. If you go into too much detail too soon, people feel pressured and back away. Have you ever walked into a shop and been pounced on by an over-eager assistant? Most people run a mile from that kind of pressure. The key to this is to sell without selling: wait for people to ask for information and supply it.

This advice applies equally to meeting individuals and having meetings with potential buyers at their offices.

FINDING CORPORATE CLIENTS

In the corporate arena, as in the private one, obtaining work is largely about networking and personal relationships. Coaches are usually hired either directly by executives or through the HR department. Most organizations are either hiring external coaches, or training their own internally, or training their managers in day-to-day coaching skills, or a combination of all three.

Equally, there is strong competition in the field. Some coaches sit on the phone calling companies until eventually they come away with a meeting. Probably the most useful person to ask for in this situation is the HR director. If you want to take this approach, a helpful way to look at it is to imagine you are throwing a dice with every phone call. Every time you get an appointment, you have thrown a six. The other calls are not rejections, just throws of the dice that did not produce a six.

The most common way that executive coaches obtain work is through contacts and referrals. To get into corporate coaching it is more important to have some corporate experience yourself than to complete an executive coaching course (in addition to your foundation skills training), not because you need expert knowledge of any particular business, but so that you can speak 'corporate jargon', thereby creating rapport and communicating comfortably.

If you do not have any corporate contacts, with a little patience and determination they can be created over a period of time. One way is by networking with other coaches who may eventually ask you to join them in fulfilling a corporate coaching contract; another is to call HR executives regularly for a chat, without focusing on selling your services, and staying in touch during periods when they may find themselves between jobs.

Going on courses is another great way of picking up coachees, whether personal or corporate. It is also an interesting and fruitful way of spending time, but can prove expensive!

It is not necessary to have printed material or PowerPoint presentations, but they can be helpful. **Corporate meetings** Never start a meeting by showing a PowerPoint presentation unless you are specifically instructed to by the potential client. Nothing is more yawn-inducing to the average HR executive than seeing the dreaded laptop come out. Both private individuals and companies are sold on their relationship with the provider concerned, not the gloss of his or her marketing tools.

It is just as important to engage the individual's interest in a corporate setting as it is in a networking situation. Follow the same pattern of asking executives about their requirements, their work and themselves, in that order, before you attempt to present your own case. While listening to their replies, you can interject sympathetic details about your own services which are specifically relevant to what they are saying. This will lead to a more general conversation where you will gradually be able to get across the advantages of working with you without overkill.

It is important to remember that there is no point in talking to someone who is not listening; coach the executive through the meeting. He or she may not be clear about what is wanted, and until that is clear you will not be able to deliver it.

> You can close more business in two months by becoming interested in other people than you can in two years by trying to get people interested in you.
> Dale Carnegie

INTERNET MARKETING

Although it is possible to start a coaching business with nothing more than a business card and a telephone, eventually you may wish to expand your marketing activities, and two effective ways of doing this are by creating a website and/or a newsletter.

Websites There are two advantages to having a website. You can refer new people you meet to it, and potential coachees may find you through web searches. A website gives solidity and stature to your business, provided it looks professional. That does not necessarily mean it has to cost a fortune; you can create your own website for a small annual fee, with the added advantage that you will be able to update it yourself. Most domain name servers or internet service providers offer this type of service. Some even have facilities for PayPal links, interactive forums and databases. Be sure to include associates and testimonials, if you have them, as well as listing what you do.

If you have the resources, search engine optimization is another way of picking up business. Search engine optimization is a way of ensuring that when people put a word like 'coaching' into an engine such as Google or Yahoo, it is your coaching website that comes up on the first page. There are thousands of small businesses on the web claiming that they know how to make this happen, and some of them may indeed be able to. The key to it at the time of writing is the number of other websites which link to yours. How highly those websites are rated by the search engines dictates where your own website will show up.

Search engines For instance, if your website has a link on six small business websites, it will not have much impact on the search engine. However, if your link is on the BBC website, that will probably guarantee you front page on Google.

Small world networks Internet networking is just like real-world PR: the more places you can get yourself or your company mentioned, the wider the word will spread and the more weight your name will carry. For instance, books by hypnotist Paul McKenna hit the top of the best-seller charts because of his television series; the series supports the books, which support his live dates, which in turn support the books.

Anthony Robbins, the American consciousness-raising guru and author of a series of best-selling books, built up his profile in a similar way. If names like this seem too extreme to compete with, remember that Rome was not built in a day and that every article you publish, or interview you obtain, or local radio slot you appear in, may lead to the next contact in your own small world network. If you are ever lucky enough to experience a big breakthrough you will have built up enough ballast through your network to capitalize on it effectively. Even if that is not your target, these small links will increase your profile enough to impress potential coachees.

An alternative to search engine optimization can be to buy a **Pay per click** pay-per-click campaign: these are the small ads which run along the top and down the side of search engine pages like Google. You enter a credit card number, decide what budget you wish to set, choose your 'keywords' (which are the words you think will be most commonly entered by people looking for your type of business), and are charged only when someone clicks on your ad. The disadvantage is that some searchers automatically discount paid advertising and pay more attention to the 'organic' lists, which are often simply a result of another part of the marketing budget.

In addition to Google, there are companies such as Overture which cover a number of search engines. These vary according to which country you are in and what parts of the world you want your campaign to cover. You can get an ad up and running worldwide or in any combination of countries on Google in a matter of days, for as long as your credit card will support it. The search engines also offer sophisticated reports to help you decide how to target your budget efficiently.

However, extreme care should be taken in organizing such a campaign as there are numerous pitfalls. It is possible to run up high bills without realizing it because the website accounts are complex. Also, competitors may click on your advert in order to drive up your account to its daily limit, when your ad will disappear.

When writing copy for your website, add weight by **Marketing copy** maximizing the use of 'hard' material, such as the names of companies you have worked for, qualifications obtained or awards won, rather than fanciful claims such as 'I can help you achieve your vision.' Of course, signed testimonials from people claiming that you did indeed help them to achieve their vision are valuable and well worth including.

An e-mailed newsletter can be useful in building up a regular **Newsletter** mailing list. Make sure your newsletter contains material of interest and use to the people whose inbox it lands in, rather than simply being a sales campaign, otherwise you may find that your subscribers rapidly unsubscribe. An interesting and well-presented newsletter will keep you at the forefront of the minds of potential coachees. There is plenty of software available for putting together a professional newsletter, which can easily be found by searching the internet. The opening lines need to be attention-catching, otherwise the recipients will not bother to scroll down, but simply delete the email unread.

Another great way of using the internet is to network by joining as many e-mail forums as possible. If you intend to operate as a personal coach (where your coachees are paying for themselves), a discreet message from time to time outlining what you do and inviting people to try a free introductory session will probably bring in a few volunteers who have no intention of paying for coaching – but that may change once they experience the value of it.

Some final advice on marketing: when I first built up a practice the last thing on my mind was picking up coachees. I focused on honing my craft, the value I could bring to others, and maximizing my enjoyment of the session by having fun, learning about other people and injecting as much humour as possible. These are the qualities that attract both corporate and private coachees.

★ *Focus on the quality and the money will look after itself.*

CLOSING THE DEAL

You have gone out and made some new contacts and found some who seem intrigued by coaching. Now, how do you turn them into clients?

Timing is everything. If you walk around offering free sessions to everyone you meet, it will devalue what is on offer. People have become suspicious of free offers – if something is worth having, why is it being given away? However, there is a very good reason to offer the first session free in private coaching, and that is, as we have touched on before in this book, because very few people understand what coaching is until they have experienced it.

Remember your networking skills: ask about the other person, be economical with the information you give out, and wait until you can see someone is seriously interested in what you have to say before offering a session. Having said that, it is essential that you do make the offer. People are not mind-readers and may be embarrassed to ask for a session, or worried about what it might cost. Also, many of us have a tendency to undervalue ourselves and what we do, and may be so focused on whether people want us that we fail to notice any reciprocal doubts about whether we would want to work with them. You may have made such a great impression that your potential client is thinking, 'Why would someone like her want to coach someone like me?'

In corporate coaching a free session is not expected. The company will usually dictate the terms, and may hire you for a series of sessions or just for one.

TERMS OF PAYMENT

Most private coaches expect the coachee to commit to a minimum number of sessions, and to make payment at least one month in advance, by cheque or through a credit card if the coach has that facility.

Organizations often pay at least 30 days after receipt of invoice, although some will agree to one-third upfront, one third in the middle of the coaching series and one-third at the end. There is no harm in asking a company for this. It makes sense to request a testimonial as part of the deal, particularly if your price has been negotiated down.

WHAT TO CHARGE

This is the part that makes coaches cringe. It helps to start by deciding what the job is worth to you:

- Are you keen to get some testimonials and experience under your belt? Many coaches start off with pro bono (non-paying) coachees in order to build up their confidence and credentials.
- Or are you so busy that you would like to have fewer coachees? In that case, put your prices up and pass potential coachees who can't meet your charges on to other coaches. If you only want five coachees a week and have access to more, setting your prices high means you will lose some but get paid higher fees for a smaller number of hours.
- Is there an organization you have been particularly keen to get into and the work is out to tender? Companies are unlikely to make a decision based solely on cost, but if they like you and you are offering to do the work for less than a competitor they favour equally, you will get the job.

Still not sure how to approach pricing? Let's start by looking at rates for personal coaching, ie where the coachees are paying you out of their own budget rather than their employer's.

Personal coaching rates

If you are new to the profession, a good way to start is to ask the coachee what he or she can afford to pay. Start off with that and raise your charges with each coachee as your confidence and experience grows. Some coaches start at a very low price per session and up the fees by say 50 per cent with every new coachee. I once trained a coach who set her fees at £150/US$300 a session from the beginning – a high fee for a starter coach – because she had been my coachee and that was my fee at the time. Within a few weeks she had no less than 11 coachees all paying that rate.

Rates for personal coaching What coachees will pay you relates more to the circles you move in than to how good a coach you are. If you are looking for coachees through friends and most of your contacts work at junior level, then your fees will probably settle at between £30 and £60 a session. If you mix with high-earning professionals, celebrities or CEOs, the sky is the limit and you will probably soon collect an array of clients whose organizations are footing the bill.

Corporate rates

Always try to get the organization to tell you its budget for the project. If you can't elicit this information, a good rule of thumb is to quote fees from £150–£400 per hour, depending on the seniority of the coachee. This is the price range an organization would expect to pay, whether in the corporate or public sector.

Corporate rates However, if the coachee in question is the CEO of a large organization, the fees may rise to £1,000 per session (and a session will be as long as it takes, probably two to three hours), or up to £3,000 per day. I know one coach whose day rate is £5,000, but this is exceptional. It is advantageous to the company and the coach to try to slot in several sessions a day. It is acceptable for the part-day rate to be proportionately higher, and higher again for a one-off session. For instance, if your day rate is £1,500, your half-day rate (for three to four hours) might be £800–£900 and your rate for an hour and a half long session £400.

If you are dealing with a small to medium-sized business, prices are as flexible as in personal coaching.

In both corporate or personal coaching, you can add reasonable travel expenses as long as they are agreed in advance. Coaches often set their fees at lower rates for telephone coaching, because this involves less time and trouble. The coachee always calls the coach, thus bearing the charges, and this should be made clear from the outset. These topics are included in the sample coaching contracts in Appendix C.

PAPERWORK

Paperwork is not a word that looms large in coaching, which tends to focus on the 'being' and the 'doing'. However, a small amount of paperwork is beneficial for record keeping, for setting out clear agreements between the parties and for bringing added insight and awareness.

In Appendices B, C and D you will find examples of:

- coach's worksheet;
- coachee's worksheet;
- personal coaching agreement;
- corporate coaching agreement;
- forms for evaluating the coaching.

These are described in more detail on the following pages.

In personal coaching, you will give a paperwork pack to your new coachee before or after the introductory session. In a corporate situation, this happens either before or after the first session. It is sometimes a good idea to wait until after, to ensure that you have won the coachee's confidence.

Coaching agreements

It makes sense to have a coaching agreement to confirm that both parties have understood what has been agreed in terms of finance, time and commitment. A personal coachee signs this after the introductory session. In corporate coaching, a representative of the organization signs the agreement, which is provided by either the coach or the organization. It is a good idea to have the agreement signed by the coachee as well, in order to strengthen the coachee's commitment to the coaching. This can be included in the corporate agreement, as in the example in Appendix C, or you could make up a separate agreement omitting the reference to charges.

Forms for evaluating the coaching

It is recommended that the coach requests verbal evaluations during the coaching series, perhaps every three or four sessions, by asking questions like 'What would you like me to do more or less of?'

The evaluation forms in Appendix D are to be given for formal feedback at the end of the series. They can be adapted for working with corporate or personal coachees.

NICHE COACHING

A 'niche' refers to a particular area in which a coach might choose to specialize, such as career, finance, the pharmaceutical industry or weight loss. Opinion is divided on whether there is any advantage for a coach to operate within a niche field. On the one hand, the title 'career' coach might cut out coachees who are not looking for that type of coaching; on the other, it will attract those who are.

Coachees tend to favour coaches with a similar background to themselves, in the belief that this will help the process. Because of this, some coaches end up working within a 'niche' area simply because it reflects the background they come from. One advantage to this is that the coach is well placed to offer occasional tips to the coachee arising from the coach's own experience. However, from the coach's point of view, I find it easier to coach someone from a business I know absolutely nothing about than from my own background in the music industry, when I have to resist the temptation to offer solutions.

PROFESSIONALISM

Acting professionally as a coach involves a number of areas, the main components of which are:

- punctuality;
- well-ordered paperwork;
- looking the part;
- respecting the coachee's confidentiality;
- fulfilling promises;
- walking the talk, ie being a good coaching role model.

MENTORING AND SUPERVISION

However thoroughly a coach has trained, the training course is only the beginning of the learning. Every session is an education, presenting new challenges and fascinating areas to explore, and I find this is as true now for me as it was when I first entered the profession.

It is recommended that coaches work regularly (say for one hour a month) with other experienced coaches to uphold their standards and support them with any challenges that arise during their work with coachees. Similar practices exist in disciplines such as therapy.

The term 'supervision' is becoming used increasingly in coaching. However, this is a term borrowed from therapy and its use in coaching is not entirely accurate, because it implies that the supervisor is somehow superior, exercises judgement and that some assessment is involved. However, in coaching 'supervision' refers to a session where one coach will support another in terms of acting as a sounding board, sharing experiences and giving advice. 'Mentoring' is a more accurate description, although this still implies that the mentor is more experienced than the mentee, which is not always the case here. In the early stages of training, the supervisor/coach mentor will indeed need to be more experienced; however, once a coach is qualified, two coaches at an equal level can provide supervision/mentoring to each other. Coaching is a peer to peer activity, and this should be reflected in the supervision/mentoring arrangement.

An additional element for any coach involved in designing corporate programmes to take into account is that if an organization wishes to create a force of internal coaches, who will require internal supervision/mentoring, executives are likely to be far more comfortable with the term 'mentor' than 'supervisor'. There is also the danger that people will take the term as their guide and start acting like traditional supervisors, instead of offering the support required here. The word 'mentor' is a more accurate guide of what is expected of them.

For this reason, throughout this book I use the terms 'supervisor/coach mentor' and 'supervision/coach mentoring', because I feel it is important that this relatively new profession of coaching develops its own terms which will not be misunderstood in the world in general. Wherever possible in my own practice, I use the term 'coach mentor' alone. 'Supervision/coach mentoring' is not coaching, instructing or assessing, although supervisors/coach mentors are likely to use some coaching skills as they will be part of their natural communication style.

In therapeutic disciplines, supervision is well defined and essential because of the nature of the work, which is not always coachee-led and may involve deeply disturbed coachees. The requirement for supervision in coaching is less exacting, but it is recommended that coaches maintain their own coaches and/or mentors in order to seek advice and reassurance when they need it.

Peer support can be provided by joining or setting up coaching networks, e-mail forums, regular meetings or reciprocal coaching arrangements. The latter work particularly well when they are tripartite: A coaches B, B coaches C and C coaches A. Supervision/mentoring groups can also be formed for the same purpose.

ETHICS

Coaching has a strict code of ethics, and being a relatively new profession, is currently grappling with some tricky questions of conflict of interest between coachee, coach and sponsor organization.

Coaches may hear information from their coachees which the coach feels morally bound to pass on to the coachee's organization: for instance, if the coachee is acting unethically towards the organization without its knowledge. The coach has a responsibility to the organization which is paying the fee; however, the coachee will have been assured of confidentiality and trusts the coach to abide by this. Deciding what would be the ethical way to behave in a case like this can be extremely difficult, and there is no simple answer. Each coach has to decide how to handle the particular situation according to its circumstances and the people involved. The best advice I can give is that there is always the door. Coaches have the right to terminate the arrangement if they feel they are being ethically compromised in any way, and this can be done openly or subtly, by pleading overwork or persuading the coachee that he or she might find another coach more suitable.

Unlike the medical profession or the priesthood, there is no protection for coaches in law against disclosure. If a coach becomes aware that a coachee is doing something illegal – stealing, child abuse, animal abuse or whatever – he or she can, and probably should, report the person. There may be other avenues available, and the best of all is to raise the coachee's awareness until the coachee takes ownership in seeking other professional help or ceasing the illegal activity.

The Association for Coaching publishes a Code of Ethics on its site www.associationforcoaching.com.

In Chapter 9 a series of moral dilemmas in the workplace has been provided by highly experienced corporate coach Gillian Jones, from Emerge. Each is taken from her own personal experience and offers recommendations on how to proceed.

Exercise

1. Working with your partner, pretend to be a potential coachee who wants to find out more about coaching. What sort of things would you want to know? Write these down, then swap over.

2. Now each make up a two-minute piece introducing what you do as a coach, based on the answers to the questions above.

3. Deliver your two-minute piece to each other, give each other feedback, and work on your talk until you feel entirely comfortable in delivering it.

4. If your interest is in corporate coaching, do this exercise as if you are an HR executive or line manager interested in bringing coaching into your organization. What will you look for in the coaches? What else will you need to know?

5. Then make up a two-minute piece that you would deliver to an HR executive if you met one at a networking meeting. Do some reciprocal practice with your partner until you are both confident.

6. From now on, if you are not already doing so, talk to as many people as possible about your interest in coaching – friends, family or strangers. Find out what they think and which descriptions work best with people.

The aim in all this is to become someone who can talk easily, authoritatively and authentically about the benefits of coaching.

7

How to create a coaching culture in organizations

Throughout this book I have covered workplace coaching in tandem with personal coaching, because the requirements are often the same, regardless of who is paying or where the coachee has come from. This chapter deals with the questions I am most often asked by HR executives: where do we begin and where do we go from there? Prior to that, the chapter tackles some issues that relate specifically to workplace coaching, including confidentiality, informal coaching and measurement of the return on investment.

WHO CAN BE COACHED IN THE WORKPLACE?

Staff may have reservations about being coached by certain categories of other staff; for instance some may wish to be coached only by those senior to them, or by those whose paths they will never cross in the normal course of work. However, provided that no one is ever forced into being coached by anyone else, the reservations often fall away because the ownership of the coaching series is in the coachee's control.

There can be a conflict of interest if managers formally coach their own direct reports, and this is not recommended. However, the managers' coaching skills, when used informally, will make them highly effective leaders.

It is recommended that coachees are allowed to choose their coaches from a selection. The essence of coaching is that the agenda is controlled by the coachee, and a selection process reflects this.

CONFIDENTIALITY IN THE WORKPLACE

It is essential that no reporting back takes place, in either specific or broad terms, without the explicit agreement of the coachee. If there is any suspicion that this may happen, the coachee will not be able to achieve the inner focus required to benefit from the coaching.

External one-to-one coaches are effective partly because their coachees feel that the confidentially factor is more secure than with a coach who works for the same organization. Therefore it is equally important that external coaches are not expected to divulge any detailed information about the content of the coaching. The organization will need some criteria for measuring whether it is getting value for money, and this is discussed later in this chapter under the heading 'Measurement in workplace coaching'.

It is also essential that the coach does not have any ulterior agenda. Coaches must not be asked to lead their coachees towards any particular outcome; let us remember that the essence of coaching is 'self-directed learning'. Paradoxically, an organization will normally have a reason for introducing coaching, and may have overall goals towards which coaching is a strategy; the organization should be open about these to both coach and coachee. It is the coachee's own goals, strategies and experiences within the coaching series that must remain confidential.

In Chapter 2, we illustrated this by saying that in normal conversation, we ask questions in order to obtain information. In coaching, the coach asks questions in order that the coachee can obtain information about him or herself. Through this process, coachees can discover for themselves the best way forward – whether that means towards the company's annual goals, or out of the door into a new career!

I have always been open with corporate clients that coaching sometimes results in resignations, and I have found that organizations recognize that a satisfied workforce is a more productive one. Coaching enables individuals to identify limiting aspects of their workplaces, and gives them the motivation to instigate change. If they are not able to make satisfactory adjustments to their current positions it is probably better all round for them to find a new path to follow.

This question of confidentiality relates back to the section on Ethics in the previous chapter.

INFORMAL COACHING IN THE WORKPLACE

As coaches in training reach a level of fluency in their skills, their emotional intelligence rises in all types of communication. Their skills will have become integrated to the point where they are used naturally with colleagues, bosses, family and friends, the milkman, the postman and the plumber; all the coach's relationships will step up a notch.

Leading from behind   New coaches will learn how to 'lead from behind' – a highly effective form of leadership which harnesses the energy of staff by giving them ownership of their work. This results in a heightened sense of job satisfaction, which surveys show to be more important than earning power to the majority of employees.

For instance, in a Gallup survey of 2,000 workers, 69 per cent indicated that receiving recognition from their bosses was more motivating than money, and four out of five said recognition or praise motivated them to do a better job (source: http://edis.ifas.ufl.edu/pdffiles/HR/HR02600.pdf). In blunt terms, what that means is that bosses can expect a higher return from employees by praising them than by paying a bonus at the end of the month. Imagine the effect of that on the bottom line.

Coaching can spread from small beginnings; if one person starts using it, the difference will be felt and ripples can grow to great waves. For example, I knew a coach who was hired by the manager of a services company. The sales of the whole organization were on a downward turn, yet over the next quarter, the department of this particular manager showed a 20 per cent increase. His director asked what was happening, and the manager credited his success to the fact that he had a coach. This resulted in a coaching programme being run out across the whole organization, bringing about a whole culture change and an upturn in the profits.

USES FOR COACHING SKILLS IN THE WORKPLACE

Coaching is not appropriate in every situation. There are times when people need instruction, advice or mentoring. As their skills become fluent, coaches will intuitively know whether to respond in a coaching style or not, and should trust their intuition in making that choice.

There are other times when the coach may feel stuck in an exchange with a colleague, boss or report, and can consciously reach into the toolkit for an appropriate response.

Coaching skills prove most useful when:

- giving or receiving feedback, either positive or negative;
- bonding teams, particularly during mergers and other changes;
- motivating staff to achieve their best with the most amount of enjoyment and the least amount of stress;
- eliminating fears which block action;
- improving assertiveness, particularly during meetings or on conference calls;
- working on areas for improvement highlighted by staff reviews or surveys.

Team coaching Coaching skills can be applied as effectively with groups as with individuals – the underlying process is the same. The coach will brainstorm with the group a session outcome – which may be within the context of an organization's wider goals – then identify where the group is at present within the context of the session outcome. Through a process of discussion, both within the main group and subdivided groups, options are explored and goals arrived at.

THE PURPOSE OF WORKPLACE COACH TRAINING

Some trainees join a coaching course in order to improve their communication skills in general, and have no intention of conducting formal sessions. Nevertheless, I have found that if participants are trained to the full extent of conducting formal sessions, the various skills and tools will be more firmly embedded than if they are simply taught how to improve their communication skills.

For those trainees who wish to become in-house coaches, some type of assessment and accreditation is desirable, such as delivering a session to a trainer and receiving a pass mark or otherwise. If the trainee is not up to scratch, the trainer can work through feedback and coaching to raise the skills to the required standard.

Trainees who become accredited coaches can act as mentors to other in-house coaches after they have amassed a reasonable amount of experience, say having conducted 60 coaching sessions.

MEASUREMENT IN WORKPLACE COACHING

There is a perception that it is difficult to demonstrate the benefits of coaching in an organization. However, there are a growing number of effective methods available.

Surveys such as 360 degrees

The 360-degree method is covered in detail in Chapter 8. Many companies have in place some sort of staff review programme which involves regular surveys, perhaps annually, and these can be harnessed to help evaluate the benefit of coaching.

Measurement of hard factors

Sales levels, profits, staff retention rates or absenteeism can be assessed at regular intervals. These work only where such figures are available and meaningful.

Recording improved performance throughout the programme

Every time the coachee says that something has improved – for instance 'I handed in my report on time for the first time this week' – the coach can make a note. He or she can then compile a report at the end of the coaching series to hand to the organization (always with the coachee's approval, to respect confidentiality). This can be taken a step further by asking coachees how much money they estimate their improved performance has made the organization. Figures such as these can be translated into hard estimates which will impress the accountants.

Values-based surveys

The Values questionnaire in Chapter 8 is an example of this, as is the Cultural Transformation Tools online values survey, which is described later in the chapter. Just as people have personalities created by their values, beliefs and habits, so an organization has a personality. We call this its 'culture'.

Organizational culture The culture of an organization is determined by the values, beliefs and behaviours of its directorship and its workforce. Asking employees to complete surveys identifying the current organizational values, as they see them personally, and then the values they would like to see in place, enables them to identify where their organization is aligned with their own values and where the culture of the organization diverges.

Through identification of these elements, a process of change will have begun. Employees will be able to see where the organization is helping them to develop and grow and where they could start to make some changes.

The results of such surveys, if spread across large numbers of staff within the organization, can be analysed to see where stumbling blocks lie. Some limiting behaviours which might show up are bureaucracy, long working hours and dictatorial management. Employees can be asked to quantify what losses they estimate are occurring, and the results can then be used to calculate what percentage of the bottom line is being lost through such limiting factors.

The resulting figures may not be strictly statistically accurate, but they offer something to show the accountants: a guide to how much the profit could rise, or costs could be cut, if the organization were able to effect changes in its culture. Running such surveys on a six-monthly or annual basis can chart the progress of the organization and highlight the effect of coaching and training on its bottom line.

COACHING ACROSS CULTURES

At corporate level, industry today is becoming rapidly more globalized. A giant corporation will have divisions all over the world, not only in the cosmopolitan hubs of London, New York, Sydney and the like, but in what were previously considered outposts, from Abu Dhabi to Bogotá.

The global picture   The worldwide organization as a whole will have a set of aims and values which it will wish to see adopted worldwide. Staff from one country will often be sent to spend time in various divisions all over the world, moving their homes and families every few years like tortoises with houses on their backs. Another factor is the increase in mergers, which may mean global board meetings with representatives from the United States, Japan, Germany, Italy and the Middle East sitting round a table together and having to agree a way forward, or teams from different divisions having to collaborate across the world.

There are without doubt cultural differences to take into account here, and although there are different degrees and exceptions to the rule, some generalizations can be made. For example, Australians and Americans may more often say what they mean, whereas to some nationalities this directness may seem over-aggressive and can be hurtful. The feelings of rejection and lack of respect it creates can produce hostility and resentment.

Italians may be voluble and display their emotions; Asian countries tend to value humility and politeness, and people communicate with tacit signals, striving to avoid causing any offence or hurt. This can be viewed as weakness by their Western counterparts.

Some nations more commonly practise an analytical approach, others a deductive one, and it may be necessary at times for an executive accustomed to one type of thinking to operate within another.

In Chapter 1 we discussed how people have their own interior cultural backgrounds, arising from the behaviour and attitudes of their parents and early influences, and how coaching respects these differences, whether they are evident or not. Coaching is a great leveller across international cultures too.

It is possible to take coachees who find themselves in stressful encounters with foreigners whose attitude seems cold, aggressive or intimidating, through exercises in clarification to identify where the mismatches lie. This type of analysis will provide clarity, and eventually acceptance that different types of behaviour and systems all have value and something to contribute. The coachee will stop taking differences as a personal affront and become able to identify and accommodate the variations.

This can be done during one to one coaching, and a team approach is also useful here; groups of executives from different nationalities can spend time identifying their styles and listening to others explaining their way of thinking. Not only will this result in greater understanding and cooperation, the team members and their bosses will start to recognize and take advantage of the different approaches instead of fearing them and putting up blocks. As in any other team, all types have something to contribute, and the global team provides a richer vein for those who have the vision, skill and courage to mine it.

Coaching across cultures   A study has been made in this subject by Philippe Rosinski, whose book *Coaching Across Cultures* (2003) was the first to address the issue. The author's aim is to raise awareness about cultural orientations, and he provides some constructive methods and tools to do this, including a Culture Orientations Framework and a Global Scorecard.

These cross-cultural differences can be complicated by the fact that people working in one sphere of an organization may view themselves as being more part of their speciality team than their national one. For example, it may be that an Italian and German IT team will work smoothly together because they see themselves as the IT team, which has its own language, traditions and challenges, even though as individuals its members reflect their respective national traits. The latter will diminish when the team bonds in the face of clashes with, say, the international sales force or the creative department.

Similarly, company leaders from different countries may work smoothly together if they are all, say, results, analysis, or action oriented, regardless of what may be quite substantial differences in national temperament and methods of communication. On the other hand, two leaders of the same nationality may clash if their leadership styles and values are a long way apart.

Taking a coaching approach, it is important to allow the participants in any cross-cultural integration programme to identify where their differences arise, and not to assume that these will inevitably be nationality-based. The benefit of such a programme is that once recognized, differences become acceptable, whether they arise from international, work or personal cultures. The danger of causing offence recedes and the various parties start to value different contributions instead of fearing and erecting barriers against them.

CREATING A COACHING CULTURE IN THE WORKPLACE

There are many organizations today that wholeheartedly embrace the concept of a coaching culture, and there are others that remain stuck in the old 'command and control' way of doing things. There is no denying that many business success stories stand upon a foundation of bullying and fear. Alan Sugar and Donald Trump are classic examples, if their recent television series are anything to go by (although we cannot help wondering how much the lure of the camera was responsible and whether they really behave like this back in the office). Jack Welch is regarded as a business guru, yet he proudly publicized his system at General Electric, where, every year, managers had to rate their staff for effectiveness and the bottom 10 per cent would be fired. He found that managers would go as far as to put the names of dead workers on the list to avoid having loyal, effective and hard-working team members lose their livelihood. The result of such a rule of fear must surely be to encourage furtive spanners to be placed in the works, and to provoke a desire to unseat the tyrant if the chance ever presents itself.

John Whitmore tells the story of an 'inner game' (Tim Gallwey's methods upon which performance coaching is based, as described on page 7) ski instructor who informed his students that this would not be the fastest way to learn but it was the most effective. One trainee asked what the fastest way would be. The instructor replied that if he told the class that at the end of the week he would line them up and shoot the least proficient, they would indeed become great skiers. However, they would be unlikely ever to go near a ski slope again. I would add to this that they would find themselves spending more energy on scheming to murder the ski instructor before he could do it to them than on learning to ski. Take that analogy back to the workplace, and we can see that a rule of bullying and fear channels the workers' energy and creative powers into ways of destroying the organization rather than building it.

The question I would put to any CEO who claims to have made a fortune from ruling by fear is, how much more would you have made if your workforce liked you?

Another story comes to mind about the distribution plant which manufactured records for Virgin in the 1970s. This was not long after Edward Heath's famous 'three-day week', when he took on the unions so fiercely that the country had to ration its power supply in the middle of winter, engendering a truncated working week and car stickers that read 'Hooray for Ted, 3 days in bed'. The factory's workers went on strike (it was not a company owned or controlled by Virgin) and we had to issue a press release explaining why we were unable to supply records. Our left-wing press officer added that he was in favour of any workers, anywhere in the world, breaking the monotony of the factory line by striking whenever they got the chance. We thought about this and came to the conclusion that people are naturally creative beings; if their work does not allow an outlet for that creativity they will use it for creating mischief, mayhem and unrest, such as strike action.

So where do we begin to create a culture which confers responsibility, engenders self-belief and is blame-free, the three key aspects of a coaching culture that we identified in Chapter 1? This is the question I am most often asked at presentations, after relating stories of the culture at Virgin to a bemused roomful of HR directors who may be up to their necks in compliance.

Below are some guidelines which should be varied according to the circumstances of each particular organization.

The goal

Ascertain what it is that the organization wants to achieve. This can be achieved through one or more of the following:

- Meetings with the HR director or CEO, who should be coached (informally) by the provider until clear on exactly what the requirements are.
- Focus group meetings with the board of directors, facilitated by the provider, until they are united on what they want to achieve.
- Surveys conducted throughout the organization to highlight trends among the staff to see what they would like to see changed. The most effective method of doing this that I have found is the use of Cultural Transformation Tools, described on page 121; for a smaller organization, the Values questionnaire on page 120 is a simpler form of this.

Notice that in all the above processes, and in those that follow, the premise is that the answer lies with the client, just as it does in a coaching session.

Some useful questions to ask during these processes might include:

- Does the organization want to bring in external coaches or develop internal ones?
- Will external trainers be required to train the managers in coaching skills, or are there people within the organization who could be trained to do this?
- Does the organization want to develop a handbook of coaching and leadership skills to be given to the managers, or to the whole staff?
- How much does the organization want to be able to measure the results of a coaching initiative?
- What terminology does it want to use? Sometimes 'leadership training' or 'management development' will sit more comfortably than 'coach training'.
- Over what time period does it want to achieve the changes?
- Does the organization want to achieve a flatter hierarchy, where all staff feel they are valued equally at whatever level? In that case, will the directors take the same training courses as the managers and other staff?

Reality

Once everyone is clear on where they are going, it is vital to find out what resources they have at their disposal. Similar processes can be used to those outlined above, using different questions some of the time. The provider can coach and prompt to ensure a broad perspective on all possible issues, asking about:

- succession planning;
- what support people are given when they join the organization, say for their first hundred days;
- whether there are staff reviews and how they are conducted;
- the current situation regarding knowledge retention;
- what training and development is currently available;
- what support is in place for embedding such training and development;
- how many internal coaches the organization has at present;
- how they are assessed and accredited, if at all;
- what mentoring or supervision is in place to support the coaching culture initiative;
- what budget is available;
- what similar interventions have been done before.

Options

With the information gleaned on where they want to get to, and where they are starting from, the managers charged with implementing the change are probably by this time bursting with ideas on how to move forward. This third stage is simply to capture these concepts, explore them, add any from the provider along with advice from the provider's experience in the field, and work out the costs and time frame. Some useful questions to ask here might be:

- How much time will the staff have available each month to be coached or trained, and to follow through on practising and embedding the training?
- What budget is available for this project? (This is often the hardest piece of information to extract, and you will usually have to work out the project, name some figures, then trim it back if the cost is beyond the organization's means.)
- If the programme involves coaching sessions and coaching skills training, will these elements happen simultaneously or one before to the other? If the latter is the case, it is better if the training happens first, giving people some insight and knowledge to take through their personal development journey during the coaching.
- How many internal coaches, coaching mentors (or supervisors) and coaching trainers does the organization want? How many external?
- How will staff choose their internal/external coaches?
- Who will be entitled to one to one coaching?
- What support could be set up in terms of monthly co-coaching or mentoring/supervising meetings?
- If the organization has more than one base, will there be a system in place where managers can select coaching by phone from other branches, either in the United Kingdom or abroad? I have successfully coached people I have never met in the United States and Australia by phone. Such interaction between organizational depots can do wonders for international cohesion.
- Will all the employees receive some coaching and training? If not, who will?
- Is it desirable to have an induction presentation where the coaching programme can be explained to all the staff (perhaps in shifts on various days) so that everyone, including receptionists and warehouse packers, understands what this new coaching programme is about, even if they are not directly in line for it?
- What assessment and accreditation is required, and will it be undertaken by internal or external assessors?
- What evaluation and measurement on the return on investment is required and how can this be achieved?

What will be done

All that remains is to tie this down into a schedule which suits the organization, the employees involved and the provider. Did you notice that we followed GROW in the above plan? (see page 35). This robust model is an excellent framework for almost anything that has to be achieved, from a single coaching session to major organizational restructuring, whether it involves coaching or not.

For a large organization that can provide the budget, you are likely to end up with these elements:

- meetings and focus groups to explore the steps outlined above;
- staff surveys such as Cultural Transformation Tools, MBTI or 360 (all of which are described in Chapter 8);
- induction presentation/s to the whole organization;
- training in coaching skills, which is extended over at least one month, including paired practice to embed the learning, where managers will be trained to:
  - exhibit coaching skills;
  - deliver formal coaching sessions;
  - train, assess and accredit other managers in the first two.
- one or more manuals/handbooks for reference regarding the coaching skills and training;
- coaching sessions.

An interesting example of how one organization tackled the question has been kindly donated by Liz Macann at the BBC, and features in Chapter 9 on page 149.

CONCLUSION

The culture in an organization can only change when its people do. Nothing can change without the instigation of at least one individual and the cooperation of others. One of the reasons for the explosive success of coaching and coach training in recent years is that a coach enables individuals to identify what they would like to change in themselves, and helps them to make that change in a positive way. By initiating change within themselves, such people inevitably trigger a transformation in their organizations: the 'happy virus' in action.

With coaching programmes becoming more common in the various fields of education – schools and universities, for instance – I foresee a time when the world will have a whole generation of leaders who communicate through coaching skills, and will consequently be capable of listening to and understanding one another.

Exercise: Competency assessment

Our final exercise is a competency assessment which you are recommended to complete in respect of your own skills and then debrief with your practice partner, through coaching each other as you have done during the exercises in the previous chapters. Use the forms to identify what you would like to change and then, using GROW, facilitate each other in setting goals and working out how to achieve them.

8–10 =   Unconscious competence – I am on automatic pilot
5–7   =   Conscious competence – I know I am doing it right
3–4   =   Conscious incompetence – I know what I don't know
1–2   =   Needs coach training – I don't know what I don't know

Establishing the coaching relationship

	1	2	3	4	5	6	7	8	9	10
Decides whether coaching is appropriate for the situation	1	2	3	4	5	6	7	8	9	10
Asks permission to coach and wins the coachee's trust	1	2	3	4	5	6	7	8	9	10

Coaching presence

	1	2	3	4	5	6	7	8	9	10
Is present in the moment and flexible in approach	1	2	3	4	5	6	7	8	9	10
Accesses own intuition	1	2	3	4	5	6	7	8	9	10
Uses humour effectively	1	2	3	4	5	6	7	8	9	10
Shifts the coachee's perspective	1	2	3	4	5	6	7	8	9	10
Is able to remain neutral when dealing with strong emotions	1	2	3	4	5	6	7	8	9	10

Focused listening

	1	2	3	4	5	6	7	8	9	10
Focuses on the coachee's agenda, not the coach's	1	2	3	4	5	6	7	8	9	10
Listens at Level Five	1	2	3	4	5	6	7	8	9	10
Clarifies, reflects and paraphrases	1	2	3	4	5	6	7	8	9	10

Awareness questioning

	1	2	3	4	5	6	7	8	9	10
Chooses questions that raise self-awareness	1	2	3	4	5	6	7	8	9	10
Chooses questions that encourage self-learning	1	2	3	4	5	6	7	8	9	10
Chooses open questions to create awareness and insight	1	2	3	4	5	6	7	8	9	10
Chooses questions that move the coachee's focus forward	1	2	3	4	5	6	7	8	9	10

Direct communication

	1	2	3	4	5	6	7	8	9	10
Is clear and articulate, speaking precisely and concisely	1	2	3	4	5	6	7	8	9	10
Gives useful feedback	1	2	3	4	5	6	7	8	9	10
Builds coachee's self-belief	1	2	3	4	5	6	7	8	9	10
Uses subtle aids such as humour and metaphor	1	2	3	4	5	6	7	8	9	10

Goals and action plans

	1	2	3	4	5	6	7	8	9	10
Supports the coachee in prioritizing goals	1	2	3	4	5	6	7	8	9	10
Stretches the coachee to aim for his/her highest potential	1	2	3	4	5	6	7	8	9	10
Helps the coachee to create a strategic plan with targets	1	2	3	4	5	6	7	8	9	10
Holds the coachee accountable	1	2	3	4	5	6	7	8	9	10
Celebrates the coachee's achievements	1	2	3	4	5	6	7	8	9	10

Figure 7.1   Final exercise: competency assessment

Part II

Advanced coaching

Tools, models and international case histories

8

Coaching tools

This chapter gives a brief summary of the most popular methods, apart from coaching, used by coaches and organizations today. References to books on each field are included in Further reading (page 224), and there is a great deal more information available on the internet. There are other systems, tools and models available to coaches and there is no significance in my not having included them all; it is just a question of space.

Although widely relied upon by consultants and organizations, the majority of these tools, skills and disciplines have no scientific basis and there is no conclusive proof that they work. Therefore, as well as illustrating what can be achieved through the use of a particular method, I have endeavoured in places to flag up the pitfalls a coach needs to be aware of when working with it.

The chapter covers:

■ transpersonal coaching;
■ David Grove's clean language, metaphor and emergent knowledge;
■ the talking stick;
■ the change curve and four-room apartment;
■ transactional analysis;
■ values questionnaire;
■ cultural transformation tools (CTT);
■ systemic coaching;
■ appreciative inquiry;
■ the Myers Briggs Type Indicator (MBTI);
■ 360-degree feedback;
■ neuro linguistic programming (NLP);
■ body language;
■ coaching by telephone;

- other models;
- the role of the coach in the organizational hierarchy;
- an organizational hierarchy of needs;
- how people and organizations change;
- the relationship between the component parts of coaching.

TRANSPERSONAL COACHING

I am grateful to John Whitmore for providing the following information.

Transpersonal psychology is the next evolution of psychology beyond humanistic psychology, upon which life and workplace coaching were based. On the surface, therefore, transpersonal coaching is the adaptation of a number of important perspectives, models and methods from transpersonal psychology to the coaching format, but its implications are far deeper than that. The practice of transpersonal coaching demands further training and the acquisition of certain techniques not previously used, a perspective shift and a commitment to the coach's own developmental journey.

Transpersonal means 'beyond the personal', although of course it starts with the self. As a whole systems approach, it recognizes the interconnectedness of individuals, families, communities and organizations, cultures and life itself. It also recognizes and works with the yearning, ingrained in the human psyche, for something beyond the personal, beyond the material and the everyday, that is often described as the spiritual.

Dr Roberto Assagioli, a colleague of C G Jung and the creator of psychosynthesis, a core transpersonal psychology, described the spiritual as 'all the functions and activities which have as common denominator the possessing of values higher than the average; values such as the ethical, the aesthetic, the heroic, the humanitarian and the altruistic'. The most important distinguishing feature of transpersonal psychology is that it does not draw a line between personal and spiritual development, but sees them as stages on a continuum.

Transpersonal coaching is at the cutting edge, and now more than ever vitally needed by business, individuals and humanity if we are to build a world we wish to live and work in that is mutually sustainable and beneficial to us all. Coaches are more frequently than ever being asked to help with issues of meaning and purpose, especially by successful business leaders who see little value in what they are doing. Indeed transpersonal coaching will inevitably assist coachees to uncover and connect with their deeper values. Trained transpersonal coaches have perspectives, models and methods that enable people to explore their deeper nature and begin to discover who they really are.

With the cracks showing in many previously reliable institutions and indicators, insecurity is everywhere and it is those who are equipped with the best tools and experience that will be able to provide much in demand coaching. Transpersonal coaching is the coaching of the future.

Sir John Whitmore
www.performanceconsultants.com

Performance Consultants pioneered transpersonal coaching through John Whitmore's industry standard, 'Coaching for Performance', has included it in its coach training for years and is actively promoting its wider adoption by the industry.

DAVID GROVE'S CLEAN LANGUAGE, METAPHOR AND EMERGENT KNOWLEDGE

David Grove is a psychologist who worked on alleviating traumatic memories in the 1980s. He discovered that when he asked patients to talk about their experiences, they naturally slipped into metaphor, and that if he facilitated their own metaphorical descriptions without any guidance or influence, they could work through their trauma and be cured of the symptoms arising from it. He developed nine questions which he found would least influence his patients, and coined the term 'clean language' to describe these. His work is documented on the sites www.cleanlanguage.co.uk and www.cleancoaching.com.

We often use metaphor to aid communication. Metaphors, like dreams, are a direct link with our subconscious which, Carl Jung theorized, does not have words and communicates in pictures and symbols.

Some common metaphors are:

- Under pressure.
- Stressed.
- On dry land.
- I can see clearly what I should do.
- A millstone round my neck.
- What's blocking me is...

When coachees deliver metaphors, whether spontaneously or because you have asked for one, honour their symbols without introducing your own. Use open questions or reflect their words back to them to help them find out more. When a metaphor is described in detail it changes and, in doing so, brings the coachee greater insight and understanding.

This technique is useful for coachees who have a block which repeatedly trips them up. As always in coaching, it is important to keep the focus positive by asking questions like, 'What would you like to have happen?' Exploring a negative metaphor, like dwelling on a problem, will make things worse.

Work on metaphors and symbols was pioneered by Carl Jung, who wrote many tracts on the subject and whose methods are still widely and successfully used in therapy today. One key difference between Grove's work and Jung's is that Jung sought to interpret the symbols and relate them back to past experiences in the coachee's life. One of Grove's breakthroughs in the field is that he realizes it is more effective not to attempt to identify the source of the metaphor. In this way, traumas which are too painful to face may be alleviated without ever having to be identified.

Since Jung's work on dreams, metaphors and symbols, a number of psychologists have developed guided visualization techniques where the coachees are asked, for instance, to imagine they are walking along a path, and reach a house, or a river, or a person etc. These exercises can be valuable, and Brandon Bays, creator of a healing technique called 'The journey', is one among many who claim success in healing patients with illnesses as severe as cancer through guided visualization techniques.

However, there is a drawback with this type of exercise. Jung himself believed that it was not possible to have a blanket interpretation of the symbols which arise in dreams, because people develop their own symbols according to events that have happened in their own lives (reference the 'cultural map' described in Chapter 1). Therefore, it is possible that the practitioner's symbols may not relate to the coachee at all, or that coachees may have a traumatic attachment which will prove unhelpful or even dangerous. For instance, if the practitioner introduces a river into the scenario and a coachee, when aged 3, had watched a parent drown in a river, introducing a river symbol could be damaging for him. Coachees often reach a vulnerable psychological state during coaching or visualization, when they are more susceptible to suggestion than usual.

Clean language is not dissimilar to the guided visualization techniques, but has one major difference: the practitioner follows the coachee's metaphor at all times instead of introducing symbols of the practitioner's own. In this way, coachees are led by their own subconscious minds, or their intuition, without any interference from the coach, or perhaps more importantly, from their own conscious minds.

In the previous example of the coachee who has had a traumatic experience with a river, the coachee may introduce this symbol at a point that is appropriate to his own healing process, and develop it in a way which will take him through the trauma and out the other side, thereby healing the scar, rather than risking the jarring effect of introducing the symbol at a time when he is not ready to deal with it.

During visualization the coachee usually enters a trance state to some degree, and afterwards coachees often feel the desire to do nothing but sleep, sometimes for as long as 12 hours at a stretch. This is because everything in our unconscious minds is related, so if a significant change has taken place, what the body wants to do is shut down while all the relevant changes are made throughout the psycho-system. Coachees will often find after a clean language session that emotional reactions they experienced regularly before the session, such as irrational fear or uncontrollable spurts of anger, have simply stopped happening, with no conscious effort on the part of the coachee – or the coach for that matter.

The process seems nothing short of miraculous, and I have sometimes had to bring a session to a halt after working with metaphor for 10 or 20 minutes, because of the profound effect it has on the coachee and their need to shut down while all is unconsciously rearranged.

My own first experience of clean language was a series of sessions with Penny Tompkins and James Lawley, who developed 'symbolic modelling' from David Grove's work, which cured my fear of public speaking in only three sessions. One of my main lines of work is now professional speaking, and thanks to these techniques, it has become a pleasure instead of something to dread. Since then I have used the techniques successfully with many coachees, and now work regularly with David Grove on furthering his work, which is always progressing into new and related areas.

Below is an example of a clean language session:

Coachee: I feel scared all the time. My life is out of control.
Coach: And when you feel scared all the time and your life is out of control, that's like what?
Coachee: I feel as if I'm on a river. It's rushing along.
Coach: And when there's a river that's rushing along, what kind of river is that?
Coachee: There's a waterfall ahead and cliffs behind.
Coach: Is there anything else about a waterfall, a river that is rushing along and cliffs?
Coachee: The waterfall is ahead. It's powerful and out of control.
Coach: And when there's a waterfall ahead that's powerful and out of control, is there anything else about that?
Coachee: It's sparkling. Silver and gold flashing in the water.
Coach: And is there anything else about silver and gold that's flashing in the water?
Coachee: The silver is calm and the gold is energy. They are what is needed to control the water.
Coach: And what happens next?
Coachee: I am riding on the water now.
Coach: And what kind of water is the water you are riding on?

Coachee: It is calm and full of energy. It is bearing me up.
Coach: And is there anything else about water that bears you up?
Coachee: It's turning into land.
Coach: And what kind of land is that?
Coachee: It's green. The sun is shining like the gold and the river is flowing gently like the silver. Everything is calm.

Note that the coach is not introducing any elements of his or her own into the scenario. As in standard coaching, the process is coachee-led and the coach is asking non-leading questions. A slight difference is that a substantial proportion of the questions are 'closed' as opposed to 'open', as described in Chapter 2, and this is probably more so than in regular coaching. This is because working with metaphor has to be even more coachee-led, as the symbols are leading directly to the coachee's subconscious mind and there is a greater danger of causing damage by leading the coachee. The closed question 'Is there anything else?' is less leading than 'What else is there?', because the latter implies that there is something else. The former question does not assume that there is or is not – it is entirely up to the coachee's metaphor (or subconscious mind) to let the coachee know.

The metaphor will usually reach a place featuring calm, positive symbols. The coachee will have worked through some anxiety on a subconscious level and will be less troubled in future. Coachees are often surprised at the number of changes which happen to them on many levels after such a session. For instance they may find it easier to speak up at meetings, or to flirt, or to sleep through the night, when the original reason for the session was around something quite different. This is the subconscious system at work; changing one element has sent a wave of changes through the others.

David Grove's work has moved into emergent knowledge, which incorporates his techniques of clean language and metaphor to explore a coachee's inner 'psychescape' using methods identified in the new science of emergence. This science explains the processes by which ants build nests without being directed by a 'leader' ant, how cities form themselves and how search engines like Google function through iterative (repeating but not exactly the same) algorithms. David Grove has applied this principle to the human psyche and uses repeating, similar questions to 'emerge' self-knowledge which the coachee may not have been able to access.

In emergent knowledge, clean language is still used but the psyche is explored by spatial, more than linguistic, processes. The coachee is literally moved around physically to uncover buried knowledge and new perspectives.

An everyday use for this is to ask the coachee to move to a different place in the room if he or she is stuck for an answer. Physically moving position gives a different perspective.

Coachee:	I can't see a solution to this.
Coach:	Is there a place in the room you could move to which might have a solution?
Coachee:	[Coachee moves]
Coach:	And what do you know from there?

David and I have been working together to develop his emergent knowledge techniques over the past two years and to train others in them. More details on our work in this area are available on www.cleancoaching.com.

THE TALKING STICK

The talking stick is a centuries-old tradition from Native American tribes, which maintained order in council meetings and ensured that everyone was heard in a just and impartial manner. The stick would be an object such as a shell, a peace pipe or a feather. The elder would hold the stick and when he had said everything he wished (of course it was always a he there and then), he would pass it to another member of the tribe, who would then hold it until he too had said his piece.

This is a useful exercise to use at the end of a group session, where everyone closes by saying what they have learnt during the day. It is also an opportunity to give thanks and feedback.

I employ a further development of this method for conflict resolution. In a meeting of two or more people; the speaker holding the stick asks the others to repeat back what she or he has said in their own words, until the speaker is satisfied that they have understood the meaning as intended.

This gets round the problem that most people in meetings listen at Levels One to Three of the five levels of listening described in Chapter 2, usually thinking about what they want to say themselves. However, in order to paraphrase what someone is saying, you have to thoroughly understand the meaning yourself, and hey presto: conflict resolved. There can be some quite emotional moments as scales fall away from eyes, and it is not impossible that the worst of enemies will end up becoming the best of friends through this exercise.

THE CHANGE CURVE AND THE FOUR-ROOM APARTMENT

One of the greatest challenges in corporate life today is constant and unwanted change; there are mergers, acquisitions and de-mergers, chief executives moving on every few years or less, new systems to contend with which may change the demographic of whole departments, and similar situations which employees can feel are inflicted upon them.

The change curve was devised by Elizabeth Kubler Ross, a therapist who worked extensively with people who were bereaved or facing death themselves. She noticed a pattern of reaction to unwelcome change, which went through the stages of:

- shock that the change is going to happen;
- denial, burying the head in the sand and hoping the unwanted situation will simply go away;
- anger at self and others, resentment and blame; at this point energy is at its lowest and it is difficult to achieve anything at all, either in a personal life or an organization;
- letting go of the old regime and accepting change as inevitable, which leads to:
- testing the new situation and discovering, in the case of an organizational change, that there may be some advantages in the new regime if one can keep an open attitude;
- integrating into a new whole which can move forward or, in the case of someone facing death, the possibility of acceptance and spending the time that is left in a valuable way.

One of Kubler Ross's contentions was that the key element needed to deal with change is time; managers today rarely have that luxury. I recently worked with 20 managers from a major financial institution who, on being asked where they were on the change curve, said that they went through the whole curve every day and that it was expected to continue that way for the next two years.

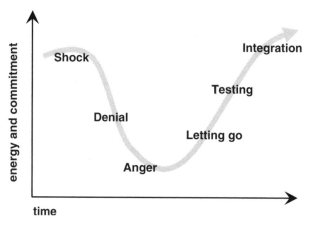

Figure 8.1   The change curve

Nevertheless, looking at the model can alleviate some of the stress when people realize that the sometimes intense emotions of anger and despair they are feeling are normal human reactions, that they can try to move forward in a more positive state of mind, and that they have a choice of how to feel about it and what action to take.

A further development from Kubler Ross's change curve is the four-room apartment model, developed by Claes Janssen (see Figure 8.2).

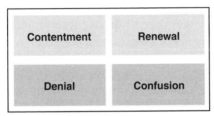

Figure 8.2   The four-room apartment

This model works anticlockwise from the top left and aptly describes the stages we go through when confronted by change. It can be used in the same way as the change curve.

TRANSACTIONAL ANALYSIS

Developed in the 1950s by Eric Berne, transactional analysis has some components that can be useful in coaching, for example the parent–child model. In the 1960s this became popular in management development, usually as a way of manipulating others; if you could identify your own state and the other person's, it was theorized that you could adjust your state in order to gain an advantage.

This exercise can be useful to help coachees to discover more about themselves. Identifying that you are communicating in, say, the child mode shown below, is a step towards being able to choose to behave in the adult mode.

Berne theorized that in our communications (or 'transactions') with others, we are playing the role of parent, child or adult, exhibiting the following traits respectively:

- **Parent**: controlling, bullying, didactic, critical, judgemental, finger wagging, use of words like *always, never, for once and for all.*
- **Child**: sad, despairing, temper tantrums, giggling, baby talk, using words like *I'm gonna, things never go right for me, the best ever.*
- **Adult**: straightforward, attentive, non-threatening and not threatened, using words like *I see, possibly, probably, disappointing* (instead of *devastating*),

I think (taking responsibility) *I believe*, and all the coaching questions, such as *how much, how many, what …*

Berne counselled that if someone is playing the 'child', the communication will be easier if you play the 'parent' and vice versa. The ideal is, unsurprisingly, when both parties behave like adults.

One of Berne's theories which dovetails with coaching is that we are all born as whole, complete and balanced individuals, which he termed 'OK'. Considerable development by other psychologists has taken place since Berne's initial work, and one widely used model has become known as 'the OK Corral', originally developed by Frank Ernst (see Figure 8.3).

NOT OK – OK	OK – OK
I am not OK with me **You are OK with me** I am not good enough I am dependent on your opinion	**I am OK with me** **You are OK with me** We are confident and get on well We can both add value
NOT OK – NOT OK	OK – NOT OK
I am not OK with me **You are not OK with me** This is hopeless We'll never manage it	**I am OK with me** **You are not OK with me** I know best You've got it wrong

Figure 8.3   The OK Corral

People who operate in the top-right quadrant tend to be optimistic, confident and easy to get on with. Of course, to some extent we move around all the quadrants at various times and situations, but most people tend to have one particular quadrant that they act in most of the time.

Coachees may be helped by looking at the quadrants and becoming aware of which they are operating in at different times in their various relationships, particularly with bosses and reports.

VALUES QUESTIONNAIRE

What do we mean by values? People's values are formed through a combination of their beliefs, behaviours, principles and personality. Your 'values' will show up when you have to act in a way that feels uncomfortable: for instance, if you are asked to fire someone at work who you feel deserves to stay. 'Values' might be the 'still, small voice' referred to in the Bible – the voice of conscience which might speak to you if you are tempted to pocket that £5 note the person ahead of you has dropped. Alternatively, your values may show up in the way that you run forward to return the note to its owner without any hesitation, or risk putting your head above the parapet to speak out for the one in line to be fired.

On a simpler level, your values represent the things in life that you value: if you like keeping healthy by playing tennis, then exercise might be a value for you. If you like to laugh, then a sense of humour would be one of your values. You might enjoy being tidy and financially secure, or living the life of a chaotic gambler. All of these qualities can be termed 'values', and the ones you live by now may not always be those you aspire to.

Organizations have values too: for example, caring for staff, maintaining ethical practices, bureaucracy and internal backstabbing are all values that may be exhibited by companies. Clearly, not all values are positive ones. Most individuals and organizations have a set of values, declared or instinctive, that they would like to practise, but it is rare to see these achieved 100 per cent.

Set out in Figure 8.4 is a list of values which you may find useful both to complete yourself and to give to coachees. The first step is to pick out 10 personal values – not the ones you aspire to, but those you (or your coachee) are actually exhibiting in your life at the moment. Then mark the 10 values most often exhibited by your organization at the moment. Finally, choose 10 values that you would like your organization to exhibit. Mark each set with a different symbol – for instance a 'P' for personal, 'C' for current organizational and 'D' for desired organizational. You can add new values which apply to you if they are not listed.

Seeing which values coincide between two or three of the sections enables coachees to discover new insights, such as how much of themselves they have to leave behind when they come to work in the morning. The exercise may prompt them to consider how they can change their work environment for the better. In some cases, the new insight may be that their workplace is so incompatible that they need to start looking for another job; then again, the survey might make them appreciate their organization all the more.

On an organizational level, this exercise can pinpoint what culture is desired and what changes need to be made to achieve that culture. Identification of common values provides a map of where the organization or the individual is now (R of the GROW model referred to in Chapter 3) and helps the coach and coachee to create a pathway towards successful change.

Whether working with private or corporate coachees, the time to hand out these sheets is either before or after the first session. They will bring clarity and insight for both the coach and the coachee. If completed at regular intervals, they will provide a measuring tool for the effectiveness of coaching.

This model was developed from Richard Barrett's Cultural Transformation Tools surveys, described in the next section.

Select values from the following list and mark them in the margins. Add more values if you wish.

10 personal values (mark with a P). These are not the values you aspire to, but those you currently live by.

10 values that represent the current culture of your organisation (mark with a C).

10 values that represent the desired culture of your organisation (mark with a D).

Accountability	Creativity	Hierarchy
Achievement	Diversity	Human rights
Ambition	Ease with uncertainty	Humility
Balance (home/work)	Efficiency	Humour/fun
Being liked	Empathy	Image
Being the best	Empire building	Independence
Bureaucracy	Employee health	Information hoarding
Caution	Employee safety	Information sharing
Clarity	Environmental awareness	Innovation
Commitment	Excellence	Integrity
Community activity	Exploitation	Intuition
Compassion	Family	Leadership development
Competition	Financial stability	Logic
Confidence	Flat structure	Long-term perspective
Conflict resolution	Forgiveness	Making a difference
Conformity	Friendships	Manipulation
Continuous learning	Future generations	Mentoring
Control	Generosity	Mission focus
Cooperation	Global perspective	Openness
Courage	Health and fitness	Perseverance

Personal fulfilment
Personal growth
Philanthropy
Positive feedback
Power
Pride
Professional growth
Profit
Reliability
Respect
Risk-taking
Self-belief
Self-discipline
Short-term orientation
Skills training
Status
Strategic alliances
Teamwork
Tradition
Vision

How many matching values do you have?

P-C [ ]   P-D [ ]   C-D [ ]   P-C-D [ ]

Ask these questions:

What have you learnt about yourself?   What is the impact of not changing?
What new insights do you have?   How would you like it to be?
What impact is this having on your life?   What would you would like to do about it?
What impact on your work?   When/where/how?

Figure 8.4 Values questionnaire

CULTURAL TRANSFORMATION TOOLS (CTT)

The CTT model was developed by Richard Barrett and is used to map the personal values of employees and their perception of the current and desired values of the organization. The model is also used to map the values of teams and any other group of individuals who share a common purpose, towards development of leadership and whole-system change.

Barratt builds on Maslow's hierarchy of needs (see Figure 8.5). The process is conducted through online surveys which can stretch to include many thousands of people all over the world. From the resulting reports, trends can be identified about the culture of the organization, such as that it allows people the freedom for self-development or, at the opposite end of the scale, that they are feeling bullied, for example, or there is too much bureaucracy.

The seven levels of consciousness

Positive focus / Excessive focus

Level	Name	Focus
7	Service	**Service to humanity** Long-term perspective. Future generations. Ethics.
6	Making a difference	**Collaboration with customers & the local community** Strategic alliances. Employee fulfillment. Environmental stewardship.
5	Internal cohesion	**Development of corporate community** Positive, creative corporate culture. Shared vision and values.
4	Transformation	**Continuous renewal** Learning and innovation. Organisational growth through employee participation.
3	Self-esteem	**Being the best. Best practice** Productivity, efficiency, quality, systems and processes. Bureaucracy. Complacency.
2	Relationship	**Relationships that support corporate needs** Good communication between employees, customers and suppliers. Manipulation. Blame.
1	Survival	**Pursuit of profit & shareholder value** Financial soundness. Employee health and safety. Exploitation. Over-control.

Richard Barrett and Associates LLC. Corp Tools (UK) Ltd. Copyright 2004. www.corptools.com

Figure 8.5   Cultural Transformation Tools

Once a trend is identified, interventions such as coaching and training can be designed to remedy any limiting values that are regularly showing up. The process can be extended into measurement through further surveys which ask employees how much of the profit, or budget, is being taken up by the limiting value. If these subsequent surveys are extended across enough people, the average figure delivered will be accurate enough to get the attention of the financial decision makers in the company.

I find this process far more effective and comfortable than 360-degree type surveys, because the latter may evoke judgement and criticism of particular individuals in the organization, whose consequent fear and anxiety will not do anything to increase their motivation or performance.

Figure 8.6 shows an example of a report from a similar survey conducted in a real organization, which estimates that over £13 million was lost in the year 2000 through limiting values, turning what might have been a good profit into a loss. Richard Barrett's ideas are explored in a series of excellent books, in particular *Liberating the Corporate Soul* (1998).

Cost of limiting values

• Bureaucracy (unnecessary)	£1,799,618
• Confusion	£3,178,636
• Empire building	£1,764,682
• Information hoarding	£1,634,045
• Hierarchical	£624,327
• Long hours	£187,909
• Short-term focus	£3,480,818
• Sickness and leavers	£834,225
• Total (potential business value)	£13,504,260

Based on staff perception of lost productivity & opportunity.
Annual income £33,000,000 and loss of –£500,000 in 2000.

Figure 8.6   The cost of limiting values

SYSTEMIC COACHING

Systemic coaching examines human relationships as a system; if one person in a system changes attitude, then others can as well. The process can highlight situations where people may be transferring childhood emotions, such as guilt, onto their current relationships, perhaps treating their employees as children or their peers as siblings. The relationships the coachee may have had with his or her own siblings may be quite inappropriate in the workplace, or in the coachee's current marriage or interaction with friends, and people who exhibit this are often unaware of the effect they are having on others who did not grow up within a similar framework.

The model works along a similar process to GROW. The Systemic Coach will start with diagnostics, to assess how well the system is functioning at present, then set goals, and then coach individual members on strategies to achieve the goals.

In common with other coaching-related practices, systemic coaching treats the individual as complete, resourceful and as having all the knowledge he or she needs. The coaching helps people to set in motion their self-directed learning, to activate their inner resources and plan ahead for future growth.

APPRECIATIVE INQUIRY

Appreciative inquiry is an organizational change methodology developed by David Cooperrider, chair of Organizational Behaviour at Case Western Reserve University in Ohio.

It takes place in four stages, shown in Figure 8.7. Can you see the parallels to our coaching GROW model? Appreciative inquiry embodies the visionary and forward-focused nature of coaching.

Discovery:	Looking at the best of what is working at the moment
Dreaming:	Envisioning the best that could happen
Design:	Working out how to achieve it
Destiny:	Allowing it to emerge gracefully, flexibly, cooperating with others, using the resources that are there

Figure 8.7 Appreciative inquiry

The model works for individuals as well as organizations. Standard coaching questions for the different parts of GROW could be used in one to one coaching. For an organization, the process parallels our 'Values questionnaire' model described earlier, and might go like this:

- **Discovery**: running surveys from the staff, setting up focus groups, getting people talking about what they like about the organization and what works well at the moment.
- **Dreaming**: asking people how they would like the organization to be.
- **Design**: working out how to achieve their vision, what systems need to be changed or put in place, what attitudes need to change and how these outcomes could be achieved.
- **Destiny**: supporting efforts to change and allowing the new vision to unfold in its own way; integrating surprises and new ideas that crop up along the way, recognizing and calling upon existing resources, particularly the various individuals within the organization.

Appreciative inquiry treats an organization as a phenomenon to be celebrated, in all its diverse and conflicting glory, rather than as a problem to be solved; every individual working there is regarded as having something of value to contribute to the whole.

THE MYERS BRIGGS TYPE INDICATOR (MBTI)

One of the most widely used personality tests in the world is the Myers Briggs Type Indicator, a psychological assessment system developed by a mother and daughter team some 60 years ago and based on the work of psychologist Carl Jung. The MBTI asks the candidate to answer a series of 'forced-choice' questions, where each choice identifies the candidate as belonging to one of four paired traits. The test takes about 20 minutes, and at the end the candidate is presented with a precise, multidimensional summary of her or his personality, classifying it into types based on four bipolar dimensions:

- Extraversion–Introversion (E–I)
  - energizes either from being with people (E) or
  - being solitary (I).
- Sensing–INtuition (S–N)
  - gathers information directly through data and detail (S) or
  - indirectly through relationships and possibilities (N).
- Thinking–Feeling (T–F)
  - makes decisions using objective logic (T) or
  - using subjective feeling (F).
- Judging–Perceiving (J–P)
  - likes to plan and organize so as to know what lies ahead (J) or
  - prefers flexibility and being open to options (P).

Cross-referencing these four categories results in 16 personality types, illustrated in Figure 8.8.

There is, however, a fundamental drawback with this and any other personality definition test: the danger is that once people have identified their types, they will be imprisoned in the boxes that the labels create. Take the case of an executive who has competently participated in meetings, given successful presentations and attended networking events when required. The executive is aware that he has no desire to join those of his colleagues who stay up half the night partying at sales conferences; midnight finds him safely tucked up in his hotel room. However, should this same executive identify himself as an introvert, through a personality profile test like MBTI, he may start to find it more difficult to summon up the energy required for the networking, assertiveness at meetings and public speaking that his current role requires. This is even more perilous in the early stages of a career, before the person has developed the confidence to perform outside of her or his natural tendencies.

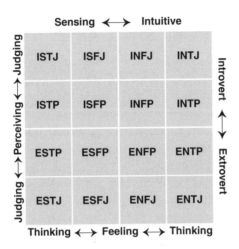

Figure 8.8   The Myers Briggs Type Indicator personality types

Despite its popularity, there has been no quantifiable research to show whether MBTI is actually effective at classifying personalities.

MBTI is another tool in widespread use in organizations which in some ways contradicts the ethos of coaching. It can be argued that such tests help to provide the Reality section of the GROW model described in Chapter 3, by offering people a chance to reflect on their inner make-up, thereby providing new insight. However, these advantages may be outweighed by the notional limitations the tests place on the candidates; labels have a tendency to create their own reality. One of the main aims of coaching is to create awareness in coachees that they have choices – of jobs, attitude and behaviour – and enable them to act upon their choices. Being labelled as what they are rather than what they want to become can be daunting. Referring back to the discussion about 'habits' in Chapter 4, and later (page 134) to 'How people and organizations change', it is hard enough to break down recurring behaviour limitations without having them reinforced.

The risk from the organization's point of view is that candidates may fake their answers to appear more suited to a certain job. Whether it is possible to achieve the desired effect this way is a moot point, but it will certainly distort the result. However, as this product is almost universally used in large organizations, it makes sense for coaches to familiarize themselves with it in order to coach efficiently the duly labelled coachees and support them in exploring new insights and dissolving any limiting walls which may have been created by the categorization.

360-DEGREE FEEDBACK

360-degree feedback is a process used by many organizations today to provide managers with feedback from all the different categories of people they come into contact with in the course of their work: for example, the manager they report to, the staff who report to them, colleagues, customers and clients. The feedback is usually delivered anonymously, and participants are asked to fill in a series of tick-boxes (often online) and make individual comments about various aspects of a manager's performance.

Sometimes the manager can choose the participants and at others the participants are selected by the manager's own boss or perhaps the HR department. The process can be helpful in the case of a manager who does not realize he or she is a bully, perhaps, or to identify the areas to work on during a forthcoming coaching programme.

The pitfalls of this type of survey are that:

- people are not always honest in case their identity is guessed;
- sometimes their identities *are* guessed;
- personal grudges, jealousy or ambitions can dictate a participant's comments;
- negative feedback can be meaningless if it is not known where it comes from;
- people tend to hear criticism louder than praise and can become demoralized by the process.

Any type of survey where some of the staff are asked to give feedback about other specific people in the business should be managed with great care. The recipient should be coached through the results rather than just handed a report. I have personally worked with a manager whose confidence was so shattered by his feedback that he was unable to go to work for a week, in spite of having previously been a reasonably happy and successful director. He later discovered that some of the blackest comments had been intended to refer to a different manager altogether – but astonishingly, this was not made clear when he was handed the results. I and other coaches continued to support this manager for some time but he has said he may never regain his confidence.

Another unwelcome side-effect is that some managers hide behind the process of written feedback in this way, now that it is available on a regular basis, rather than confront a colleague, boss or report with their grievances. I worked with a senior manager of a multinational who intensely resented the fact that some scathing comments from her own direct line manager had gone the rounds of HR and various directors before she had even seen them. To add to her sense of injustice, the manager had never raised any hint of displeasure with her directly; in fact, the situation was quite the reverse and she had thought she was highly regarded and doing a good job.

What rankled the most was that she was not even told who had seen the report, or what would happen to it in the future; for instance, would it be stored on her file so that future staff would see it? She felt humiliated and had become too disheartened by the whole process to raise these questions at all. She felt that she was not being shown the basic humanitarian respect and courtesy that any individual deserves and requires to flourish in an organization.

Surveys such as these fly directly in the face of the principles of building self-belief and creating a 'blame-free culture', as described in Chapter 1, both of which are fundamental to the ethos of coaching. Nevertheless, they have taken a firm hold in many companies whose stated aim is to create a coaching culture, so coaches need to know how to handle their effects.

In situations such as I have described, the guideline to follow is to get the individuals involved talking. Coach them on how to have a non-confrontational, inoffensive conversation, offer to facilitate a meeting, or give them some training in coaching skills and concepts. Find a way to get the conflicts out into the open, off the paper, and into direct communication.

NEURO LINGUISTIC PROGRAMMING

Commonly known as NLP, this model works on the theory that you can programme the brain to change its habits by visualization, use of words, or changing the position of the body. A number of coaches are committed exponents of NLP, and some of the processes show parallels with coaching, such as mirroring the coachee's words and noticing the coachee's body language. This is because NLP and coaching developed from some of the same sources.

NLP was founded by Richard Bandler and John Grinder in the 1970s. Later the pair fell out catastrophically and spent much of the next 20 years involved in a lawsuit over who owned the name. During that period, many splinter groups were formed either using the name NLP or creating variations, such as neuro associative conditioning, which was developed by consciousness-raising guru Anthony Robbins.

Some coaches successfully base their entire practices on NLP techniques, and the discipline has aficionados who regard it as having cult status. There is also a wide body of criticism aimed at the subject, mainly that the claims of NLP have not been scientifically verified.

One example of this is the NLP premise that people are either visual, auditory, kinaesthetic or olfactory; ie they process information best through seeing, hearing and speaking, touching and feeling, or through their senses of taste and smell. It is claimed that you can tell which of these categories people fall into by watching which way their eyes move when answering a question. However, there has been no scientific proof of this at all, and in my experience the majority of people process information in all these ways. Very occasionally, however, I have come across someone who, rather than falling predominantly in any of the categories, appears to be unable to process information in one of them. For instance, the question, 'How do you feel?' can elicit a complete blank and has to be rephrased in a different way. According to the laws of categorization, you could say 'How do you see your situation at the moment?' or 'What can you tell me about that?' However, the ones who cannot answer questions about how they feel are usually men, and the cause may be more to do with culture or the different wiring that, it is now accepted, men have from women.

I met one participant in a training room once who said she could not grasp the concept of metaphor at all. When I talked about 'interior landscape', for instance, all she saw was the phrase 'interior landscape' written in letters before her eyes. I discussed this with metaphor guru David Grove (see page 111), and he suggested this is the result simply of a blockage, and that when he works with such people they eventually become able to see metaphors as well as anyone else.

The field of psychology is moving at an astonishing rate, with new discoveries being theorized and proven every day. I recommend the best policy is to keep in mind John Whitmore's phrase 'This is not the truth', mentioned in my Introduction, and remain open to all theories and experiences.

Although the tools can be effective, some NLP practitioners take the 'sticking plaster' approach, working with the symptoms rather than the cause. Personally, I believe that bringing about change at core level – working from the inside out – results in more lasting and congruent benefits, and this is the approach that good coaching takes, whether or not the coach uses techniques from the field of NLP.

There is such a broad amount of information available on NLP elsewhere that I shall not go into further detail here. One of the areas that the discipline places great emphasis on is body language, which is discussed in the next section.

BODY LANGUAGE

Words are only part of the story in human communication. Albert Mehrabian premised that:

- only 7 per cent of meaning is in the words spoken;
- 38 per cent of meaning is paralinguistic (the way that the words are said, including tone and pace);
- 55 per cent is in facial expression and body language.

Mehrabian's theory has been taken out of context over the years; the percentages listed above, particularly the first, are not intended to be applied indiscriminately to any form of communication anywhere. They specifically refer to a conversational exchange between two or more people.

It is evident that when people are in rapport, they tend to mirror body language: for instance, cupping a hand under the chin, crossing the legs or tilting the head to the same side.

Have you ever been in a situation where you kept shifting your position by crossing and uncrossing your legs, or taking your elbows on and off the table, or wanting to lean back when you were forwards and forwards when you were back? What this tells you is that you are uncomfortable in the situation – perhaps you are feeling criticized, not respected or aggressive towards the person. Dip into coaching skills to relieve the situation and create some understanding with the person. Asking awareness questions starting with what, where or how is likely to have the effect of relieving tension and making you both warm towards each other.

Great emphasis is placed on the use of mirrored body language in the practice of NLP, ie deliberately copying the other person's position or gestures in order to get into rapport. However, deliberate mirroring is to be used with caution because it can appear awkward and unnatural. When having a conversation, it is worth noticing whether the body language of yourself and the other person is similar. If not, rather than forcing yourself into an unnatural position, ask yourself why you are not in rapport and address that root cause rather than the symptoms that are showing up. Using coaching questions is more likely to achieve comfortable rapport, and a natural mirroring of body language, than deliberately altering your position, which will in any case take up part of your concentration and prevent you from listening at Levels Four and Five.

COACHING BY TELEPHONE

There is no separate model for telephone coaching, although at least 50 per cent of coaching probably takes place in this way. I am often asked the question 'How is it possible to read body language over the telephone?' The answer is that telephone coaches 'hear' the body language in the coachee's voice. Coaches who work by telephone become increasingly sensitive to tone, pauses and silences. A small shift in the voice communicates almost telepathically with the coach, and can prove more effective at a deeper level than the reading of body language.

Organizations usually require coaches to visit their premises and conduct sessions face to face. However, even in the workplace, telephone coaching is becoming more popular. Coaches often deliver the first session face to face, thereby winning enough of the coachee's confidence to agree to a telephone session. Although doubtful beforehand, many coachees find they prefer working by telephone. There are fewer distractions, no one has to travel and sessions can be slotted in more easily at odd times or across widely spread locations.

OTHER MODELS

Other models that the coach may come across or wish to explore (and which can easily be traced on the internet) are:

- Johari window model by Ingham and Luft;
- Bruce Tuckman's forming, storming, norming, performing team development model;
- Hershey-Blanchard situational leadership model;
- Thomas-Kilmann conflict mode instrument;
- Reuven Bar On Eqi;
- Insights personal profile;
- Belbin team role model;
- Schutz's Symlog and Firo B on interpersonal behaviour;
- Kolb and various other learning style and communication style inventories and quadrants;
- group and team coaching;
- perceptual awareness;
- spiral dynamics;
- DISC profiles;
- Apter motivational styles;
- Tony Buzan's mind mapping;
- Dilts' Logical Levels.

The key for a coach working with any of these models is to approach them in a coaching style, acknowledging people's right to privacy and respect, and using them as tools to evoke the three principles of coaching in the coachee: awareness, responsibility and self-belief, as opposed to judgement of self or others.

This is by no means an exhaustive list. Happy learning!

THE ROLE OF THE COACH IN THE ORGANIZATIONAL HIERARCHY

Figure 8.9 shows the typical functions of the HR director and the coach in relation to the hierarchy between the stakeholders in a coaching intervention. For example, the HR director will monitor the coach but support the CEO to whom he or she reports. The HR director will support and develop the other directors and monitor, support and develop their reports.

The coach's role is always a supporting and developing one. In the example used in our diagram, the coach is not actually coaching the CEO, so her or his role is shown as a supporting one. If the CEO were being coached, the coach's role would involve development as well.

A diagram such as this can be useful in early meetings about a potential coaching programme, to assist the decision maker in deciding what type of coaching programme to run, and in identifying who is responsible for monitoring and evaluation.

AN ORGANIZATIONAL HIERARCHY OF NEEDS

Figure 8.10 has been developed from Maslow's hierarchy of needs. It illustrates the various stages through which an organization passes, and is relevant to all types of business, from start-ups to global corporations.

- **Profit**: no organization can run if it is not in profit (or in the case of the public sector, achieving its remit within budget). Therefore this is placed at the base of the chart, from which all the other areas will become possible.
- **Systems**: an organization may experience sudden leaps in profitability, particularly at the start-up stage. It is essential then to have efficient systems in place for invoicing, collecting payment, monitoring costs and future financial planning. In today's world, the organization is likely to have to develop its IT systems, as well, and there may be some work to do on compliance in HR, finance and the legal department.
- **Relationships**: once the finances and systems are flowing well, attention turns to relationships. In order to maintain financial equilibrium and move

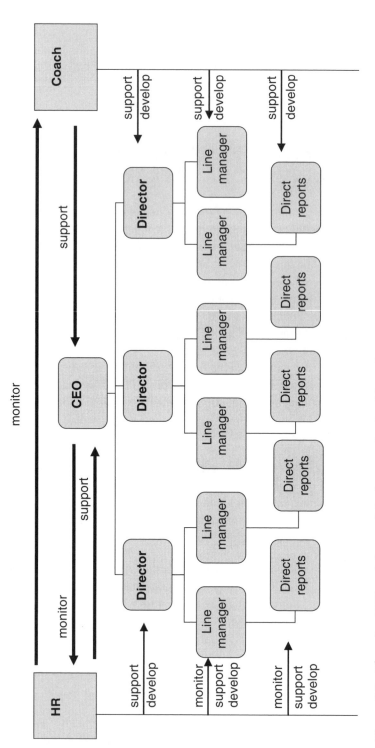

Figure 8.9 The role of HR and the coach in the organization hierarchy

Full potential	■ The organization enables itself and its workforce to reach their full potential in terms of development, satisfaction and financial results.
Loyalty	■ All employees taking pride in the brand and feeling they are part of the best team. Working for the company is a privilege.
Relationships	■ Managers and employees support each other. Good role models. Managers listen.
Systems	■ Work is supported by sound but not limiting financial, IT and hierarchical systems.
Profit	■ Private sector: revenue covers expenditure Public sector: able to achieve objectives within the budget.

Figure 8.10   An organizational hierarchy of needs

forward, the organization will need to be working as a cohesive whole in terms of its teams, departments and leaders.

■ **Loyalty**: a combination of all these factors will raise the organization to a level of momentum where employees feel they have a personal stake in moving the brand forward. This may be not about profit sharing (although that is likely to be a part of it), but more concerned with a feeling of ownership of the organization and the sense that each individual can make a difference to the whole. This is exemplified by great loyalty towards the company and pride in the brand. For instance staff may turn down offers of better-paid work elsewhere and go above and beyond the call of duty in carrying out their roles. The early Virgin Records was an example of this, and it is quite common in successful companies during their first few years.

■ **Full potential**: this type of organization is likely to become an entity which functions at a much broader level than making money. It will actively contribute to wider issues such as sustainability and the welfare of the wider community; will become a safe environment where people can take risks to stretch themselves; it will concern itself with research, ethics and philosophy, and all while remaining extremely profitable. A contender for this might be Innocent, the smoothie company, which proudly cites the company's focus on ethics, environmental responsibility and charitable work, plus development, freedom, fun and rewards for the staff. The antithesis of this is Enron, where ethics were absent and systems not rigorous enough to identify the debt-shuffling practised by the management, which eventually caused thousands of employees to lose their jobs and retirement funds.

HOW PEOPLE AND ORGANIZATIONS CHANGE

Figure 8.11 tracks the way that coaching works, and how the coach achieves each stage, and is best explained by an event which actually happened to me. I was once driving down a motorway when my car stopped without warning. To my horror and embarrassment it had run out of petrol. Now, this was a new car and for five years previously I had driven a car that gave an audible beep when the petrol gauge reached a certain level – and another beep, and another, as the levels dropped. Without being aware of it, over five years I had developed the habit of never looking at my petrol gauge.

This account illustrates how insidious habits can be; sometimes we are not even aware that they are there. Habits are powerful things and what they want is to drag everything back to the status quo. So it is possible to experience a one-off coaching session in which the principles of awareness and responsibility described in Chapter 1 hit like a floodlight, leaving you highly motivated to make sweeping changes; but six months down the line you find everything is just the same.

As described in Chapter 4, it is recommend that coaching takes place in a series of sessions over three to six months, in order to identify old habits, break them down and put new ones in place. This process leads to lasting action, success and self belief rather than a short-lived epiphany.

What the coach specifically does at each of these stages is shown in the list to the right of the triangle.

THE RELATIONSHIP BETWEEN THE COMPONENT PARTS OF COACHING

Figure 8.12 sets out all the different components involved in coaching and shows how they work together to achieve results. For instance, the 'coaching techniques' enable the 'coaching principles' to happen, and are used by the 'coaching models'.

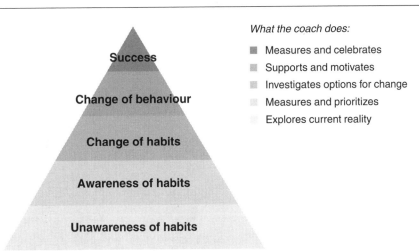

Unawareness of habits: Obtain an overview using the first part of the introductory session described in Chapter 4, with questions about the culture of the company and how people relate to each other.

Awareness of habits: highlight the coachee's insights by reflecting back words and clarifying.

Change of habits: support the coachee using the **GROW** model. Having recognized personal or organization habits, the coachee finds that ideas for change are already surfacing.

Change of behaviour: tie the ideas for changing habits down to actions. Work out an inspiring vision with the coachee, break it down to what can be achieved in three months, and work through a coaching series to achieve it.

Success: Measure how far the coachee or the organization has come. Celebrate with positive feedback.

Figure 8.11   How people and organizations change

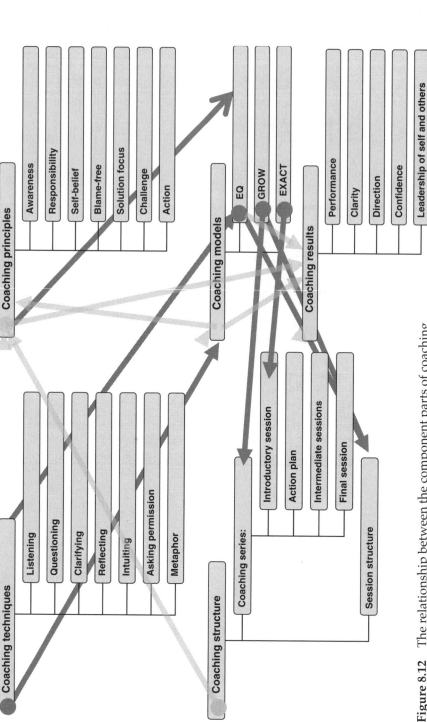

Figure 8.12 The relationship between the component parts of coaching

9

Case histories

I am immeasurably grateful to my kind colleagues worldwide who have contributed these studies to this book. I have chosen to leave them largely as they were submitted, in a multitude of styles varying from storytelling to the academic. The views of the contributors do not necessarily reflect my own, but on the whole they do, because the writers were selected from experts in this field whom I admire, trust, and in many cases, have learnt and am still learning from.

The case histories are:

- Delegation and responsibility (by Carol Wilson and James Wright).
- Coach training at the NHS (by Carol Wilson).
- Evaluating coaching at OFGEM (by Wendy Oliver).
- Career development in corporate finance (by Bill McDermott).
- Building confidence and self-esteem (by James Wright).
- Creating an in-house coaching service at the BBC (by Liz Macann).
- From Beijing to Belgium: Coaching the global nomad (by Katrina Burrus and Philippe Rosinski).
- From Macedonia: Increasing sales through the HRDF Project (by Viktor Kunovski).
- From California, USA: Career coaching an environmental scientist (by Jo Miller).
- From Australia: Management development at Orica (by Anne Stanley).
- From Abu Dhabi: Corporate Coaching in the United Arab Emirates (by Michael Daly).
- From Australia: Leading for Performance; Building a Values-Driven Organization in IT Services (by Niran Jiang and Alex Feher).
- From Japan: Management Styles and Succession Planning (by Paula Sugawara).
- Moral dilemmas and coaching challenges (by Gillian Jones).
- Coaching for performance (by Tiffany Gaskell).

DELEGATION AND RESPONSIBILITY

I designed and delivered the following intervention with my associate James Wright. The focus was to give the managers the skills to enable their own teams to take responsibility for decisions.

A national organization located HR managers in 10 different areas throughout the country, and each manager headed a local team. We were consulted because managers found that the local teams would ask for solutions and then blame the manager if the result left anything to be desired. The managers wished to learn coaching skills in order to help them enable their teams to take responsibility for decisions.

We designed a course encompassing foundation coaching skills, with the emphasis on enabling the managers to learn how to 'ask' their teams for solutions rather than 'tell' them the answers. The group of managers met for three consecutive days face to face, then continued the training through eight fortnightly conference calls.

At the start of the first day, there was some cynicism among the managers towards the training; not all had volunteered for the programme. One declared that her way of working was to tell her staff what to do and they would do it: that is what they expected from her as manager, she said.

We demonstrated a simple coaching technique of 'asking' rather than 'telling', and then paired the participants up to try it for themselves. From that moment on the group's interest was captured, including the opponent, mentioned above, who eventually became the biggest supporter of coaching.

By the end of the three days, all 10 in the group were 100 per cent committed to coaching. Over the next few weeks, feedback came in that not only did the teams prefer the new way of working, but that the managers found that they liked it better too. Teams were taking ownership and responsibility, and growing in confidence, as the managers had wished, and they were thriving on it.

This project illustrated the 'feel-good' value in coaching – as soon as people experience it, either as coachee or coach, they find that their communications improve at home and at work and the bar is raised on their performance. No incentive is needed to continue to practise and perfect the skills: if something feels good, people naturally want more of it.

Feedback at the end of the course was 100 per cent positive that the desired outcome for the project had been achieved and that the 10 managers were now successfully using a coaching style with all their teams, with the result that the teams now offered solutions to problems instead of asking the managers to solve them.

Carol Wilson
www.performancecoachtraining.com

COACH TRAINING AT THE NHS

In 2004, the NHS 'Charter for Change' led to the widespread implementation of coaching projects throughout the organization. One of the projects I worked on as part of this initiative was to train a team of six managers from St Marys Trust in coaching skills.

The training took place over three days and was supplemented by six conference calls at two-week intervals, during which the participants were paired up to practise with each other and embed the skills. Managers attended by choice and for a variety of reasons; there was no specific problem, and all the participants were already good communicators who were interested in acquiring new techniques.

The style of the training was highly interactive, and delivered by group coaching more than a standard instructional mode. During the first two days of the training I modelled coaching skills, with either my assistant trainer or a volunteer participant. Then I asked the group to comment on what techniques I was using and what the benefits were, while I highlighted the points I thought would be most useful to them and added anything extra I thought they needed. Then the participants went into groups of two or three to practise the skills themselves.

Although we had not been requested to teach the group how to deliver formal sessions, by the second day they requested this, so we fitted it into the training. By the end of the course, all the participants had enlisted a coachee from within the organization to practise on.

During the weeks that followed, we met on a series of six conference calls, where the training continued in the same interactive style. I added one more element, which was to have them coach each other on the call, then give themselves feedback and receive it from others.

This, and the practice sessions they had in between the calls, embedded the learning, enabling them to integrate the techniques into their daily working life.

After the training, I ran some mentoring/supervision calls to support the participants in any challenges they might come up against and to build their confidence by highlighting their achievements.

Participants reported finding the training enjoyable as well as useful; its interactive and experiential nature meant that their attention was fully engaged at all times and that they had fun practising with each other and joining group discussions. This is one of the great benefits of coach training which, at its best, is delivered in a coaching style so that trainees have ownership and control of their learning experience.

In practical terms, the group reported that the skills helped them to help their staff and enabled them to approach their work with more clarity and decisiveness.

On a personal level, trainees said that coach training had enabled them to learn more about themselves and that they found coaching in-house coachees an uplifting experience.

One interesting reported benefit was a breakthrough in communication between a hospital patient and a doctor. A coach-trained manager acted as intermediary and revealed that some aggression being levelled at a doctor by a patient was in fact arising from the patient's relationship with a relative who was present at the time. The manager specifically used the clean language and metaphor techniques described in Chapter 8, which made it possible for her not only to uncover the core of the problem but to bring about a resolution to the conflict between the relatives.

Carol Wilson
www.performancecoachtraining.com

EVALUATING COACHING AT OFGEM

This case history shows how a return on investment was not only achieved but clearly identified. The organization, OFGEM (the government regulatory body for the gas and electricity market) wished to increase staff retention.

Wendy Oliver, who undertook the work, is the founder and MD of Oliver Purnell, a consultancy which provides leadership development through corporate and executive one to one coaching, team coaching and group facilitation with CEOs, MDs, directors and managers in businesses and government. She also supports organizations in creating a coaching culture and trains executives to be more effective coaches. In addition, she is dedicated to working on a voluntary basis with teenagers who are underachieving and on the verge of expulsion from school.

In March 2004, Wendy Oliver put in place a coaching programme for OFGEM together with some associates. The programme was triggered by an 'Investors in People' report which found that individuals at OFGEM, especially in the higher pay bands, were struggling to find time to train and consequently were not attending the management and leadership training courses already in place. As such, their personal development was not progressing as it might. In addition, an internal feedback report identified that there was a need for training and development to be 'more specific and linked more closely to individual Business Plan objectives'.

The Learning & Development team within OFGEM identified coaching as a potentially ideal solution, particularly because managers would be able to attend short sessions tailored to their own specific needs and style in line with the business's objectives.

Prior to designing a scheme all parties recognized that evaluation of any programme was important to assess whether this was a viable learning intervention giving a return on investment. With this in mind the coaches and HR department defined the objectives of the scheme as an integral part of any post evaluation. Aims on a number of levels were identified:

- Organizational aims: the key organizational aim was to increase retention.
- Departmental aims: the main group identified were the leaders and managers and the key aims were to facilitate their career advancement within OFGEM and to improve the managers' people management skills in line with the organization's leadership competencies and business objectives.
- Individual aims: to encourage self-awareness and personal development.

OFGEM decided to set up a pilot scheme. A lunchtime meeting was arranged where Wendy and three other coaches engaged to do the work led a presentation on what coaching is and how it can be used, the aims of the scheme, the coaches' backgrounds and styles of coaching, the coaching process and what would be expected from the coachees. Seven participants signed up and were asked to submit a business case which outlined the outcomes they wanted to achieve from the coaching. They created this in alliance with their directors so that the business needs were taken into account and there was agreement as to the leadership competencies to be developed and goals to be achieved. The directors were now in a position to identify and encourage changes in behaviour and contribute to the evaluation at the end of the programme.

In March 2004 the coaching series began. Each person received a two-hour coaching session each month for six months from their selected coach. During those early months more people joined the scheme until there were 22 people being coached, which represented 12 per cent of the whole. At the end of the coaching series, the results were evaluated through going back to the original aims and noting what had happened. Evaluation was conducted by looking at the statistics; through questionnaires and through a series of meetings with the coaches, coachees and the coachees' line managers. The types of questions asked of all groups were:

- To what extent were goals achieved?
- How had that contributed to business objectives?
- What were the changes in behaviour (particularly in relation to the management competencies) and what evidence did they have/had they seen?
- What difference had coaching made to their individual and department objectives?

- How did coaching compare with other management interventions?
- What worked, what didn't?
- What changes would they make to the process?
- Did they consider the scheme to be value for money?

The coaches' competencies were also assessed by the coachees, where their ability was rated from 1 to 5 covering a whole range of coaching competencies.

The evaluation showed that for those that were coached the following results were achieved.

Organizational aims

Retention of staff increased, which was evaluated through looking at the statistics: only 5 per cent (one person) of staff being coached left OFGEM during the coaching period, compared with 26 per cent of their peers who did not receive coaching.

Departmental aims

Career advancement within OFGEM increased dramatically. This was also evaluated through looking at the statistics: 32 per cent of the people who received coaching either moved within OFGEM or were promoted, compared with 12 per cent of their peers who did not receive coaching. Feedback showed that coachees were able to identify which competencies they needed to work on and develop the new behaviours with the support of their coaches.

People management skills improved in line with the organization's leadership competencies and business objectives. This was evaluated by coachees' self-assessment and achievement of goals, their director's observation and noted evidence of changes of behaviour in line with the leadership competencies. One hundred per cent of the participants were able to give evidence as to how their behaviour had developed in relation to the competencies, and areas included:

- delegation and trust;
- managing relationships assertively and influencing upwards;
- developing strategy and seeing the bigger picture;
- running and participating in team meetings;
- coaching;
- managing team performance;
- presentation skills;
- sharing knowledge;
- time management.

A number of their directors said that coachees had requested meetings with them and expressed their views on situations, which they would not have done without the support of a coach. This had helped to resolve a number of internal frustrations.

Individual aims

There was an increase in self-awareness. Personal development: managers reported in the evaluation that participants' attitudes had shifted, they had benefited from the personalized nature of the support, gaining more self-awareness and focus in their roles and future careers, more confidence in their abilities, and had become generally more proactive. The individuals themselves took greater responsibility for making decisions in their professional and personal lives, and took action on things they had previously tended to avoid. There was also an increase in assertion, motivation, confidence, time management and risk taking, and seeing situations from others' perspectives.

As a result of the evaluation some valuable changes have also been made to the process – individuals can now be flexible on where the sessions take place and over what duration. Coaches have also been able to analyse and develop their coaching skills through analysing which competencies they are receiving the highest and lowest gradings on.

The evaluation reported that the main aims of the programme had been met. Coachees found that their expectations had been exceeded and short sharp sessions over a period of time were a very effective use of their time. Managers found that the majority of the objectives set out in the coachees' original business cases had been achieved, and hence development was in line with the business objectives of the organization.

It was concluded that coaching had been the most successful leadership intervention ever undertaken and good value for money.

Without having some very measurable objectives before starting the scheme, which were agreed by all parties, these happy conclusions may never have been drawn. The coaching scheme is still in place today and over 35 people have now passed through the programme.

Wendy Oliver
Director, Oliver Purnell
+44 (0)20 7272 0100 / 07768 693304
wendy@oliverpurnell.co.uk
www.coaching-consortium.com

CAREER DEVELOPMENT IN CORPORATE FINANCE

This case study concerns a senior corporate banker whose career had stalled. He was feeling demotivated and thinking of leaving the organization, which was keen to retain him and reawaken his commitment and enthusiasm.

Bill McDermott, the coach in question, is co-founder of People Plus Solutions, specializing in development, career and performance coaching with corporate and individual clients across the commercial, banking, SME and public sectors. Having an extensive career background in high profile, international leadership, humanitarian, and operational management roles, Bill has had significant exposure to different cultures and ways of working, often operating in challenging situations.

James was a 45-year-old corporate banker who had been a senior managing director in a global bank for many years when he discovered that a role he was expecting to inherit had been awarded to a junior colleague who had been more aggressive in his approach to winning the post. James was more than a little downhearted by the episode.

In spite of not promoting him, the bank remained extremely keen to keep James. He was regarded as a big hitter, liked by the leading corporate players and effective in winning business. James, however, felt uncertain of what he wanted to do next.

Bill McDermott was invited to coach James through this stage, to focus him on next steps, to stay with him through the transition and to work with him until he had decided on his next role or otherwise, as appropriate. The management believed he had not succeeded with the appointment because he was not demonstrably ambitious enough; he could be 'too nice' and was not always heard in the competitive melee that is typical of corporate culture.

Bill first met his coachee in the lead up to Christmas, when James was feeling emotionally tired and bruised. He had dismissed the first two coaches presented to him and Bill had been warned that he would not be an easy prospect. First of all, Bill took time to listen. James was very angry and had much to get off his chest: he felt cheated, others had been dishonourable, in his view, and he was uncertain what to do next. It was clear that he needed to offload to someone and he found Bill a suitable candidate. They gradually found some common ground, and Bill was able to determine how they could work together. Bill filled James in on his experience, how they could work in unison, what James could expect from the relationship and that it would be entirely confidential.

They agreed to meet every week for the first month in order to develop short-term goals and then to focus on going further as the programme developed.

Initially, James was only interested in the 'now': how to react to the various pressures he felt, how to deal with not getting the role he had expected and to decide his future with the bank. He wanted to work with someone who would challenge him, could stand up to his forceful personality, could help him to develop goals for a new role and support him in transitioning into it.

First of all, Bill had to determine what his coachee wanted, what issues and challenges were present and what shifts needed to occur. These were identified as:

■ clarity and focus about where he should go next – either to stay and seek an internal role at the right level or to seek an alternative solution outside the bank;

■ to get through his angry period, to relax and to avoid feeling and talking about being a failure;

■ to re-establish his confidence, sense of humour and strong, forceful demeanour in order to be convincing as the corporate heavyweight he in fact was.

Bill also identified what strengths James had that could be useful as coaching tools. He was well read, versed in coaching, enjoyed people relationships and extending himself; he was creative, imaginative and a good communicator. This meant they would be able to be ambitious in the coaching programme, push out the boundaries and challenge James's thinking and habitual behaviours. Bill realized that he would need to be flexible, demanding and direct in his communication style.

The coaching tools used to help James achieve his desired outcome included:

■ A structured format to ensure clarity and completeness and to demonstrate process and competence. James was not impressed by general statements and wanted to be held to account; if not stimulated by the interaction, his attention span would be short.

■ Following the customary introductory details, Bill and James embarked on a goal-setting exercise to get James focused on determining what issues he was dealing with at this time in his life. Together, they identified the areas for coaching, which were initially around how to get a new role, how to prepare for it and the strategy and actions required for success.

■ Once a role had been secured the goals were altered to focus on:
   – increasing James's learning and understanding of his new areas of responsibility;
   – developing his team and building his department;
   – identifying new business activities.

■ In establishing the programme Bill used 'values' tools to ascertain what would be acceptable or otherwise to James in his next role.

■ Bill used a coaching model to explore, define, improve and agree on how to stretch the goals and to keep the forward momentum.

James was also given some homework to complete: a communications survey in order to review his behavioural traits, his communications style, to see where he was most comfortable and to determine how others might work best with him. Bill provided feedback on where James needed to develop, to be aware, to be flexible and particularly where he was overstretching himself into his discomfort zone and giving too much of himself. This process enabled coach and coachee to work more effectively together, and highlighted to James what was required in order to move forward, especially regarding his next role option.

During the process all the coaching core competencies played their part, but it was initially important for Bill to establish sufficient trust, confidence and rapport with James to be able to progress. 'A difficult bear of a man who could intimidate many' was how he was described, and Bill found that he lived up to that description.

Bill's credentials and coaching presence were crucial in establishing the relationship and becoming accepted. Bill's ability to communicate directly, and specifically to understand James's style and to deliver appropriate powerful questions were instrumental in moving James on towards winning a big role in the bank. Bill asked questions like:

> How do you think your boss would react to you calling on him now to discuss your future?
> What is stopping you from doing it?
> When will you do it?

The immediate effect of the coaching was that James felt motivated enough to go straight to his global head and ask for the role he really wanted. The result was that he won the role: all his bosses had been waiting for was for James to demand it and display his commitment. In this case, direct communication and creating the awareness to take action were crucial to the successful outcome. Consequently, Bill has been retained as James's coach to work through other goal-setting programmes and manage James's continuing forward progress.

The coaching also provided a learning experience for James, in that he is now better able to value his own skills, to empathize with the potential outcomes of his actions, to appreciate his need to communicate more effectively and directly and to 'just do it'. Once James made the effort, he discovered the door was wide open and success achievable. The process reinforced his already positive relationships with senior colleagues.

As a coach, Bill's own learnings were:

- to trust the process;
- to follow one's instincts;
- that, with the coachee's permission, it is acceptable to push out the boundaries;
- that clarity of purpose is vital;
- an awareness that purpose can keep changing as matters develop, so it is important to remain flexible;
- to hear beyond and behind the coachee's words in order to discover what is not being revealed.

Bill McDermott
People Plus Solutions
coaching@peopleplus.org.uk

BUILDING CONFIDENCE AND SELF-ESTEEM

This case history relates the story of a single mother who was bullied at work and how, through coaching, she mustered the inner resources to stand up to her bullying boss and forge new opportunities elsewhere.

James Wright is an executive coach, trainer and speaker who also works as an associate for various organizations including Alpha Coach Training and Sir John Whitmore's Performance Consultants International. He has joined me as a lead trainer for many years on our public performance coach training courses at Performance Coach Training.

James worked with a private coachee who was a young single mother of two autistic boys and worked as a teacher in a special needs school for autistic children. An intelligent, aware woman with a PhD in the field of autism, she was eminently qualified for her job. However, she encountered sarcasm, inappropriate comments and general lack of support from her principal.

James helped her to set three goals, with the intention of working together over a 12-week period, meeting once a week. One was aligned specifically to her work situation and two others concerned other personal issues. Her work goal was centred around proving her worth to her boss, and she worded it provocatively: 'I'm going to show him!' She insisted on this wording in spite of James's concern that the outcome was to some extent controlled by a third party, namely the principal.

During the second session, James helped her to work out a set of strategies, commencing with a written account of her precise current situation and her emotions surrounding it, as well as a written vision of how her life would look when she had achieved the goal. Subsequent strategies were centred on issues of confidence and self-esteem, and it was here that the insights came thick and fast. However, it was proving difficult to create a really strong 'energy' about this goal despite its provocative title.

In the fourth week of coaching James received a phone call from the coachee saying she had 'something important I need to discuss'. The upshot was that she had realized, during her exploration of her own confidence and self-esteem, that she did indeed value herself and her undoubted academic and professional achievements, as well as her remarkable energies as a single working mother to two demanding autistic boys. She had asked herself a number of confrontational questions over the previous 10 days about what was truly important to her, writing down her responses and posting them up on the walls of her home as affirmations in various strategic places.

Through this, she had started to see her life from a different space. In this space, she became the centre of her new world, very different from her old world that had as its centre other people's perceptions of her. She said that her previous goal, 'I'll show him!' no longer fitted, and she had asked herself the question, 'How can I make this goal all about me?' She found that a revised goal had come naturally to her and she worded it in the present tense:

I am an amazing educational consultant.

James was impressed and when he asked what she intended to do about this, she replied, 'Well, I hope it's all right but I already took action. Yesterday, I went into school, demanded a meeting with the principal, told him what I thought of him and his methods and attitudes, and told him to shove his job! I handed him a resignation letter I'd brought with me and walked out there and then. I drove straight to the local education department and told them what I had done. They congratulated me and told me they were impressed I had lasted even 18 months with that principal, because his misogyny was well known. Then they offered me 77 days of consultancy on the spot at £750 per day, with more to follow.'

When asked what she had learnt from this, the coachee reported that she felt elated and that when she centred the goal specifically around herself, she was able to 'take back the reins' and 'chart her own course', with immediate and life-changing results. 'In future', she said, 'any time I have doubts about what to do, I'll just remember to make it personal, remember who I am, what I can do, and nothing can stop me!'

So the simple but practical learning here is that when your coachees are setting goals, get them to make the goals *personal*. If this proves challenging, get them to ask themselves confrontational questions about what is truly important to them and display their responses as affirmations in strategic, visible places around their home/office. These actions will allow them to place themselves in the centre of the dilemma and a strong goal will always follow.

James Wright MSc
+44 (0)113 226 1702
jameswright@ntlworld.com

CREATING AN IN-HOUSE COACHING SERVICE AT THE BBC

By the end of the last decade, coaching proliferated throughout the BBC but there was no real cohesion or quality control. Liz Macann relates how she tackled the challenge of creating a robust structure for training internal coaches and maintaining standards.

Liz Macann is the co-founder of the BBC's in-house Executive, Leadership and Management Coaching Network and co-creator of the BBC Coach Foundation Course. Liz is responsible for the selection, professional training and development of 80 coaches and the service they provide. She continues to develop her own coaching practice by working with a diverse client group of senior executives and leaders, and supervises less experienced coaches both inside and external to the BBC. Through her coaching partnership, Liz has delivered coaching to senior executives and their teams and worked with organizations in both the private and public sectors to implement cultural change.

Nationally, Liz takes a leading role in the development of coaching as a profession, participating in the activities of the European Mentoring and Coaching Council, the Association for Coaching and a number of think tanks and focus groups aimed at shaping the future of executive coaching. She is a speaker at national and international coaching conferences and seminars.

As well as being an accredited coach, Liz is trained in brief therapy, constellations therapy, coach supervision and is qualified to administer, interpret and give feedback on a number of psychometric instruments. Liz's belief in the basic tenets of coaching originated in her work with communities in developing countries and also with traumatized horses.

In the late 1990s some of our very top executive tier were receiving coaching from an assortment of expensive external coaches whose selection, standards, ethics and success criteria were not scrutinized or monitored. Our aim was to provide evaluated executive coaching to all leaders and managers at a standard equal to or better than that which was available from external providers – and at a lower cost! At this stage in the development of the coaching profession there was little written about what and how to do it, so we simply coached ourselves through what we wanted to achieve and how we could achieve it.

We established that there was sufficient interest from the staff to have this strange new process called coaching by piloting short coaching programmes, from which we learned that we needed:

- coaches to believe in the process and have thorough skills training – enthusiasm is not enough;
- a shared understanding of the coaching objectives by the line manager/client/coach;
- structure around the coaching offering;
- quality control.

As the demand for coaching slowly grew we knew that we needed to expand our small number of trained coaches, especially when it was decided to incorporate coaching as an integral part of the corporate leadership programme, which caused the demand to rocket. Having failed to find externally the level of training we wanted our developing network to have, we created our own course and devised a selection procedure which ensured that anyone who we invested in already had a high level of the competencies we required.

Selection criteria

We wanted coaches to come from all over the business, not just the people professions, so we posted flyers in strategic places and were astonished at the level and spread of interest in something which most people knew little about. Applications came from programme makers, engineers, techies, professional services – all categories of staff are now represented in our mix. We currently have 74 coaches, all volunteers from the ranks of established and senior leaders and managers who fit their coaching activities into already demanding diaries and who receive no reward for this work other than the sense of fulfilment that it gives them.

Over time the details of the infrastructure have evolved, but because we began with nothing to copy and simply started with the end in mind, what we created in those early days remains largely the same.

Selection process

The selection process begins with a purpose-built application form asking only for information which relates to someone's suitability to train as a coach; other corporate considerations are disregarded. The shortlisted applicants then go through to a role play assessment, based on the five main competencies we regard as important for our coaches to possess:

- building and maintaining relationships;
- communicating;
- analysing;
- planning and organizing;
- self-awareness – the big one!

Those achieving the required standard are then invited to attend an interview for final selection for a place on the Coach Foundation Course.

Training

Twice a year, 12 senior managers/leaders are trained as coaches by two senior coaches and an external tutor, the course being divided into three modules over a four-month period.

The Coach Foundation Course
Module 1:

- Pre reading.
- Three days skills training, input, practice, observation and feedback.
- Six weeks fieldwork supported by coach mentor.

Module 2:

- Pre reading.
- Three days' psychological underpinnings, practice, observation and feedback.
- Six weeks fieldwork supported by coach mentor.

Module 3:

- Pre reading.
- One day of final observed assessment plus tools and techniques.

The Coach Foundation Course is currently being assessed by the European Mentoring and Coaching Council as an accredited training course.

Trainees who are deemed to meet the standard necessary to be a BBC coach are then required to coach a minimum of three clients at any one time and enter into continuous professional development by attending one to one supervision every other month, and in the month in between, attending a Shared Learning Session; and attending a number of master classes, workshops and refresher sessions held monthly.

Coaches who wish to can, after 60 hours of logged and supervised coaching sessions, apply for externally assessed BBC Coach accreditation. At that stage a growing number of our coaches go on to take advanced or specialized coach training external to the BBC. This is not a requirement and the BBC does not fund it, but it is increasingly something that our more experienced coaches want to do for their own personal development.

The portfolio

We have grown from offering short informal coaching sessions to having a portfolio of four different offerings:

- The Executive Coaching Programme – for established and senior leaders and managers with objectives agreed with line managers. The duration of the programme depends on the level of the executive but is never longer than 20 hours contained within one year.
- The Leadership Coaching Programme – for anyone attending the corporate leadership programme with objectives derived from the client's 360-degree feedback.
- The First One Hundred Days – for established and senior leaders and managers transitioning into a new role or entering the corporation from another organization.
- Coaching Skills for Managers – as the value of coaching is increasingly recognized, many managers who do not wish to be a coach want the basic coaching skills to enhance their management style. This is a three-day, two-module course which teaches them the basic but all-important coaching skills of active listening, open questioning and the GROW model. This short course is being credited with accelerating the organization's shift to a coaching style of management. Still a long way to go!

Evaluation

Meaningful evaluation of coaching is notoriously difficult but we have run four studies which have shown that the coaching provision is a much-valued intervention which has benefited both the individual and the business. We have also carried out three evaluation pieces over time which produced the following findings.

The appropriateness of internal v external coaching

We were astonished to find that the staff were completely comfortable with the notion of internal coaches (provided they are rigorously trained) and thought external was preferable only for those in particularly high-profile, outward facing roles.

Leadership coaching impact

The most interesting aspect of this was the extent to which challenges were considered to have been largely or completely resolved by using coaching. The topics which showed the highest success rate were:

- confidence building;
- transitioning;
- dealing with uncertainty and change;
- career issues;
- performance management;
- building relationships;
- managing upwards;
- creating strategies;
- resolving business issues.

The least successful areas were generating creative thinking and managing resources. Interestingly, established and senior leaders reported largely the same level of impact for the same topics.

The BBC coaching provision

This produced the following quotes, which are representative of a large number received:

> I'm much more aware of my personal strengths and weaknesses – and how my style and behaviour impacts on others.

> Allowed me to explore how I have operated as a manager in the past and helped me find techniques to adopt alternative approaches.

> It was an effective means to think out loud with someone who having no vested interest in my department was able to facilitate my working through a troubled relationship with my boss.

> Very thought provoking. Each session was intellectually stimulating and quite demanding.

> It helped me to diagnose the issues, to articulate the key challenges, to prioritize where I needed to put my attention, and come up with a realistic action plan.

What's next?

It has been an amazing learning journey during which we have had to have enormous self-belief and resilience in the face of internal opposition, external competition and massive restructuring of the whole organization. In order to respond to this, we have continuously developed the network, its coaches, its structure and the coaching it provides, and by partnering constantly evolving business needs, we will continue to support the change programme and help to embed the coaching culture as the preferred management style within the corporation.

In those early days the BBC buzz words were; 'Just do it', 'make it happen'. And we did.

Liz Macann
Head of Executive, Leadership and Management Coaching
Liz.macann@bbc.co.uk

FROM BEIJING TO BELGIUM: COACHING THE GLOBAL NOMAD

The case history that follows is an amalgamation of various cases Dr Burrus has been involved with, and was originally prepared for the workshop 'Leveraging Multiple Perspectives; Practising on a Concrete and Complex Case' co-facilitated with Philippe Rosinski at the ICF European Conference, Brussels, in May 2006. The nominal client is given the fictional name of Marie and the coach involved is referred to as the Coach. The account starts with a description of the reason why the Coach was called in and is followed by an essay from Philippe Rosinski on his recommendations for handling the situation.

Belgian coach Philippe Rosinski is an expert in executive coaching, team coaching and global leadership development, sought by leading international corporations. He has pioneered a global approach to coaching that leverages multiple perspectives for greater creativity, impact and meaning. The Harvard Business School chose his groundbreaking book Coaching Across Cultures *(2003) as its featured book recommendation in the category of business leadership. A Master of Science from Stanford University, he is also the first European to have been designated Master Certified Coach by the International Coach Federation.*

Dr Katrina Burrus specializes in coaching global executive nomad, high-potential, and abrasive senior managers in telecom, banking, food, perfumes, non-profits and the pharmaceutical industry throughout Europe, Asia and the

United States. She founded MKB Conseil & Coaching and is affiliated with a network of international experts and scholar practitioners.

Dr Burrus was the first ICF Master Certified Coach in Switzerland; she is a past president and founder of ICF Suisse Romand, a past board member of ICF World and Switzerland, and is currently part of the credentialing commission. She is a senior secretary for the International Federation of the Red Cross and Crescent Societies, holds masters' degrees in international management and human development and has a PhD in the strategic effect of global financial markets on Swiss private banking.

The Coach's account

Marie is the business developer for Asia of a prestigious global consumer service company with headquarters in the United Kingdom. Marie's boss suggested that she work with a coach, which was unusual; her company seldom invests much in ongoing training for its people. Marie was thus surprised, and felt privileged to benefit from a coaching programme. The Coach was highly recommended to her, but lives in Europe; Marie, a US citizen of Anglo-Saxon descent, asked to be coached in Beijing, where she had lived for the past year.

Marie said that she wanted to use the coaching to become more effective in developing the business in the region. In a few years, she wanted to have established the Asian region as one of the main business centres for her company. She also mentioned that she was constantly working, and could never relax enough to simply be; she always had to be doing something: work, reading or study. She wanted to share more time with her husband.

With Marie's approval, the coach talked with her functional and regional bosses (she reported equally to both in a matrix format) to determine what they expected from a coaching programme. Through these two direct supervisors, the Coach learned the following.

Marie's regional boss Joe, a British citizen living in Beijing, described Marie as an outstanding professional with an incredible workload capacity who had to deal with multiple complex situations. 'Marie,' he said, 'is devoted to the success of the business and obtains outstanding results. She has been sent to difficult, emerging markets in Eastern Europe to troubleshoot problems and has been able to get projects through, resolved and in a timely manner. Socially, she is charming and pleasant, but at work she is very pushy when promoting her ideas. When she delegates, she relentlessly comes back to her direct reports to see what has been accomplished.' Joe reported that this too was perceived as pushy.

Joe continued, 'Her Asian teams, from Japan, India and Beijing, tend to shy away from working directly with her. She has been known to shout at her direct reports publicly and humiliate other colleagues in front of their bosses. Even clients have been subject to her wrath,' Joe whispered. 'She needs to create a team spirit and have people happy to work with her.'

Joe paused to think and then continued, 'After an argument, Marie might try to make amends with the person she has upset, but she cannot stop herself from competing to win the argument, even if it will cost her the relationship. Many of her colleagues think she has a need to compete and have the last word.'

'What has surprised more than one of her colleagues is that Marie's self-confidence at work contrasts noticeably with her submissive attitude with her (functional) boss, Jane.' Joe then paused, and continued, 'I have noticed that she walks briskly into the office. She looks tense. When she is annoyed with a discussion, she rolls her eyes and walks away.'

Marie's functional boss, Jane, an American based in the United States, summarized Marie's attitude as, 'She lacks confidence. Marie remains silent in meetings.' She continued, 'She wants to impress people and overcompensates. She tries to impress people that she is bright, and what would we do without her? When she encounters resistance with her direct reports, she becomes aggressive, hierarchical, very top-down. She has little to no empathy or social radar. She is perceived as having little sensitivity to what is required by others.' Jane paused and said thoughtfully, 'She does not know how to profile herself to engage people.'

Marie herself told the Coach that she was 42 years old, had been married for 12 years, and had no children. She was raised in the eastern United States, and came from a traditional, middle-class family. Her husband was a very successful Swiss banker, who had been promoted every few years and changed countries with each promotion. Marie said that she has usually found a way to follow him while continuing to pursue her own career or studies. She also mentioned that her husband admired her achievements but complained sometimes that she relied too much on him to make decisions.

When Marie gave some information on her background, the Coach learnt that she had an elder brother who was the apple of their parents' eyes. All hopes were focused on his career, until he decided to quit the business life to live in a retreat. She was an average student at school, but once her brother left the business world, Marie began to achieve outstanding results.

Marie talked proudly about what she had achieved and her constant travels. She confided in the Coach that she was driven by her own agenda and would get upset when anything got in her way. She knew that she was perceived as pushy and wanted to learn how to inspire rather than impose. Her company had given her the opportunity to receive coaching in order to work on developing her emotional intelligence, which she understood to mean developing her interpersonal skills. With this background information from Marie and her two bosses, the Coach's assessment of the coaching situation began.

Philippe Rosinski's recommendations from multiple perspectives

As far back as I can recall, I have always been fascinated by multiple perspectives. For example, when I studied electrical engineering at Stanford University, I took all my electives in the humanities (with the exception of a windsurfing class!). I had captivating classes in history, literature, sociology and philosophy as part of my Master of Science degree. I found these radically different perspectives inspiring and enriching. My fellow students usually preferred computer science, which they viewed as a more natural and practically applicable prolongation of electrical engineering.

Later, this same inclination led me, as an executive coach, to introduce the concepts of global coaching and coaching from multiple perspectives. I wondered in particular how to take advantage of new angles (notably political, cultural and spiritual), which had not been part of traditional coaching. In my experience, this leads to more creative, powerful and meaningful coaching.

In my view, the executive coach's mission is to facilitate the coachee's journey towards high performance and high fulfilment, towards sustainable and global success, for the benefit of the coachee himself/herself and for others he/she can impact.

In practice, executive coaching today (still) tends to be reduced to its two traditional perspectives: psychological and managerial. These are certainly fundamental, but usually insufficient to unleash the coachee's full potential.

However, as coaching is establishing itself as a new discipline, I am pleased to notice that many of the 'scholars' who are contributing to the 'institutionalization' of coaching, have adopted the view that coaching should be enriched by multiple perspectives for more relevance and impact. In 2006, two books illustrate this shift: both *The Evidence Based Coaching Handbook* (Stober and Grant, 2006) and *Excellence in Coaching* (Passmore, 2006) propose a diversity of approaches in coaching and exemplify the richness of adopting multiple perspectives. Linda Page has well summarized this evolution: 'There is a growing consensus that the field of coaching studies should be cross-disciplinary, multidisciplinary, or interdisciplinary – that is, a hyphenated field rather than one that is 'owned' by any one existing academic discipline' (Page, 2006).

Coaching, if it integrates multiple perspectives, is a powerful vehicle for enabling sustainable and global success (for oneself and for others). I use the term 'global coaching' to refer to this broad and inclusive form of coaching.

Coaching from multiple perspectives assumes an enlarged mission for the executive coach, and implies the readiness to engage in a lifelong learning journey.

I have found the general perspectives mentioned in Table 9.1 to be particularly useful. Each general perspective itself includes multiple perspectives. The *Evidence Based Coaching Handbook* (Stober and Grant, 2006) clearly illustrates, for example, how various schools, theories and models within psychology can contribute to coaching. These include adult development, cognitive psychology, psychoanalysis and positive psychology.

Reality is multifaceted and the various perspectives are interconnected. Recent research in neurosciences is notably paving the way towards an understanding of the mind–emotion–body connections. Coaching is an art in that it implies choosing in any given situation an approach that is most likely to generate insights and foster progress. For the coach, it means the ability to juggle with multiple perspectives and, even more powerfully, the capacity to seamlessly link and possibly leverage these alternative viewpoints for addressing the coachee's challenges.

Marie's case

In this section, I examine how these ideas can apply to the case written by Katrina Burrus. It makes good sense to work with Marie by focusing primarily on the psychological perspective and by taking into account the cross-cultural dimension clearly apparent in this cross-continental situation. However, let me briefly discuss how other perspectives could open additional possibilities and growth opportunities for Marie.

Spiritual

Marie wants to learn how to inspire. Beyond coping, the spiritual perspective is a useful avenue here. To really be able to inspire others, Marie needs to come into closer contact with a deeper sense of purpose and meaning. She has to develop a strong and calm presence; this implies becoming comfortable with herself, developing an eagerness to give, to touch people, to affect them in a positive fashion.

In the Jewish mystical tradition, the Kabbalah literally means 'receiving'. It suggests that an essential spiritual quality is the ability to receive light: warming up to a child's smile, rejoicing at melodious music, or welcoming a colleague's encouragement. You have to let the light in before you can inspire others, that is, shine and reflect the light you have received in the first place.

It seems that Marie is harsh not only towards her co-workers but also often with herself. The coach could help her develop instead a loving acceptance of herself. Sometimes, it takes hardship and a trauma to move further. The challenging

Table 9.1   General perspectives on coaching

Perspective	Definition/explanation	Two essential qualities fostered by the particular perspective
Spiritual	Spirituality is an increased awareness of a connection with oneself, others, nature, with the immanent and transcendent 'divine'. It is also the ability to find meaning, derive purpose and appreciate life.	**Meaning and unity:** See comment in section below ('Cultural').
Cultural	'A group's culture is the set of unique characteristics that distinguishes its members from another group' (Rosinski, 2003). External characteristics include behaviours, artefacts and products. Internal characteristics include norms, values and basic assumptions.	**Diversity and creativity:** In our complex, multicultural and turbulent environment, it is increasingly essential to learn how to embrace diversity, bridge cultural gaps, learn from cultural differences for more creativity, live meaningfully, act responsibly, overcome divisions and strive for unity (internally and externally).
Political	'Politics is an activity that builds and maintains your power so that you can achieve your goals. Power is the ability to achieve your meaningful, important goals. Politics is a process. Power is potential and it comes from many sources' (Rosinski, 1998b).	**Power and service:** Politics is inherent to organizational life and essential for leadership. Politics becomes constructive when it also works in the service of others. As power gives impact and leverage, service can guide your actions.
Psychological	Psychology is the study of individual personality, behaviours, emotions and mental processes. Psychology differs from culture in that its primary focus is the individual rather than the collective 'supra-individual'.	**Emotional and relational quality**
Managerial	'Management is a task that consists in focusing resources on the organization's goals, and then monitoring and managing the use of these resources' (Campbell, 1991).	**Productivity and results**
Physical	'Of or relating to the body as opposed to the mind' (Oxford Dictionary, 1998).	**Health and fitness:** Health and Fitness are fragile foundations that can easily be taken for granted but should be actively nurtured instead. 'Mens sana in corpore sano' (a healthy mind in a healthy body).

situation can be reframed as an opportunity to grow on her hero's journey. The coach could help Marie put her reality into perspective, and develop a sense of gratitude for the gifts of life she may currently take for granted. This attitude of appreciation will help her feel the inner calm and peacefulness that will naturally lead her to change what can be and accept what cannot.

Coaching from a spiritual perspective means facilitating unity. To help Marie become more united with herself, the coach needs to gently help Marie confront and embrace her shadow, her demons and her vulnerabilities. Carl Jung described how the self emerges when the ego meets the shadow. To help Marie become more united with the world, the coach could invite her to meditate on her power, right and responsibility. When culturally appropriate, the coach might quote the Talmud here:

> The man who saves one man saves the world entire.

It is also written that 'Every man shall say: "It is for me that the world was created."' And again, 'Every man shall say "the World rests on me".'

The coach could then challenge Marie to reflect on the legacy she wants to leave behind and determine specific actions for improving the world at her level. Replacing her current destructive communications with benevolence and respect towards colleagues would be a good start.

Cultural

Marie can benefit from learning and hopefully accepting and embracing alternative cultural ways whenever her own norms, values and beliefs have proved inadequate for addressing her challenges.

For example, several dimensions in the Cultural Orientations Framework set out in my book *Coaching Across Cultures* (2003) seem to be at play here. I mention only a few of these below.

- **Humility versus control**: the coach can help Marie give herself permission to do the best she can, while accepting that not everything is under her control. Marie can learn to let go and be more detached.
- **Indirect and hierarchical**: in such a culture, Marie may not get the feedback she needs. She should not take this absence of feedback as de facto approval of her abusive behaviours. She should instead remember that bruising people is the number one derailment factor for executives, as the Center for Creative Leadership's classical research has shown. Marie should realize the alienating impact of loss of face, which is particularly problematic in indirect cultures.
- **Being versus doing**: the coach could challenge Marie that, somewhat paradoxically, more being is usually necessary to ultimately get more doing. Her goals in the being realm could include becoming more serene and developing

closer interpersonal relationships. This will help her create the supportive and constructive environment necessary for sustainable high performance.

Political

The coach can help Marie to reflect and devise deliberate actions to build internal alliances. Rather than estranging herself from her colleagues, she should realize the self-defeating impact of her competitive stance: what is the point of winning an argument at the cost of ruining relationships with potential allies? These colleagues could instead help Marie in building her business in the Asian region, thereby raising her profile and influence in the organization.

Psychological

Referring to transactional analysis (see page 117), Marie is 'playing psychological games', adopting various roles in the 'dramatic triangle', from Persecutor (OK–not OK when she shouts at her direct reports) to Victim (not OK–OK in her submissive attitude towards her boss). As a priority, the coach should help Marie become assertive instead, adopting an OK–OK mindset.

Interestingly, the cultural and spiritual perspectives can be viewed as a natural prolongation. At a deeper level, OK–OK means accepting herself and others, loving herself and others. Accepting and even embracing alternative cultural ways will bring Marie closer to other cultures, while giving her an opportunity to grow and become more united.

Managerial

The coach could help Marie to systematically review the various projects she is engaged in, possibly discovering with her additional opportunities for increased productivity and results.

Physical

Marie is still fairly young (42 years old) but her body may soon no longer be able to sustain the high level of stress she has become accustomed to. Fortunately, she has apparently not suffered yet from a major health condition (and hopefully never will!). The global coach should invite Marie to take care of her body, as a way to increase her well-being and calmness, reduce her stress, and develop her resilience (which includes her ability to effectively deal with stress). She has the privilege of still being able to adopt a preventive approach rather than the remedial one that is necessary if a breakdown occurs. With her coach, she could set specific targets and determine activities for promoting healthy habits, including fitness routines, adequate nutrition, sufficient sleep, having fun (lightness and laughter would help!), etc. Marie might benefit from a medical check-up and personalized programmes with experts (such as a physiotherapist and nutritionist).

Examples

I have not coached Marie, or even met her. Nonetheless, let me illustrate how some of these multiple perspectives have informed my coaching in two recent situations, which to some extent connect to Marie's circumstances despite clear differences.

Like Marie, a goal for one of my coachees was to become more assertive (having what transactional analysis refers to as an OK–OK mindset and behaviours). In his case, this was particularly necessary for dealing with unfair criticism and conflict. Relying on cognitive and behavioural psychology, including using the coaching safe environment to practise engaging in his challenging situations through role playing, this executive notably learned to connect with anger (which he tended to mute when treated unfairly), and to give up a self-imposed and self-defeating standard of perfection. My coachee executive experienced no difficulty, however, in stepping back from his daily work environment in order to see the big picture and take effective action. His marathon training routine, several hours of running a week, was a source of well-being and an opportunity to reflect calmly.

On the other hand, another coachee had no issue with asserting his position, yet he was feeling uneasy. He was treading a complex terrain with multiple stakeholders, trying to negotiate the best possible agreements, with the goal of setting up a new business venture in the most effective way. Coaching from a political perspective proved very helpful here. Still, it was not enough to increase his sense of satisfaction and fulfilment. The spiritual perspective helped him to keep sight of his larger mission: the highly financially profitable enterprise he wanted to create was meant to serve society by making breakthrough biomedical findings available in medical treatments. He learned to connect with himself, significant others and his mission at a deeper level.

On one occasion, sensing his stress, I proposed something I had never tried before in a coaching session: spending half-an-hour walking in the forest of Soignes nearby. Uniquely, this wilderness extends into parts of Brussels: you might encounter a deer if you silently walk by. My coachee welcomed the invitation, and a few minutes later we were in the forest of Soignes.

He was still busy talking when I asked him if he had noticed the beautiful surroundings. He admitted he had not paid attention to them. I invited him to look attentively. I also suggested he touch the trunk of a huge tree, focusing on feeling and internally visualizing the tree, his body, and the contact between the two. In just a few minutes, my coachee had calmed down and felt a sense of serenity. The half-hour spent was quickly 'regained' by his increased clarity in the last part of our coaching session for creatively addressing some of his complex challenges. He commented about the fact that nobody else was walking in the forest, despite its proximity and beauty. This short detour became for him a metaphor for stepping back, regaining perspective, noticing and appreciating. I can imagine a similar activity would be equally beneficial with Marie.

Promoting positive energy does not mean burying unpleasant emotions such as anger, fear and sadness. It does imply however the ability to express anger assertively rather than aggressively, since that is usually a more effective way. It implies choosing one's battles and taking a pragmatic approach: avoiding conflict can sometimes be best. A boxer will want to first acquire additional technique, force and resistance, rather than engage in an uneven contest. Likewise, an executive might decide to gain new knowledge and build new alliances rather than fight a battle that is likely to be lost. It could also be that the stakes are not important and the issue is really not worth the time and the energy.

Being both in healthy contact with one's emotions and having adequate distance from them equates to acting with a cool head and a warm heart. This exemplifies the notion of unity, which I see as a form of completion, wholeness or globality, achieved through the synthesis of differences (psychological or cultural), and not to be confused with uniformity, a bland version in which disparities have been eliminated.

Möbius strip

Reflecting on my practice of coaching executives, I tried to further conceptualize the notion of multiple perspectives. I wondered how best to represent graphically the relationship between the various perspectives (my former engineering background may have incidentally popped up here!). The Möbius strip then stood out.

The Möbius strip, also called the twisted cylinder (Henle, 1994), is a one-sided surface obtained by cutting a closed band into a single strip, giving one of the two ends thus produced a half-twist, and then reattaching the two ends (Gray, 1997).

The artist M C Escher has created famous representations of the Möbius strip, notably one with ants crawling on the one-sided surface forming an 8-shape (which happens to symbolize infinity). Amazingly, the Möbius strip paradoxically represents unity and infinity at the same time: it has only one side and one edge, and ants could crawl on it forever. The mathematically inclined might even want to enhance the model by weaving fractals into the strip, thereby actually producing an edge of infinite length.

The multiple perspectives could be imagined as diverse viewpoints lying on a Möbius strip. Of course, I do not think we can know the ultimate representation of a complex reality, and I doubt a single representation even exists. Multiple representations can coexist, each with its merits and limitations. This Möbius strip representation is merely an attempt at highlighting certain characteristics that seem important: unity (one side and one edge) and at the same time, infinity.

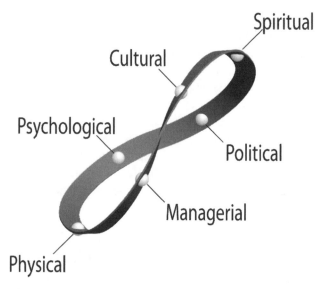

Figure 9.1   The Möbius strip

The one-side and one-edge property evokes the concept of unity we discussed earlier. Moreover, the 8-shape visually combines dilation and contraction, mirroring exploration and openness together with focus and closure, all necessary for creative coaching.

Finally, the duality unity–infinity inherent to the Möbius strip is a powerful reminder for global coaches that everything is interconnected. It is an invitation to leverage diversity and foster synthesis.

Philippe Rosinski
www.philrosinski.com

Katrina Burrus
www.mkbconseil.com

FROM MACEDONIA: INCREASING SALES THROUGH THE HRDF PROJECT

This case history deals with the challenge of developing a programme to improve the sales techniques of a leading travel company in Macedonia.

Viktor Kunovski works as a business and organizational development coach in Macedonia. His managerial approach is based on inclusiveness and systemic coaching. He is a pioneer of coaching management culture in Macedonia and is an associate of Performance Consultants International for the Balkans, where he also writes and lectures on coaching and leadership.

As part of the developmental assistances that the European Union offers to its future Member States, the HRDF (Human Resources Development Fund) project started in Macedonia. One of the main goals of the project was to develop enterprise competitiveness through upgrading the skills of managers and staff.

After an extensive selection and internal assessment process, 30 small and medium-sized enterprises (SMEs) were selected from over 60 candidates. The project had two main components:

- **Learning groups**: educative training where the managers and staff had a variety of lectures and training by the consultants and were learning from each other's experience.
- **In-company projects**: where companies chose a goal to be developed internally, through means of coaching and consulting.

The whole €1 million project was managed by the EAR (European Agency for Reconstruction) and ECORYS BV from the Netherlands, with 15 local consultants, including myself as the coaching specialist.

The client

City Travel was one of the 30 chosen SMEs. It is a leader in corporate travel in Macedonia and the first ISO 9001:2000 certified air travel company in southeast Europe, one of the rare few that hold the certificate at present. At the start of the HRDF project the number of employees was five and rose to six, including the management: two managers plus four highly skilled and trained air ticket salespersons. City Travel currently serves more than 200 corporate clients through air ticket sales (90 per cent of City Travel's business and 4 per cent of the market share in Macedonia), hotel reservations, insurance and car rental.

After the assessment, the management of City Travel concluded that the strongest driving force in the company was the partnership with the sales staff. In order to maintain a leadership position in what is a difficult market, strengthen customer satisfaction skills, cope with a recent change of company image and increase sales, City Travel management identified several segments of its business functions that needed to be improved.

It was decided to put a particular focus on the improvement of the communications skills of the staff with the customers, and to improve customer service skills, promotion, sales and marketing skills. In addition, the direct marketing capabilities for acquiring new corporate clients needed to be reinvented and stepped up.

After the assessment, the management of City Travel set up an objective for their work with the project. This was called In-company Project Goal.

The In-company Project Goal

We created a SMART goal to be achieved over a period of one year:

> To increase the sales and profit of City Travel by improving the communications skills, customer relations and performance management.

The end goal of increasing the sales and profit was reliant on achieving the second part of the goal, ie improving the communication skills, customer relations and performance management. The In-company Project Goal was created after a strategic review (a company assessment which included a SWOT analysis and a needs assessment for further growth and development). The process was tele-scoped from session to session, with the main goal being constantly in the fore-front. The sessions covered the following themes:

1. The company's presentation and presentational skills.
2. Follow-up activities with communication skills training.
3. Team assessment in communications skills.
4. Win-win-win culture in communicating, presenting the company, sales, customer care and in all other activities.
5. Soft skills coaching for improvement of sale skills.
6. Boundaries between client and staff during the sale and communication process, exploration of polarities of patience and impatience, passive and aggressive sales.
7. Focus on work with brand new clients, communication and targeting new clients.
8. Action plan for some marketing activities.
9. More focus and continuation of the work with new clients, and special marketing activities for them.
10. Conclusion and next steps for City Travel.

The process and experience

During the whole 12 months the work was based on team coaching (with some individual coaching work in the group) rather than classical old school consult-ing. The methods described in the GROW model were used, with a transper-sonal and systemic approach. Company alignment and performance improvement were two of the end results of this work.

It could be said that this was a self-consulting improvement process because the consultation input from myself, as the coach, was minimal. My main role and responsibility has been to act as a 'goal holder' facilitator, motivator and guide in the development/learning process of the team and towards the fulfilment of the goals, and to keep the goals of the company in line with the actions of its members.

The aim of the coaching was to guide the team towards the achievement of the determined goals. This was done by increasing the team's awareness regarding a particular issue that was chosen for improvement and development, identifying the necessary individual and team responsibilities that were needed in order to reach the chosen goals, and taking constant consecutive actions.

During this process of performance building of the team, particular importance was placed on the full participation and input of all the team members. This promoted the sharing of responsibility as a corporate value. The growth of the team was stimulated and encouraged by the process of sharing of experiences and knowledge of its members. The team was guided towards the goals the team members had set themselves.

Key empowering, evocative and positively constructed questions were constantly used in order to guide the team towards the achievements of the goals and solutions. The coaching process always followed the priorities of the team, and the team was left to hold the responsibility for its development. This was perceived as very empowering and helpful for staff confidence.

Each consecutive session was designed from the results of the previous session. In this way the continuity of the process was preserved. Some sessions ended with the completion of certain small goals, and we did not have time to set a new goal for the forthcoming session. In the absence of current goals, the team was encouraged to trust its intuitive needs and determine a goal for the session, and in cases like this I ran what I called 'free style sessions' (popcorn intuition). I would ask each member of the team to choose a developmental issue as a new small goal for the current session which was in line with the end goal. From the joint list, we as a team would choose the most important issue and work on that.

It has been interesting to observe how this process unfolds systemically and organically, and to notice that what sometimes seems to be missed, omitted or forgotten in the course of current work, eventually emerges on the surface as a priority need for improvement.

It is to be noted that for the first two sessions only the two managers were present on the consultations. For the rest of the sessions the whole team was included. The newest employee also joined the sessions at a later stage in the process (session 7).

The results: the benefits of the 'systemic organic coaching development'

As a result of the whole HRDF project, the learning group processes, the openness and the sharing methods of the coaching process in the In Company session, several things emerged as noticeable improvements and benefits:

- Enlarged involvement – shared responsibility of all members of the team behind the company's strategies, and goals for continual development.
- The non-managerial staff became aware of their own part and responsibility for the growth of the company. It seemed that their initially high involvement and responsibility reached new organizational levels.
- By the end of the process, the management style of the two managers became more coaching-oriented and inclusive of the staff. This was noticeable in the way the managers were asking questions through which they were trying to elicit cooperation, awareness and responsibility from their staff.
- The improvement of the communication style and the level of openness of all employees were also reflected in their relationship with the clients as they shared, preserved and enlarged knowledge within the team. By sharing information the team was able to understand more about each other and to realize the importance of their openness and cooperation in the process of improvement of the company as a whole.
- Improvement and understanding of how communications affect sales, customer care and satisfaction.
- Increased awareness of the basic needs of customers (particularly new clients) and how the advertising and marketing efforts need to be designed in order to follow the clients' needs.
- Maximization of all working efforts, marketing, sales and promotion.
- Improvement of the general work conditions within the agency, which resulted in additional employment and enlarging of the working space.

Conclusion

In my first contact with the two owners of City Travel, I realized that I was working with the top professionals in the industry. They were not just good managers; they were something of self-actualized ideal models of executives, with incredible values, organizational skills and openness for this coaching managerial style of work. I would describe this company as a self-evolving, self-aware, learning, responsible, win-win-win organization.

The coaching work ended after 12 months, during which time 10 three-to-four-hour in-company coaching sessions were run. It was my sense that this team is at the developmental stage, where the learning is and will be continually practised, revisited and improved.

Before the project, City Travel reported sales growth by 7 per cent in 2004/05. In the year they worked with the HRDF project (2005/06), sales rose by 15 per cent.

Annex: the importance of the language and the words we use in the coaching process

Language and words have extreme importance in the coaching process. It is the language and the words that hold the focus and guide us towards our goals and objectives. Apart from the focus, the words hold lots of energy within them.

For example, if I posed a question, 'How could we do the work without a single error?' I would have set myself and the team I coach a trap. The trap is in the last four words: 'without a single error'. Coaches and leaders have to infuse their questions with superlatives and passion. Creative, empowering, superlative-infused questions will evoke similar energy from the coachees, saving money and generating added value.

Sometimes, especially at the beginning of a big project or task, it could be of crucial importance to sit and simply create the best possible question; this might determine the focus and the energy levels for the rest of the project. Let us take a plain coaching question such as 'How could we do that?' as an example. The answer to this question will most of the time match the energy that is in the manager's voice and passion, plus the energy that the question brings with itself. Plain questions will mostly get plain answers and correspondingly plain actions that do not reflect the fullest potential of the performers.

If for example we empower the above question with passion, superlatives and creativity, it could look like: 'How could we do that in order to achieve the best possible results?' We could add other superlatives that would empower the question even more: 'How could we do that in order to achieve the best possible results, learn from the process and have an enjoyable time while doing the work?' The difference in the energy is self-evident, even if you simply say the question out loud to yourself. When creating questions as coaches, I suggest you experiment with them. Write them down and speak them out loud. Monitor the levels of energy they infuse you with and how they radiate through your body. You will know instantly which is the most powerful.

In addition to this, on a managerial and psychological level, in order to create superior questions, coaches, leaders and managers have to think in superlatives and believe in superlatives and hold themselves to their highest personal levels. Imagine how this would be reflected on the team they are guiding!

Viktor Kunovski
+389 70 956977
victorkunovski@performanceconsultants.com
www.skyisthelimit.org

FROM CALIFORNIA, USA: CAREER COACHING AN ENVIRONMENTAL SCIENTIST

This is the story of a young technician, who aspired to a corporate management role, and how she achieved her ambitions through the support of a specialist in leadership coaching for women.

This coaching assignment was undertaken by Jo Miller, CEO of Women's Leadership Coaching Inc, headquartered in Silicon Valley. Jo has developed coaching and seminar programmes that have benefited women worldwide, and has logged thousands of hours coaching women who are in (or aspire to break into) corporate executive and management positions.

Nancy had had a 20-year career as an environmental scientist in the energy industry in the south-western United States. In her own words, she had 'started at the bottom' as a lab technician, and now held a position as environmental scientist with a merchant power generating company. With her two eldest children approaching college age, she was able to increase the focus on her professional development, as she knew she had greater potential than to work in a lab for the rest of her career. She undertook a Master of Science degree in environmental management, and soon after having completed it, realized that the graduate degree alone did not guarantee her career progression.

Nancy sought out coaching to learn how to move from her role as scientist in a regional plant into a corporate leadership role. She contacted me for tips on how to strategize a career plan to move up.

Ready to challenge herself more, Nancy wanted to know what behaviours would demonstrate that she was ready for a leadership role, understand what would be expected of her when she became an executive, and strengthen her leadership skills. Nancy also wanted to ensure that she was doing the things that would get her noticed as an emerging leader and be perceived as a change agent, capable of performing at a higher level than her current role. Suspecting she was underpaid, Nancy also wanted to become a better negotiator and realign her salary with the marketplace:

- to become widely perceived as a capable leader;
- to move from her scientist role into a corporate leadership position;
- to get a salary increase.

The Women's Leadership Coaching program, which I created, was developed as a result of interviews with over 1,000 women, who were asked about their leadership aspirations, the skills they wished to develop and the roadblocks they faced. I discovered a common set of challenges faced by women wanting to advance their careers, and a specific set of 12 competencies necessary to break through those roadblocks. For Nancy, the most relevant competencies were negotiation, organizational awareness (or better understanding the dynamics of power within her organization), growing her network and becoming more visible.

Using the 'G-R-I-P' process (Goals–Roadmap–Ideas–Practice), I helped Nancy to formulate a project plan, or road map, for each of her goals. In subsequent sessions we brainstormed to find the best ideas for moving forward with the next step in the plan, which Nancy then put into practice by committing to complete specific action accountabilities between sessions.

As a first step, I recommended books on negotiation tactics and how women unconsciously sabotage their careers with their reluctance to initiate and engage in negotiations. Nancy devoured the books, and started looking for opportunities to practise. I set her a challenge to seize every possible opportunity to negotiate. As an immediate consequence, Nancy started asking for, negotiating, and to her surprise getting, more of what she wanted at work. 'I had no idea it was this easy,' she commented on a number of occasions.

As a first step toward changing how she was perceived, we discussed the necessity of having 'friends in high places', and becoming more visible to senior-level leaders who had decision-making power to impact the course of her career. Nancy rarely interacted with her company's senior executives, and needed to become known to them if she was to widen the range of opportunities for her career advancement. Nancy started proactively reaching out to introduce herself, with the objective of building relationships, in the hope that this would ultimately lead to a promotion.

This included setting up meetings with her new vice-president, introducing herself to C-level executives at company events, and establishing long-distance rapport with others outside her plant. She made a point of understanding who was who at company headquarters on the east coast, and requested informationals with a number of senior-level leaders, especially women, to learn how they had achieved successful careers. Over time, Nancy became closer to the environmental executive director, and asked her to become a mentor and sponsor.

During this time, I encouraged her to seize all opportunities to present to her superiors in meetings. Nancy planned and strategized diligently to make sure she was well prepared, and presented her information at a strategic big-picture level. With the increasingly favourable feedback received from the presentations, Nancy felt that her true worth and value were becoming better recognized, and her confidence soared. Feeling emboldened, she took even greater steps to being more visible.

While part of her motivation was using these opportunities to build relationships and demonstrate her leadership capabilities, she also got clearer about her career goals and never missed a chance to send a clear message to her superiors about her aspirations to move into a corporate leadership position.

After a coaching discussion about not waiting to be handed opportunities to demonstrate her leadership capabilities, Nancy decided that taking on special projects outside her normal job responsibilities was a way to showcase leadership skills that were not always apparent in her day-to-day work. To free up time for her development, and to hone her leadership skills, she trained two lab technicians to take over parts of her role.

Nancy felt capable of representing her plant to corporate headquarters on matters relating to her areas of expertise, and representing her company to an outside regulatory agency. With my criteria for selecting special projects most likely to favourably enhance her profile, Nancy looked for opportunities to join groups at state and national level where she could assume the lead role, showcase her leadership skills, and further refine her public speaking and presentation skills.

One such example was that when leadership roles opened up with her company's charitable fund, Nancy was forthright in asking to be elected as fund president. When confirmed to the vice-president role, she committed to using the opportunity to be a strong advocate for the fund, make a significant contribution, and model the style of people-oriented, collaborative leadership she wished to be known for. When an opportunity arose to travel to corporate headquarters to present to senior executives, Nancy seized it. Prior to the trip, she identified who she wanted to network with and set up social gatherings and informational meetings to maximize her time with key executives. She made plans to stay in contact after she returned to her plant. After diligent preparation, the presentation was received even better than expected, confirmed when the CEO suggested that her group's plan be used as a model for charitable giving, company-wide.

Nancy conducted a self-assessment of her skills, strengths and accomplishments to understand better where she fell in the marketplace. After gathering salary data and comparing her job classification with her skills, she initiated what became a series of meetings with her manager, building a case for a promotion and a raise. Her manager and VP became convinced she was deserving of both.

After six months of coaching, reflecting on the process so far, Nancy said, 'I am exactly where I wanted to be.' Having seen how closely Nancy aligned herself with what her leaders at corporate headquarters were trying to accomplish, they now viewed her as their representative in her region when it came to environmental matters.

Nine months into her career development plan came a new assignment that reflected the profile she had built in her organization. Nancy explained, 'I have developed a very good relationship with the environmental executive director. I think very highly of her and she thinks very highly of me. She asked my manager if I could be the project manager for implementing an environmental information management system and he said yes. So I am managing the project of implementation at 100 facilities!'

Pleased with her expanded network and new skill set for leading and influencing, Nancy had become clear that her ultimate career goal is to become an environmental director. She was having fun at work, and reported that coaching had given her the courage, strategies and self confidence to be successful.

Eleven months after starting her coaching engagement came the big opportunity she had been going after:

> I was contacted by our Corporate Environmental Group and offered a position. I increased my salary by 10 per cent which puts me in the range of my goal and will receive a 25 per cent annual bonus plus stock grants! I will be one of three corporate environmental employees and will be responsible for developing corporate policy, managing environmental risk and promoting our corporate vision. This is the career move that I have been looking for.

Jo Miller
Women's Leadership Coaching Inc
Campbell, California, USA
www.womensleadershipcoaching.com

FROM AUSTRALIA: MANAGEMENT DEVELOPMENT AT ORICA

In this case study, we learn how a consultant developed a strategy for improving customer service delivery at a multinational company in Australia through a programme of team coaching and development.

Anne Stanley has lived and worked in four countries across the disciplines of secretarial, office management, office automation consulting, training development/delivery, project management, technical writing, process re-engineering and management training. She is also a qualified sports and remedial masseur with particular sporting interests around real tennis and motorsport. This breadth of experience helps Anne in her coaching services to assist individuals and corporations in enhancing their performance and achieve their goals.

Orica is a publicly owned Australian-based global company, which is currently ranked in the top 40 on the Australian Stock Exchange based on market capitalization. With some 14,000 employees in 50 companies, the businesses of Orica (Orica Mining Services, Orica Consumer Products, Chemnet and Chemical Services) all enjoy market leadership in their particular areas.

Orica's IT Shared Service (ITSS) is the division responsible for the support and development of the organization's computing platform. As part of the division's cycle of continuous improvement, 2006 was the year for reviewing its approach to the delivery and management of customer service. A basic customer service delivery workshop had been provided to the team about seven years ago.

As I have had a consulting relationship with Orica since 1988 (when it was ICI Australia), in a variety of capacities, I was engaged to develop and deliver a customer service delivery workshop to the 120 management and staff in the division. At the outset I decided that the style of workshop would be a coaching format, and it would take a holistic view of service delivery, as all those attending were already well skilled in the basics, such as telephone techniques and use of the system which supports the division.

To this end the management team agreed to a goal statement of 'The delivery of end-to-end, consistent and coherent services to the ongoing approval of our customers', and to allow the play on words of ITSS becoming 'IT Seamless Service'.

The workshop was initially delivered to ITSS's Management Team, who then signed off on the content. Some 10 workshop sessions were delivered to the remainder of the ITSS division. I ensured that the participant mix contained a spread of attendees across the various teams within the division for two reasons: to establish relationships across team members who might not interact frequently, and to share customer service delivery experiences across the teams. To encourage freedom of expression, I also agreed with the Management Team that there would be no management or team leader level personnel present in the workshops.

During the workshops participants were encouraged to apply the coaching model of:

- 'W' – where were they currently in relationship to the stage goal for customer service delivery.
- 'I' – investigating the options for change within themselves, their teams and management.
- 'N' – name the actions to be taken.

This structure was applied to two main topics: the impact on Orica's businesses of actions taken by ITSS, and the quality of ITSS's communications with its customer base.

The discussions during the workshops produced various insights from the participants. They agreed that as a division they were totally committed to providing excellent customer service, but that they faced some challenges in that endeavour which covered the following issues:

- Internal communications needed review given that the nature of their business had now changed significantly following the settling of a major organizational restructure some five years earlier. This included:
  - communications within teams;
  - communications across teams;
  - communications to/from management.

  Participants also believed that they had many opportunities that had not yet been explored, and the take-away from the workshops was that they were going to act individually and within their teams to address the above three areas.
- Participants expressed a desire to extend their knowledge of the workings of each of the Orica business platforms. They felt that this would significantly impact the quality of the services that were provided to their customers.
- General recognition that attention needed to be paid to cross-skilling within and across teams due to the changing and more integrated nature of the company's computing platform.

The output from the workshops was that all participants wrote their own personal action plan for how they intended to change their own ways of working; what ideas they would bring to team meetings, etc. They took their own copy and provided me with a sealed copy. The plan is to give these plans back in the future for participants to review their progress.

One of the most satisfying aspects of conducting these workshops was the generosity of the participants in the way that they freely presented their ideas and expressed their concerns. It showed that we had a group of people who were committed to re-engineering their ways of working in a collaborative manner.

The challenge for me was to present the results of the workshops in a measurable and workable format. After each workshop I wrote up bullet point notes of ideas, comments, issues etc. At the conclusion of the workshop series, I worked through these notes and developed a list of main topics and sub-topics. Thereafter I went through each of the bullet points and allocated it to a main or sub-topic until I could build a spreadsheet of results. (An example of how to do this is featured at the end of this case history.)

The next step was to present the spreadsheet to the ITSS Management Team and then meet with them individually to assess their reaction. This culminated in a Management Team meeting to jointly agree the way forward. The main points of agreement were that the time was right to revisit ways of working in order to exploit the organization's current operating conditions, and that they should take the opportunity to harness the enthusiasm of the team, as generated by the workshops, to effect change.

This is to be achieved by the formation of a joint working party comprising management and staff team members who will be invited to take the contents of the spreadsheet and select the items to be worked upon. It was further agreed that members of the team would be rotated in order to gain the widest form of buy-in from both management and staff.

Achievements to date

Whilst I am no longer directly involved with the working party I understand that a working group of 19 was formed (3 management and 16 staff volunteers). They split into three groups, each of which took a topic to work on – using the coaching model I had given them. They have presented their plans for each of their topics to the acclaim of their peers, and I am confident that this process will be ongoing until all items on the spreadsheet have been addressed and contributed to the division's goals for customer service.

Feedback

The management team felt that the spreadsheet format constituted a thorough 360-degree survey, and provided data in a form that allowed action to be taken and measured. A few weeks after the workshops the IT Manager for Orica Consumer Products reported that he had been receiving feedback from his customers that there was a distinct improvement in customer service levels.

On a recent visit to the client I was approached by several of the workshop participants, who said they were very happy with the activities arising from the workshop. In addition, they were grateful for the opportunity of participating in the workshops and having their ideas/concerns recorded and presented.

As an external entity I am delighted to have been able to act as a conduit for this emerging culture change within the client environment, and am very grateful to Orica for the opportunity of working with them in this way.

Annex: using a spreadsheet for converting assessments into measurable data

Frequently you will have narrative information from discussions, interviews, workshops etc, which needs to be converted into summarized measurable data. Such data would then be used as the basis for further activities, and subsequently measured in terms of change, success, etc. Set out below is a template process, using a spreadsheet that you may find useful.

- Convert your narrative material into bullet-point statements, each of which is a line item in your spreadsheet.
- Read through all your bullet points several times to get a sense of the content.
- Develop main category (A–Z) and subcategory (1–99) headings, eg, issues, improvement suggestions, team development.
- Work your way through your bullet-point lines and allocate them to either a main or subcategory by entering the appropriate number for the category. In reality you will allocate both a main and subcategory reference number.
- Sort your spreadsheet on the main and subcategory items and you will have all your data displayed in order of priority. This will give you your highest priorities displayed at the top of the list. From here you can then develop goals and action plans to address them.

You can then add additional columns to your spreadsheet to cover goal statement, action plans etc, including times, dates, and who. Alternatively take each one of the goals and develop a separate worksheet within the workbook.

For reasons of confidentiality, the data in Figure 9.2 are not the spreadsheet results from Orica; the table is shown as an example only.

Anne Stanley
ALS Directions Pty Ltd
+61 (0)416-24-295
stanleys@cosmos.net.au

FROM ABU DHABI: CORPORATE COACHING IN THE UNITED ARAB EMIRATES

The client company in this case history was formed during the 1980s as a wholly owned subsidiary of a regional trading company. Initially successful, it had gradually lost market share until in 2005 it posted its first negative profit statement. The owners decided the company needed a basic examination of business model and strategy. Instead of commissioning a typical business turnaround the owners decided to try corporate coaching to produce a sustainable change in business performance.

Michael Daly, MBA, Master Practitioner NLP, is a highly experienced international coach and mentor. He has worked at a senior level in British Aerospace, GEC and Hanson and SMEs in the United Kingdom and overseas. His specializations include corporate strategy, business start-up and executive coaching.

Cat #	Category	Sub-cat #	Subcategory	Issue or observation	Goal	Action plan	Who	When
A	Communications	1	Across the division	Would like updated organization chart to better understand responsibilities across div.				
A	Communications	1	Across the division	Need a formal introduction process for new starters				
A	Communications	2	Inter teams	Believe it would be good to meet regularly with other team members at other sites				
A	Communications	3	With business group	Not sure who to contact within the businesses - need clear visibility of contact points for particular systems/products				
A	Communications	4	With customer-individual	Suggest relaunching the online program for customer self-help				
B	Management	1	3rd party mgmt	Request visibility of 3rd party contract arrangements and how they impact internal support levels				
B	Management	2	Change Control Process	Need centralization of the comms around change control so all can access the details				
B	Management	3	Complaints handling process	Believe process needs review and updating to suit changed business conditions				

Figure 9.2 A sample assessment spreadsheet

Methodology

I needed to understand the company with which I was dealing without being adversely affected by its past performance. It is better to accept what you have as the starting point without delving too far into previous problems which can lead to apportioning blame and having low expectations of future performance.

The senior executives were given a number of psychometric tests to improve their self-awareness and to better understand their colleagues. The systems I used included Belbin team roles, DISC profiles and Apter motivational styles. Each executive was asked to share his or her results, which some were reluctant to do initially. The reports helped everyone to understand why they needed to tailor their communications with certain individuals, and explained some of the past problems and personnel conflicts.

The Belbin system allowed 360-degree feedback and the Apter system allowed 180-degree feedback, which helped the executives appreciate the impact their style was having on the motivation of their teams.

Each executive was then asked to complete a subjective assessment of the company's performance using a simple balance wheel chart. The assessments were carried out independently and anonymously, with the results being displayed at a joint meeting. There was a reasonable amount of variation in the assessments, which averaged out to produce the profile shown in Figure 9.3.

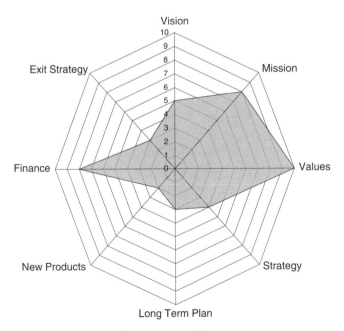

Figure 9.3   Company performance profile

The overall assessment suggested that although the organization had strong corporate values, and thanks to the parent organization was financially strong, it lacked vision and hence direction.

The next technique that was used was appreciative inquiry. This helped everyone understand that the company is good at some things and that these should be concentrated on to provide some much-needed motivation. Most of the business executives had received a typical western business management education which focuses to a large extent on identifying and then solving problems. A significant focus on problems can give the impression there are only problems and this is a 'problem organization'. This type of negative feedback can be very demotivating and does not fit well with a coaching culture.

Appreciative inquiry is a four-stage iterative process:

- **Discover**: everyone talks to everyone to discover the times the organization is at its best, metaphors are developed.
- **Dream**: people are encouraged to imagine the organization as if the times found during Discover happened most of the time.
- **Design**: a small team is empowered to design ways of creating the Dream organization.
- **Destiny**: implement the changes.

As I am based in the United Kingdom the logistics of coaching an organization a few thousand miles away had to be agreed. The project was divided into phases, with the first phase comprising the psychometric tests, for which I visited the UAE for one week. During this week the tests were completed and feedback given during a series of one to one and group sessions.

Over the following two months the implications of the psychometric tests were considered during a once per week conference call. We used VOIP for the conference calls. VOIP allows voice communication over the internet and the use of low-cost web cameras.

Phase two comprised the appreciative inquiry section, for which I again returned to the UAE for one week. This was followed up with the regular weekly conference call.

Phase three was the change implementation and monitoring phase, which also involved visits to the UAE and weekly conference calls.

Outcome

The outcome from the psychometric tests, including the 360-degree and 180-degree feedback, was an acknowledgement that the organization still employed an old fashioned command, control and coerce management style. This produced demotivated employees who did not feel they were allowed to contribute to corporate tactics and certainly not to corporate strategy.

It was also at this point the executives realized I was not going to provide them with answers like a consultant or mentor, but instead I was going to help them find their own answers by questioning. I did however suggest they did some background reading, and recommended *The Art of War* by Sun Tzu (Michaelson, 2001) and *The 36 Stratagems for Business* (Von Senger, 2006).

Coaching

I started by using an NLP technique of 'value elicitation' to assist the executives to articulate their corporate values and define the type of organization they wanted. The background reading they had completed suggested they had been managing and not providing leadership; they decided they would like to have leadership at all levels of the organization.

From the mass of results and feedback I guided them to identify three main goals and the strategies they would use to implement them. The first main change in approach occurred at this point, when they decided to delegate the tactical plan and actions to more junior staff. This freed the executives to concentrate on strategy and to start putting into place new commercial agreements with suppliers and customers.

Subsequent coaching sessions concentrated on moving towards the strategic goals and ensuring the tactical plans were aligned with the goals.

Results

Using corporate coaching, an organization that had been performing badly for a number of years turned itself around. Managers became leaders, new markets were entered, individuals worked as team members, absenteeism disappeared and hierarchical structures were dismantled. Sales and profits increased to a point that the return on investment for corporate coaching was greater than 10 times within the first year.

Future

The company continues to grow and some of its strategies are being adopted by the parent organization. Individual executives continue to receive one to one coaching and are interested in introducing a coaching culture into the organization. A mixture of coaching and mentoring is being used as part of succession planning to develop future executive leaders.

New goals continue to be developed in consultation with all the employees and increasingly with customers. The company is considering developing operations in Europe and the Far East.

Michael Daly
www.ecam.nu

FROM AUSTRALIA: LEADING FOR PERFORMANCE; BUILDING A VALUES-DRIVEN ORGANIZATION IN IT SERVICES

The client in this case history is one of the largest, and fastest growing wholly owned IT services company in the Asia Pacific region, with more than 500 people, competing successfully with its dominant global competitors. The Institute of Human Excellence (IHE) was engaged in mid-2005 by the top management team of this organization, with a brief to design and deliver a change programme to expand their leadership capacity and to build a high-performance culture. The business objectives behind this were to sustain performance, retain talents and improve shareholders' value. On top of that, the director of the organization clearly stated that they wanted to go for the extra mile beyond performance excellence to create 'happiness' in their work environment.

Niran Jiang is a co-founder of the Institute of Human Excellence in Sydney and an internationally accredited cultural transformation tools consultant and trainer. Formerly an executive at Coca-Cola and S C Johnson, Niran specializes in culture change, leadership and innovation. She has an MBA from the University of California and taught in the business school of Shenzhen University in China.

Alex Feher is a director and partner in the Institute of Human Excellence, and his executive coaching expertise is supported by a solid practical grounding in running businesses and managing change processes with large teams. He has a BSc Mech Eng and an MSc Ind Eng.

Through one on one interviews with all senior managers, a range of issues were identified, including structural impediments, hidden/limiting values, resource misalignment, change weariness, inconsistent management language, rocky communication and minimal collaborations.

Three key areas of focus for change were identified:

- Develop values-based leadership capability as a foundation to activate culture change in the organization.
- Shift senior managers' focus from managing results to managing people, and broaden their performance management spectrum to include the intangibles.
- Balance individual excellence with teamwork excellence, and create a shared culture identity and organizational cohesion.

An initial organizational development programme was designed and delivered, which included the following three stages.

Stage I: Leadership values assessment

The objective was to understand the performance drivers and barriers of each senior manager for their individual leadership development. We used the values-based leadership assessment tool developed by Richard Barrett and Associates (cultural transformation tools: see page 121). It provided a diagnosis of the values profile of each individual and the individual's team. Through this 360-degree leadership assessment, each one was able to identify his or her leadership development areas, focus and pathways.

We set up a confidential environment to give the managers their own individual control for the assessment, debriefing and development process. No reporting back to their own managers was undertaken in order to protect the confidentiality. This significantly increased the buy-in and the ownership for the programme, and put the managers in the driver's seats of their own leadership development.

Stage II: Leadership retreat

A two-day offsite retreat for leadership training and team building was conducted to link the individual development process with the group work process. Individual strengths were explored and built upon within the leadership team context. A consistent leadership framework, language and measurement system was established to activate the development of the leadership team.

Group vision, goals and action plans were created for the next 12 months, and almost all of them stated that the managers were experiencing authentic connections with each other, and a real sense of being a team, for the first time.

Stage III: Tailored leadership coaching

Each manager had the option to elect 12 ongoing sessions of individual coaching on a volunteer basis, and paid for these coaching sessions from his or her own budget. The coaching programme was tailored for each individual, based on the individual's assessment results and developmental goals.

The individual coaching sessions were combined with a group training session. In the middle of their coaching programme, a two-day inner game (following the principles of Tim Gallwey's inner game techniques mentioned on page 7) training session was delivered for the management group to build their people management capabilities and skills. We used sport as a learning metaphor on the training programme for communication, teamwork and management via coaching.

Key qualitative results of IHE's initial programme

Most senior managers at the company gained confidence and self-belief in their capacity to lead and manage people by example, with their increased self-knowledge and authenticity. They developed a robust sense of meaning and purpose in their work. Through IHE's interventions, they were equipped with models, techniques and skills with which to understand and guide the process of their staff, team and organizational development and transformation. They built strengthened and consolidated relationships, trust, openness and integrity within their team, and thereby created a high level of performance and enjoyment at work.

There was significant increase in the morale and motivation level in the whole organization. A significant impact of the new leadership competencies gained was increased concern and caring for staff, which directly led to better customer care and higher staff retention. As an organization, they developed the capacity to prepare their staff and teams to embrace change rather than fear it. The positive change in their leadership and culture led to increased customer retention, revenue growth and substantial cost savings.

Key quantitative results of IHE's change programme

At the start of IHE's programme, a full scale Gallup workplace engagement survey was conducted for the whole organization. This same study was repeated 12 months later. During this period of time, IHE's programme was the only external organizational development programme used by this company.

The Gallup study showed a statistically significant improvement in the overall workplace. There were significant increases in the measurements around people management capability, especially improvements in 'recognition', 'cares about me', 'opinion count' and 'best friend'.

Market analysts had identified the company as a significant contender to become the leading non-multinational IT services company in the Asia Pacific region. The company rapidly grew in its financial numbers, customers and locations. Profits were above target and client retention was excellent. Management team collaboration started to occur at all levels, and the balanced scorecard was recently introduced.

Current status

IHE has been working with this organization for over 18 months now, and has been further engaged by the organization for the next phase of its organizational development work, such as leading mission and vision, developing values-based decision-making capacities and training managers in coaching skills.

IHE's programme has been spreading both horizontally and vertically within the organization with its senior management team's support. IHE is also facilitating the organization to embark on a courageous corporate social responsibility (CSR) programme with an organizational objective to make significant social contributions in the community.

Niran Jiang
+61 (0)2 9400 7018
niran@ihexcellence.org

Alex Feher
+61 (0)2 9363 4870
alex@ihexcellence.org

FROM JAPAN: MANAGEMENT STYLES AND SUCCESSION PLANNING

This case history describes two separate interventions in different organizations. All the names of individuals have been changed. The first case concerns a very real problem in Japan today, that of the tradition of 'micromanaging' and how to move forward into modern methods of delegation. The second is about the challenges of succession, and how a manager succeeded in integrating his predecessor positively and how he prepared for his successor.

Paula Sugawara is based in Tokyo, Japan and runs her own coaching and corporate training company, Tokyo Coaching Services. As an executive coach, coaching in both Japanese and English, her clients range from foreign financial institutions to Japanese manufacturing companies. Her career in the financial industry and the fact that she has lived in Japan for over 18 years give her a good insight into many of the issues her coaching clients face. A firm believer in the potential of people, her favourite phrase is, 'Failure is only failure if you fail to learn from it'.

Adapting from micromanagement to coaching in leadership

Takashi is a junior level manager in the Tokyo office of a global investment bank. Although he is a high performer in his specialist field, I was brought in to help him work on issues such as relationships with his team members and direct reports, time management and organizational issues. Takashi had a number of issues with his team: how to improve communication with them, how to manage an underperformer and how to manage his relationship with a senior team member.

In order to work on improving his communication skills with his team members, an early conclusion was that it might be useful to adopt a coaching style rather than a telling/instructing style with them. When coaching Japanese managers, I often see many examples of how junior managers believe they have to micromanage people, in the sense of having all the answers themselves, giving orders, being in charge and focusing primarily on the task in hand to the extent that soft skills or people skills are given a lower priority. This sometimes ends up in creating a boss/subordinate relationship with limited communication and a fear on the part of the subordinate to ask for any help, advice or input from his or her manager.

As a result, we reached the conclusion that the first step to help Takashi improve his people and communication skills was the use of basic coaching techniques. Instead of telling and giving orders, Takashi decided to use coaching skills to ask effective and open questions, give more responsibility to team members where appropriate and support them in goal setting.

In order for him to make progress in giving them more freedom and responsibility in setting their own goals, I was curious to find out to what extent he felt he could trust them and be confident in their decisions. Did he believe in them and their ability to do their job? Was he able to connect with them on a personal level? Asking questions of this nature helped him realize that he was not as confident in them as he felt he should be, and that by micromanaging he had not even given them the opportunity to show the full extent of their capability.

In light of the different types of people and needs in Takashi's team, we explored the use of Ken Blanchard's Situational Leadership model and how he might be able to use it to work with the people in his team. During one of our sessions I asked him to consider the different learning level of each of his team members. Reflection here showed him, much to his surprise, that there was a major difference, even between those junior members who he had assumed were largely the same. This helped him to realize that he would need to take a very different approach towards each person in order to get the best out of them.

Situational leadership techniques demonstrated to him how he could modify his approach depending on the level of experience of each employee. One issue he faced here was that of a 'veteran employee' known as Shoichi. In many non-Japanese companies where promotion is based on performance and ability, it is not uncommon to find a manager who might well be younger or have been with the firm for a shorter time period than the people he is managing. For some Japanese people who are used to the seniority system at traditional Japanese companies, which dictates promotion based on the number of years of service with the company or the age of a person, this situation can be difficult to deal with. This was the exact problem faced by Takashi, who had a team member who was older than he was, had been with the firm longer and was frustrated that he had been passed over for promotion in favour of Takashi.

Our coaching conversation on this subject focused on looking at the positive contribution this 'veteran' might be able to make to the team, instead of the negative aspects such as how to neutralize his effect or how to control the person. We brainstormed some of the ways he could harness the qualities and experience of this person and how he could actually get him to adopt a specific role in the team. Further discussion focused on situational leadership and the type of approach that might lend itself to this case.

This led to the conclusion that this person was an S4 type (according to the four types in Ken Blanchard's situational leadership model), experienced and able to operate independently. Accordingly the approach to be adopted was one of delegating and giving him an independent function. Takashi decided to harness his experience and skills as a mentor and trainer for the younger and less experienced members of the team – this would give Shoichi his own independent role while providing a meaningful contribution to the rest of the team and the organization as a whole. It also helped to give Shoichi a new purpose and offset the feeling that he had been overlooked in favour of Takashi.

With Shoichi now contributing to the team and being a source of support for Takashi, it helped Takashi to change his own mindset towards him and to see him as an ally rather than a competitor. Additionally, it enabled Shoichi to use his experience in a positive way, giving him freedom to work independently while maintaining a position of respect in front of others. It also alleviated some of Takashi's work burden and enabled them to create a much more positive relationship.

Another problem area in the team was that of Jiro, an underperformer. However, this situation had been exacerbated by the fact that the underperformer largely refused to acknowledge his weakness and actually thought he was performing well. The challenge here was to provide some developmental feedback in order to make Jiro realize that he needed to improve his performance, without making him feel demotivated. The fact that Jiro felt he was actually a very strong performer and was sometimes boastful of his achievements was somewhat frustrating for Takashi, and he accordingly found it difficult not to get emotional in one to one conversations with Jiro.

Our coaching conversations focused on how he could remain objective and unemotional during their discussions but be firm in giving feedback. At the same time, Takashi decided to try to use more positive thinking and to improve his attitude towards Jiro, as he had realized that he was probably letting his emotions colour his judgment in this relationship. By stepping back and giving him the benefit of the doubt, and focusing on his strong points rather than weak points, he felt he was able to change his attitude toward Jiro. Once Takashi was able to do this, Jiro also started to open up about his own weaknesses and areas for improvement. Clearly focusing on the positive elements had helped Takashi and Jiro to establish more of a collaborative and conciliatory relationship, rather than a stand-off where they were reluctant to admit weaknesses to each other. Now that Jiro felt Takashi was on his side he was finally able to ask for input and support in improving his areas for development.

Overall, although some of the coaching techniques I used here were quite simple, they were extremely effective in creating a change of mindset in Takashi and helping him to transform two potentially negative elements into sources of positive contribution and support. This development in turn helped to build a team with greater levels of rapport and communication.

Succession planning

Mike was the head of the Tokyo branch of a major US financial institution. His assignment to Tokyo was the first time he had lived in Japan, and when I first met him he had been here only for approximately six months. As one of a handful of non-Japanese within the Tokyo office, I was called in to help him deal with a hierarchical situation as well as a succession issue regarding who would take over from him when he returned to the United States.

Although Mike was the president of operations in Japan his predecessor Jun, who had stepped aside, was still chairman of the organization. Although Jun was not overtly overstepping boundaries, neither was he making a particularly large contribution to the organization, which was a source of concern for Mike.

Our initial coaching conversations focused on what Mike wanted to get out of Jun and how he could create a meaningful role rather than just having him there as a figurehead. We looked at ways he could harness his capabilities, and Mike came up with suggestions, such as focusing on high-level corporate relationships, improving industry contacts and adopting the role of mentor to young managers. Not wanting to start the relationship on an aggressive footing by giving orders, Mike started with a softer approach of finding out what the chairman would like to do and how he personally felt that he could contribute to the organization. Although Jun came up with a number of ideas similar to those of Mike, he unfortunately did very little to implement any of them.

Mike then decided to take it to the next level, and tried a more direct approach of telling Jun what he would like from him and how he thought Jun could help him. Although Jun appeared to make some efforts over the following weeks, again these were somewhat half-hearted and were of little contribution to the organization as a whole. Mike's position was becoming even more difficult since he did not want to develop a negative relationship with Jun, but it was getting more and more difficult to justify the expense of a chairman at the top of the salary scale who was making only a minimal contribution to the organization.

Mike's next step was to sit down with Jun and work on an agreement with him as to what his role could and should be. Having reached a mutual frame-work, Mike felt that he had to include an additional element of accountability in light of the fact that Jun had not lived up to his promises so far. He decided to set up a meeting for Jun to report to him about his efforts and progress; however, he framed it as an update meeting, focusing on industry trends and key clients. By including other directors in the meeting it reduced the impression that this was a meeting for Jun to report back to him. For me, this approach showed how taking a softly-softly approach to relationships can prevent them from deteriorating very rapidly. In light of the cultural and perceptual differences that obviously existed between Mike and Jun, starting off with laying down orders for what Mike wanted Jun to do and having him report back would probably have resulted in their relationship starting off on the wrong foot. The structure he finally created between them enabled him to keep the chairman in a meaningful role until he finally retired the following year.

Another issue facing Mike was that of finding his successor and dealing with the fallout expected from his inevitable return to the United States. Since Mike's stint in Japan was for a limited period of time, we used his expected departure date to work back from and create deadlines for when he had to identify a successor. This enabled him to clarify when he had to start and how long he had to find somebody to take over from him.

The first step was to come up with a 'job description' for the new candidate in order to help Mike identify the qualities and characteristics a potential candidate would need to offer. Once he had the list, he then prioritized these to simplify the selection process, which would commence when he started to find potential candidates. One of his hopes was that the candidate would be able to come into the organization and keep things running as they were. Mike had spent a lot of effort in rebuilding and improving operations and wanted to hand it over in a smooth and perfect working order.

He considered what else he had to do in order to hand over operations in optimum condition, and identified factors such as making some organizational changes at the local level, adding some functions, changes in the management structure and changes in strategy and product focus. With these changes already starting to be implemented, Mike felt increasingly assured that he would be able to hand over operations so that they would run smoothly with the minimum of input from the new president.

As Mike made progress with his list of candidates, he realized that his next step was to foster their interest in the position of president. For many non-

Japanese, the prospect of a move to the very different working culture and environment of Japan, not to mention the linguistic challenges, is daunting to say the least. When it also involves the move of a spouse and other family members then it can be a major process. Mike started to think how he could make life easier for any new arrivals and enlisted his own family to put together the 'ABC of life in Japan'.

As he started narrowing down the field of candidates, Mike also realized that he would have to take action to manage the expectations of those who were already excluded from the list, as well as alleviate the concerns of the rest of the employees in the Japan office.

At the time of writing, Mike has already successfully identified his successor, who is eager to come to Japan and run the Tokyo office. They are now waiting for the official announcement of the appointment. Coaching helped Mike work through the process logically and effectively without waiting until the last minute to make a decision and find he had chosen 'just any old candidate'.

Paula Sugawara
Tokyo Coaching Services
+81 422 51 9283
info@tokyocoach.com
www.tokyocoach.com

MORAL DILEMMAS AND COACHING CHALLENGES

Gillian Jones, a highly experienced corporate coach and director of Emerge, shares some moral dilemmas and challenges which she has come up against during her years of coaching in organizations.

In most of the examples given, there are a number of possible routes the coach could take to help the client, and Gillian has listed the different options she would recommend. The situations are real but all names and identifying elements have been changed.

Emerge Development Consultancy has specialized in developing individuals and organizations for over 10 years now, and in the last three years Gillian has extended her coaching experience by focusing on helping organizations to implement a coaching culture. Gillian's experience draws from 17 years of coaching individuals and working with executive boards to improve relationships and achieve results.

Moral dilemmas

The sponsor client is deceiving the coachee

You have been coaching a manager for two months. During a meeting with his director, the director reveals to you that the board does not think the manager is going to make it in the company, but the director wants to continue the coaching anyway. He says that the other board members want the manager out and therefore he has to make sure that the manager has had sufficient coaching to protect the organization legislatively. The other board members feel that because the manager is quite devoted to his family he does not put in the hours the others do, nor does he appear dedicated to the organization.

The manager is unaware of how the board feels and is desperately trying to work on the behavioural issues that were identified to be in the coaching plan. During your session he reveals that he has been headhunted this week for a great job. He does not know whether to take it but is thinking he will probably stick it out with his current company because he needs the money for his children.

Suggestions

There is a case here for going back to the director and challenging him on the board's motives. The discussion should be around the purpose and intent of the coaching, specifically that coaching should always have a positive intent and you only enter into a coaching relationship on the basis that you will successfully help the other person to change his or her behaviour. This should be an interesting conversation to have with the director, as the question is, if the board are set on finding a way to get the person out, how will they feel if the coaching successfully changes his behaviour?

Your integrity as a coach is at stake here, because if you collude with the board, then it will be very difficult for you to give your all in the coaching sessions and undoubtedly your incongruity will start to leak through. However, you do also have a responsibility to the manager as you have started to work with him.

For this reason, you may decide to continue with the coaching sessions, on the basis that the manager's changed behaviour will help him wherever he is in his career. In this case, if you feel fairly sure that he does not have a future with the organization, you may feel a responsibility to help him to move on. When he brings up the subject of the job offer, you could take time to discuss this with him, asking some challenging questions about his future with the current organization and weighing up the pros and cons.

In situations like this, you can sometimes say a lot without many words, by your tone, or the look you give a person or what you don't say as opposed to what you do. If a direct question was asked, such as 'Do you think I should take the job?', a very direct look in the eyes with a controlled statement such as, 'It sounds like an extremely good opportunity,' can send a strong message. Other statements such as 'You need to do what is best for you and your family,' or even questions such as 'Tell me how you see your future with this organization,' followed by some sturdy probing, may start to get the message across.

Ironically, if the manager decides to take the job, this gives the organization the outcome it required. However, I would want to have a discussion with the board about how the situation arose and was managed. It would certainly put a question mark for me over whether I wanted to work with any other managers in this organization in the future.

The bully

You are coaching two peer members who are both senior managers. Jim used to work for John and says that John bullied him so badly that he lost all confidence. When he was promoted to peer level he felt better, but finds that working as a peer with John is still incredibly hard, as Jim feels he has been internally damaged. He still talks in anger about John and about the incidents, and he cannot get rid of the feelings, which are affecting his work. Jim and John have to work together and can barely speak to each other. You feel that if Jim were able to tell John how he had felt, it would get rid of some of the emotion and give them a stronger foundation to build on.

John is completely unaware of all this and cannot be bothered, because he thinks Jim is a complete waste of space and pathetic. John appears to have no idea that he is a bully.

Suggestions

This is one of the difficulties in coaching members of the same team; you become exposed to opposing points of view about people, based only on their own experience, and it is impossible for you to validate these with evidence unless you see any of the behaviour during a coaching session. It is, of course, highly unlikely that John will display any bullying traits during a coaching meeting. I never cease to be amazed at how compliant and polite 'problem people' are when being coached, which is a very good reason for coaching not to be used as the sole remedial solution here.

There are many approaches to helping John understand more about his 'blind spot', such as conducting a 360-degree audit, getting feedback from his manager or finding a situation where you can observe him and give feedback. If you were discussing his relationship with Jim, you could get him to take a good look at Jim's perception from a different angle. Using 'spatial position-ing' can help here – this means asking John to sit in a different chair and imagine he is Jim, and then to think hard about what Jim might see, hear or feel when working with John.

From Jim's point of view, this has clearly been a deeply disturbing relationship and he has two options: either to talk it through with you in such depth that he is able to exorcise his feelings and put them behind him by using positive tools, or to be coached to the point where he can have a full discussion with John. The decision on which way to go will be driven by the strength of feelings that remain after Jim has expressed everything he needs to, in the safety of a session with you, and by checking on how he is feeling before and after the discussions. If he is still experiencing the same strength of feeling as before, he needs to understand that this will always hold him back until he can find a way of letting go.

Techniques that help people understand that behaviour is a choice can be extraordinarily useful here. Hearing the saying, 'No one can make you feel inferior without your permission,' by Eleanor Roosevelt can be a life-changing moment. You could ask Jim how, if he is still choosing to feel hurt and damaged, would he need to change his behaviour in order to feel differently? Working with Jim to help him understand that he can choose to continue feeling this way for as long as he likes, possibly inhibiting his potential and using a huge amount of negative energy, or could choose to leave it behind, could be the turning point for him.

The coachee needs additional professional help

You have been asked by her manager to coach Jane because her performance has dipped and the manager has no idea why. Coachee Jane has lots of personal problems – financial challenges, marriage difficulties and bringing up three young boys. You have built a deep rapport with her and she really values your sessions, sometimes saying she doesn't know how she could get by without you. During a session she confesses to you that she has a drink problem, to the extent of drinking before work. The company has a 'dry' policy during working hours.

Suggestions

We all agree confidentiality with our coachees at the beginning of a relationship but there are times when that agreement can be compromised. You must remind yourself that you have a responsibility to both the coachee's organization and to the coachee. The confession that Jane has made appears to contravene company rules (although you might want to discreetly check the wording here – rules regarding alcohol are sometimes not very explicit and can simply refer to no drinking on the premises or at lunchtime). When someone confesses something like this to you it is often a cry for help, and unless you have ever run an AA group, it is unlikely that you will have the skills to deal with the situation. Therefore it is critical that you facilitate her to seek the right type of help for her problem through heightened listening, empathy and questioning skills.

You also need to think carefully about your relationship with Jane. She has said that she sometimes doesn't know how she would get by without you, which implies an unhealthy dependence on the coaching relationship. A coach has a responsibility to nurture self-dependence in the coachee and to take care not to get into situations where the coachee feels so dependent.

Although it may seem cruel at first, it might help Jane if you tell her that you are unable to continue with any coaching sessions until she has sought help for her alcoholism and has it under control. It is very likely that at some point the manager will ask you for a progress report, and if you have not made any business progress, the manager will want to know why. It is appropriate and ethical for you to let the manager know that you are not coaching Jane at present until she has resolved some personal issues, and to encourage both parties to talk to each other.

At this point, you may also wish to reflect on your coaching skills and analyse how and why Jane became so dependent on you. It may simply be circumstantial; with her marital difficulties she may have felt lonely and needed someone to talk to, and even on reflection, you cannot see that you could have done anything differently. However, it may alert you to some behavioural deficiencies in your own style that affect the balance between empathy and business focus. It is always worth checking in on skills!

The coachee is deceiving the sponsor client

You have been brought in by a manager to coach a 'high potential' in order to prepare her for her next role, as the company has high hopes for her. You have had two good sessions and then the coachee tells you she has been headhunted and is going to leave. She is not giving notice for another four weeks, as she wants to finish a course she is doing and the new company is happy to wait two months for her. She wants to use the next two coaching sessions to prepare for her future role.

Suggestions

This is a true moral dilemma because, had she not told you she intended to give notice in four weeks, you would have continued with the next two sessions, but now you know she is going you have a decision to make! In this situation, my responsibility as coach would lie with the organization paying for the coaching, which is clearly investing in the person for very good reasons. It seems unfair that they should invest money that will then benefit another employer.

You might suggest to the coachee that once she has handed in her notice, if her manager is happy for her to continue then you would be delighted to book the last two sessions. Alternatively, asking some strong questions encouraging the coachee to look at it from the manager's point of view can be enlightening too. Would she be happy to pay for development if it were a member of her own team who was leaving?

Another option is to suggest that she pays privately for the next two sessions to prepare her for the next role. Finally, you could suggest that during her negotiations with the new company she asks for funding for the last two sessions, in order to help her transition into the new organization.

The coachee does not know her employment rights

You have been coaching a director for six months and she has been promised a vice-presidency position. At the beginning of the coaching you met with her manager, who outlined what she needed to do differently in order to get the promotion, and you put a solid plan together. At two three-month reviews with the director's manager, following some very good feedback, you checked whether she was still on track for promotion, and the manager said 'yes'. She then received an end of year bonus for exceeding expectations.

Suddenly she is told that she will not get the VP position as her 'face doesn't fit' with the German parent company, and she is being offered a sideways move into a job that is not suited to her qualifications. She is told to 'take it or leave it'.

From the details you have heard and your own observations you estimate that she has a constructive dismissal case. However, she has no knowledge of employment legislation.

Suggestions

It is hard to believe nowadays that people are not aware of their legal rights as there is so much information on the web, radio and in the newspapers. However, some people believe so strongly that their company will do right by them that the thought does not cross their mind.

In this situation it would be very hard for the coach to walk away knowing that the manager could have had some negotiating leverage. Once again, the conflict of responsibilities to the organization and the coachee kicks in, and it would be unethical for you to spell out her rights. If you try to approach the company to discuss this it is likely you will be blocked from coaching in future, because it will appear as if you are siding with the employee. In addition, if you tell her why you think she has a good case, you may be called as a witness for her at a tribunal because of the discussions you had with the manager about performance improvement.

So what can you do? When the coachee first talks about the issues, you could ask questions such as, 'Have you spoken to anyone about the legal implications?' or 'Is it worth speaking to the Citizens Advice bureau about your rights?' or 'Have you asked HR to go through your legal rights with you?' If the coachee quizzed you further, you could profess to be no expert and therefore unable to comment in detail, but suggest in any of these situations it is always worth checking the legal position with an expert.

The coachee has become dependent

You have completed six months on a coaching assignment with Chris and covered all the issues you were contracted to do. Chris enjoys his conversations with you and says he needs to continue to see you each month to motivate him, even though there is nothing specific to work on – and he suggests you do it over lunch in future. He says his manager has agreed to fund another six months if you could put something together to demonstrate what further issues you need to work through.

Suggestions

This is another opportunity to examine your coaching style and check whether any of your behaviour has encouraged dependency! The comment 'needing to see you to motivate myself' is a worrying indicator, and I would want to have a discussion with him about techniques he could use to motivate himself.

Of course, coaches welcome the opportunity to coach people over a prolonged period of time, but any professional coach knows that there have to be clear and measurable objectives. Therefore a simple solution to this dilemma is to flip back responsibility to the coachee for putting together a plan demonstrating objectives, measurements and need. If you tell Chris that once he has had the plan approved by his manager you would be delighted to continue with the sessions, then the action lies with him.

You can then tackle the question of having sessions over lunch. It is impossible for a coach to give full value in a coaching session in such a situation and in a public place, so it is your choice whether you offer a coaching session before or after lunch and tack on a quick sandwich as an unpaid added extra!

Coaching challenges

The coachee needs to be more assertive

You have been asked to coach director Jack, who needs to increase his credibility. His manager says he needs more presence and impact and that Jack is OK at presenting information when asked, but not good at building rapport and chatting before meetings. The manager has also noticed that Jack does not get a great hearing at meetings as he is quite quietly spoken. Jack is a financial director and not naturally gregarious. His Myers Briggs profile is ISTJ. (For more information on Myers Briggs see page 124).

Suggestions

In a situation such as this it is important to check Jack's motivation to change – being told to 'get noticed more' can sit uncomfortably with some people. Asking questions around Jack's model of beliefs, desire and ability will help to flush out whether he really wants to change, believes he can and has the ability to do so. For example, is there any situation in which he is able to be more outgoing? If the answer is 'yes', then the coach can help him to transfer the skills he uses in that situation.

Aligned with this is Jack's thought process and how he sees himself. If he has always been labelled as shy or introverted, and he talks about himself in this way, he will need to reposition that view in order to get a true change in behaviour. Sometimes I have worked with people who say 'I am only a ... so they probably won't want to hear my ideas.' In this situation you could work with Jack to build confidence by ensuring that he sees himself as important and integral to a meeting or situation, by strengthening his internal dialogue.

It is critical not to push Jack to make changes too soon. Helping him to find small situations in which he can practise to start off with will build his confidence. You might work with him to devise statements or comments that he could make which feel natural with him; having introductory comments 'up his sleeve', which he has practised before, will give him an imaginary 'comfort blanket' at meetings.

Another method that might work well here is to encourage Jack to 'act as if'. For instance, he could be asked to think of a person who would be successful at such a meeting and model his behaviour on that person. Suggest that he has been asked to play the part of that person in the meeting, and invite him to practise with you. He is likely to find the practice extremely uncomfortable but it is critical that he has this opportunity before attempting it in the real world.

Visualization also helps tremendously. Neural pathways in the brain can be activated to allow us to believe that we have already done something we have in fact only visualized. This one activity could make all the difference to whether Jack will achieve his goal. There is more on this on page 48, in the section on 'The reticular activating system'.

To help Jack get a better hearing during meetings, and to ensure he is not talked over by more assertive people, he could be asked to think about his body language, his tone and how he frames his statements. The longer people take to speak up at meetings, the less likely it is that they will say anything at all. People who are introverted often prefer to wait until they are sure they have something of real value to add, refraining from speaking for the sake of it.

Jack needs to find statements he can make, such as 'That sounds like a good idea,' or 'I'd like to hear more about that,' which will give him the appearance of making contributions while his confidence grows. If one of the reasons he finds meetings difficult is because he needs time to construct his responses, he could be asked to come up with some 'holding statements' to use while finding the right words. Teaching him the skill of reflecting, which is detailed on page 26 in Chapter 2, might be particularly useful.

The coachee lacks confidence

You are working with a senior trainer called Sheila, who struggles with inner confidence. Sheila tends to internalize feedback and has an 'inner chatterbox' that takes over, so that whenever she gets a less than excellent evaluation she really takes it to heart. Most people have internal dialogue which can be healthy or unhealthy – like a little voice that drones on in our head criticizing us (or praising us if we have a positive inner dialogue) or reinforcing messages about ourselves. This voice is our unconscious thoughts emerging, and can be described as an 'inner chatterbox'.

Sheila has had a few bad experiences with groups who were negative and attacking, and more recently, with a group who refused to do practice sessions because, they said, this activity was 'false'. She is now finding it hard to ask participants to practise at all, and is getting into a nervous state before some courses.

Suggestions

With most people, their current behaviour is driven by experiences, and negative experiences affect some more than others. We can all be sensitive at times, which can impact on the way past experiences affect future behaviour. In this situation, Sheila clearly needs external positive feedback to do a good job and therefore takes negative feedback very much to heart. I have rarely met a person who doesn't have an internal chatterbox that can either help or hinder, and in this case the chatterbox seems to be taking control in Sheila's evaluation of her performance and giving her some extensive and destructive criticism.

It is critical to get Sheila to a point where she has a technique for evaluating her performance, internally congratulating herself on what she has achieved (first and quite specifically), and then learning from the criticisms. This is healthy. If she continues to dwell on the criticisms, or they keep popping into her mind and reminding her of the negative situations, she needs some techniques for silencing the inner dialogue.

Sometimes it can help to get the coachee talking about this internal chatterbox, describing what it looks or sounds like. (For more information on working with metaphor, see page 111.) Most people, when asked, can describe some shape, size, colour and/or sound, and once identified in this way, the chatterbox tends to lose its power. This relates to the way problems seem to shrink when they are shared; what is happening is that in describing the problem to someone else, the person sees all the issues clearly for the first time. Once everything is out on the table, the person can usually see the way forward. This experience is heightened by coaching because coaches are trained to help coachees examine all the issues in the Reality section of the GROW model mentioned in Chapter 3. Working in metaphor is another way of exploring the coachee's present reality.

An extension of this technique might be to ask Sheila to imagine the chatterbox sitting on the table in front of her and how it feels now. Invariably when people are distanced from the chatterbox they feel better about it. Coachees will often relate an urge to flatten the imaginary image when it says things they do not like! You could also ask Sheila to visualize ways of stopping the internal dialogue – some coachees come up with an imaginary box to put the negativity in, or a bin, or a door to put it outside.

It will also help Sheila to talk the situation through in detail, and at each stage to verbalize what she will do differently when faced with it again. She needs to learn how to evaluate her own performance; it is quite possible that she performed very well but that the groups she was training were badly behaved and she is internalizing their behaviour.

An explanation of the 'beliefs and experience circle' may help, ie when you have a belief about yourself, where does it come from? The answer is clearly that it comes from experience so, in order to change a belief about yourself, you need to give yourself another experience which supports the old proverb of getting right back on that horse! Some very positive inner dialogue will be required to ensure that Sheila sets herself up positively for the next experience, and it may help if you work with her on getting some perspective. For instance you could ask how important this is to her. If she has a less than satisfactory session, will she still have a home? A family? A job? Her health? Of course she will, plus she will have learnt some more valuable information for her next attempt!

The bullied

Robert, the manager you are coaching, has a deep personal conflict with another manager, Paul, with whom he is expected to work quite closely. Robert clearly has some behavioural issues himself but sees it all as being Paul's fault. He knows that they should sit down together and resolve the issue, but he cannot manage his own emotions well and feels he will break down or become aggressive. You have had feedback from other people you work with at the same organization that Robert can appear quite direct and even 'bullying' at times.

Suggestions

In a situation like this it is vital that Robert becomes able to see Paul's perspective, and using 'spatial positioning' can help here. It is almost impossible for people to 'see' someone else's point of view while sitting in the same chair from which they have just described their own perspective. So a useful technique here would be to ask Robert to describe in depth how he feels about the situation, then ask him to move to a chair opposite and to take on the role of Paul. Encourage him to get really into Paul's shoes and to imagine he is looking at himself. Now ask Robert to describe how he sees the situation in depth. Ask some really insightful questions about Paul's perspective.

A useful extension of this exercise is to ask Robert to move to a third chair and give himself some advice on how he should now interact with Paul, based on what he knows now. People are normally far more honest than you would ever have expected!

Another intervention which might help here is 360-degree feedback (which is described on page 126). It will make a huge difference to acceptance of the behaviour that needs changing, and finding a way to make it as honest and anonymous as possible will mean that the person gets some real perspective on the situation. When reviewing this feedback the coach needs to question insightfully, and as objectively as possible, to ensure that the coachee thinks deeply.

If feedback cannot be obtained, this is a situation where the coach may need to move into a more direct mode. For instance if Robert displays any behaviour (verbally or non-verbally) that is inappropriate, the coach can give feedback immediately on how it felt to be on the receiving end. This can often be a turning point; most people who have been described as 'bullies' have never been challenged about their behaviour in a non-confrontational way and will normally be quite surprised by the feedback. This in itself creates the desire to change.

The midlife crisis

You are working with a director, Bill, who reveals that he is not sure where his career is going. He does not know whether he wants to continue in the role, or to leave and be a consultant. He is unsure whether he has the skills or motivation for that role, and wonders whether he is just having a 'midlife crisis'.

Suggestions

In this situation, it is possible that Bill is struggling with his values, and it can be worth exploring this by doing a values exercise to check whether his role is congruent with his values. As our lives change and grow, our values can change quite considerably. It can be very revealing to work through this and take an audit on a current situation. This can be supported by some questions that are designed to encourage the coachee to think deeply, such as 'What three things would you change today if you were able to?', 'Who do you know who has a life that you admire and why?' and 'What is your heart telling you about what you should do?'

One exercise that works very well in situations such as this is a neuro linguistic programming one, created by NLP authority Robert Dilts, called Logical Levels (see page 127 for more information on NLP). This exercise works on the grounds that in order to identify your vision clearly, you need to clear any blocks that are holding you back. Such blocks can occur at many different levels and Dilts lists these as possibly being: environment, capabilities, behaviour, values and beliefs, and identity. These will be explored before even discussing the vision of where the coachee wants to be.

This exercise works because it allows the person's unconscious mind to project thoughts that would not necessarily come through if direct questions were being asked.

You start by asking Bill to walk through all the levels, using the spatial positioning we described in discussing Jim and John (page 192). This time, the levels are positioned in a line on the floor. You ask Bill to stop on each level and speak openly and freely about anything at all that comes into his mind. It is critical that the questions are open and not too specific, so that Bill will not feel restrained in his answers, and that he is assured that whatever he says is right. Some people find this uncomfortable as they feel that there must be a right or wrong answer, or they are anxious to give you the answers you are looking for. Therefore, you need to ensure that your questions will enable Bill to open up freely. This will be achieved more easily if you stand behind Bill as he walks through each level, saying very little but making notes of anything that he says. Very few questions are needed at each level, and often simply by asking for 'Anything else?', deep and useful information is revealed.

People may become emotional at a certain level, and this is because they have uncovered there the source of a block. Once you have extracted all the information from Bill at each level, he may be able to see a clear vision of what he wants to achieve. Even if he cannot do that at this stage, if you play back to him some of the key things he said during the exercise, he will get more clarity on how to move forward. It is important to bear in mind when coaching in this situation that it may not be possible to achieve an outcome in one session. Allowing people to reflect can be an important part of this process, so you should be skilful at judging when to push and when to hold back.

Another exercise which might help Bill to determine whether or not he has the right skills would be for him to list the qualities he feels a consultant needs and rank them in terms of criteria for success. If he then lists his own skills and rates them, it will provide a useful starting point for him to see whether he is well matched to the role.

You could also ask Bill to list the factors that are critical to him in terms of job satisfaction, then he can match up both his current role and the role of a consultant with these new criteria, and you can ask him what observations he can make. In this situation, coaches must use all their skills in holding back to ensure they do not lead the coachee at all through any of these discussions.

Gillian Jones
+44 (0)2392 792222
www.emergeuk.com

COACHING FOR PERFORMANCE ROI

In this case study we hear the story of how Tiffany Gaskell, an ex-derivatives trader turned organizational development specialist at Performance Consultants International, developed a tool for their clients to be able to measure the return on investment (ROI) for mindset and behaviour change interventions.

Tiffany Gaskell is an executive director of Performance Consultants International and lives and works in London. She has a background in invest-ment banking and has been in the OD field for 7 years. Tiffany is a qualified coach and has an MBA.

Overview

In business it is often said 'If you can't measure something, you can't manage it.' This case history relates the use of a tool called *Coaching for Performance ROI*, which measures the return on investment for interventions that affect behaviour change or mindset shift.

The client's needs

We were invited by the managing director (MD) of a fully owned subsidiary of a multinational company that had about 150 employees to run a one-to-one coach-ing pilot for the leadership team. The challenge the MD gave us was to measure the impact of the coaching on the business – he wanted to be sure that he knew that a tangible value could be linked to his investment. He felt that once he had evidence of an ROI he would be able to invest more in this area and justify the investment up the line.

How does *Coaching for Performance ROI* work?

Coaching for Performance ROI is designed to help clients estimate what impact a change in behaviour makes on the bottom line. It consists of a five-step process that is spread over the course of the intervention and which enables the calculation of an ROI. The tool works in line with coaching principles, so it allows clients to find the answer for themselves, with the coach holding the frame.

Step One: Goals and time frame

Our first step was to clarify goals and time frames:

- Each coachee was facilitated in understanding the goals agreed with the manager and what was required of him- or herself.
- We ascertained when the coachee wanted us to have achieved each goal.

Step Two: Benchmarking

We ascertained where each coachee was starting from, benchmarking both intangible and tangible goals. An intangible goal is one that is typically difficult to measure and might be a behaviour change or a new skill such as 'I want to learn to delegate better.' A tangible goal is a hard business goal such as 'I want to reduce my direct reports from 8 to 5.'

Step Three: Keeping records

We kept records over the course of the coaching engagement to ensure that we had enough information and data to calculate the ROI.

We used different ways to do this, such as:

- regular summaries to the client;
- debriefs;
- peer and management feedback on progress.

Step Four: Review

After 3 months we reviewed, with the manager and the coachees, the initial goals, the benchmark and the records we kept during the coaching engagement. From this, we were able to estimate the monetary impact of the changes in behaviour over the period.

Step Five: Calculating the ROI

We took the tangible information that was generated from the process to calculate the ROI. The tool's ROI calculation has an in-built adjuster that reflects the probability that a particular impact is related to a particular intervention.

Interview with the Coachee

'What I really like about the tool is that it quantifies the impact of the coaching. For me, knowing this makes me feel more comfortable. Overall, it was a very structured approach that delivered the tangible information that was required. I valued the idea of putting a number on the coaching, and that my manager got to see all the work that had been done, on the basis of which he could give his feedback.

On a daily basis, the tool was an easy reference that I could use to see what I needed to concentrate on. You can just flick it open, go down the columns and see a numerical value for where you were and where you would like to be.

The real question is: Would we continue the coaching without the tool proving the tangible benefits? For example, I would say that the coaching has given one of my guys more focus and confidence, and he is certainly more commercial than he was 2 years ago. On a new project he is working on now we are saving £20,000 to £30,000 a month. But is this really due to the coaching and can I trust the tool's measurement? The formula adjusts for any uncertainty, so my gut feel is that the figure it comes up with is about right, so this does add to our appetite for further interventions. My conclusion is that the tool is a pretty good way to calculate a monetary value for something that otherwise would remain intangible and so it is an important factor in our decision-making process.'

Result

We have been working with this client for 3 years now. The client has recently been confident enough to embark on a company-wide transformation programme and is in the process of rolling out performance coaching to managers. Our conclusion is that through measuring impacts, you can help clients both to manage and to value their investment.

Tiffany Gaskell, MBA, CPCC
Executive Director
Performance Consultants International
+44 (0)20 7373 6431
tiffanygaskell@performanceconsultants.com
www.performanceconsultants.com

Appendix A

Awareness questions

In this appendix you will find listed many questions which are efficient at helping people to gain new perspectives and insights. First there is a random list, then some questions for specific situations, then some questions grouped according to where they fit into the GROW model.

There are two key points to remember when choosing questions. First, whereabouts the question fits into the GROW model is more important than the content of the question itself. Trainee coaches tend to agonize over which would be the 'right' question, yet this is something the coach cannot possibly know, because of the differences in individual cultural backgrounds described on page 8 of Chapter 1.

Second, never concern yourself unduly with where you 'should' be within the GROW model during a session; this is a time for handing over to your intuition. However, if you feel stuck as the coach, it may help to ask yourself where you are now and to adjust your position consciously. Right from the start we encourage our students to forget the rules and follow their intuition while coaching, then to go back afterwards and analyse their performance and get some feedback from others. In the early stages, it is often revelationary to them how the part where the coaching stalled was where, in retrospect, they were not in the most appropriate part of GROW. Later, as they absorb the principles through practice, they are delighted to discover how frequently they landed in the right place purely by using their intuition.

COACHING QUESTIONS

What do you want?
What is the dream?

What's the ideal?
What is this costing you?
What are you attached to?
What is beyond this problem?
What is ahead?
What are you building towards?
What has to happen for you to feel successful?
What's stopping you?
What are you afraid of?
What would make the biggest difference here?
What are you going to do?
What do you like to do?
What is the impact of doing that?
What is the impact of not doing that?
What do you hope to accomplish by doing that?
What benefit/pay-off is there in the present situation?
What's the first step?
What's important about that?
What would it take to treat yourself like your best client?
How do you best re-energize?
What do you expect to have happen?
What's the ideal outcome?
What would it look like?
What's the right action?
What's working for you?
What would you do differently?
What decision would you make from a position of abundance?
What other choices do you have?
What do you really want?
What if there were no limits?
What are you getting out of this situation?
What is missing here?
What is it that you are denying yourself right now?
What question would you like me to ask you?
Is there anything that needs to be said that has not been said?
What are you not facing?
What are you not saying?
What else do you have to say about that?
What is that?
What comes first?
What consequences are you avoiding?
What is the value you received from this meeting/conversation?
What motivates you?
What does that remind you of?
What is behind that?
What part of what I said was useful? And how?
What is this person contributing to the quality of your life?

What do you need to put in place to accomplish this?
What is the simplest solution here?
What are you avoiding?
What is the worst that could happen?
What are you committed to?
If you knew, what would it be?
What's your heart telling you?
What are you willing to give up?
What does this feeling remind you of?
How do you feel about the fact that you did that?
What did you do differently that made this happen?
How does that impact how you feel about yourself?
How has this been a breakthrough for you?
What will you do differently now you know you have the power to do this?
Where else in your life could you be taking action rather than waiting for things to happen?
What has this taught you about yourself?
Is this something that you might be doing in other areas of your life? Where else?
What impact is this having on you?
What's on your shoulders?
Is this something you want to do something about?
How can you tackle it this week?
What else do you need to do so you can move forward on this?
Are you clear you will be able to do that this week? If not what are you willing to commit to?

QUESTIONS FOR SPECIFIC SITUATIONS

Measuring a goal

How will I, your coach, know when you get there?
Imagine yourself having achieved this goal: what will you see/hear/feel around you?
What elements will be in place which were not present before?
What will you be able to do that you could not do before?
What tangible changes will there be in your life/work?

Setting actions

Is there an action you would like to take around that?
How will you do that?
When will you do that?
Is there anything you need to do before that?
What would you like to do about that?
Is that an action you can commit to?
Could you do more?

How many?
How much?
How often?

Reviewing uncompleted actions

How do you feel about not having completed that action?
How important is it to you?
What is the impact if you don't do it next week?
Can I ask whether it was about not having the time, or might you have put other things in the way to avoid having to do this?

First aid

Is there a question you would like me to ask to help you with this?
What do you need to say to help you feel better about this?
What needs to be in place to move you forward on this?

GROW: Goal

What would you like to have happen?
How would you like it to be?
In an ideal world, what sort of things would you like to see in place here?
How would it look three months from now?
Can you say what you want in one sentence?
How would you like it to be in an ideal world?
How do you feel when you say that goal out loud?
How challenging is it?
What is your insight about this?
Imagine you have achieved what you want in 12 weeks time:

- What elements are in place?
- What can you see/think/feel?
- What tangible changes are there in your life through achieving this?

GROW: Reality

How important is this to you?
How do you feel about this?
What impact is this having on you?
What's on your shoulders?
How nervous are you, out of 10?
If an ideal situation is 10, what number are you at now?
What number would you like to be at?
Can you tell me what is happening for you at the moment in this area?
How does this impact other areas of your life?

What does that tell you about yourself?
What do you know now that you did not know before?
What is your insight about that?
What are your three greatest insights about that?
What can you do now that you could not do before?
What have you learned about yourself during the coaching series?
What were the major breakthroughs or turning points?
What will you do differently now?
What do you know now that you did not know before?

GROW: Options

What has worked in the past?
What steps could you take?
Would you like to brainstorm the elements you would like to see with me?
What else could you do?
If there were something else you could do, what would it be?
Is there anything else?

GROW: Will

What will you do about this?
Can you commit to that?
How will you do that?
When will you do it?
Who will you speak to?
Where will you find that?

Closure

What did I do well as your coach?
What would you like to see more of?
What would you like to see less of?
What would you like me to have done differently?
What tangible benefits did you get from the coaching in terms of money, position, relationships, etc?

Appendix B

Worksheets

Coach's worksheet: Introductory session

Date:	Time:	Coachee

	Time
1. Set the scene: Check the coachee is comfortable and will be undisturbed for the session	Time 1m
2. What will happen in the session: ■ Set an outcome for the session ■ looking at all areas of the coachee's life/work ■ identifying areas the coachee wants to change ■ setting a goal in each area	1m
3. Ask coachee to set an outcome for the session	1m
4. Get an overview of the coachee's life and/or work – a sentence on each area	7m
5. Reduce it to the areas where change is required and prioritize the goals	5m
6. Set two or three complex goals: ■ **EX**citing ■ Assessable ■ Challenging ■ Time framed	30m
7. Coach and coachee prioritize and note simple goals	5m
8. Closure	5m
9. Discuss whether to continue	
10. If continuing, explain paperwork and arrange next session	

Coach's worksheet: Session 2

Date:	Time:	Coachee	

		Time
1.	Set the scene	1m
2.	What will happen in the session: Revisit the goals Creating a strategic plan for the goals	1m
3.	Revisit the goals	1m
4.	Set an outcome for the session	1m
5.	Goal 1: create plan and one or more actions	15m
6.	Goal 2: create plan and one or more actions	15m
7.	Goal 3: (if any) create plan and one or more actions	15m
8.	Review list of simple goals, set actions if required	5m
9.	Review values questionnaire or other paperwork	5m
10.	Closure	1m
11.	Arrange next session	

Actions:

Coach's worksheet: Transitional sessions

Date:	Time:	Coachee	
			Time
1.	Set the scene		1m
2.	What will happen in the session: reviewing the goals		1m
3.	Revisit the goals		1m
4.	Set an outcome for the session		2m
5.	Go through the goals in turn, reviewing last session's actions and setting new ones		45m
6.	Get the coachee to repeat back all the actions		3m
7.	Closure		2m
8.	Arrange next session		

Actions:

Coach's worksheet: Final session

Date:	Time:	Coachee	
			Time
1.	Set the scene		1m
2.	What will happen in the session: closing on the goals		1m
3.	Revisit the goals		1m
4.	Set an outcome for the session		2m
5.	Go through the goals in turn: Review last session's actions Measure achievement as a percentage Ask insightful questions		45m
6.	Closure on the session and the whole series		2m
7.	If both wish to continue the coaching, arrange another goal-setting session		

Coach's worksheet: Strategic plan

Date: **Coachee:**

Goal 1:

Goal 2:

Goal 3:

Coachee's worksheet: Goals

Date:

Complex goals:

1

2

3

Simple goals:

4

5

6

7

Coachee's worksheet

Date: **Time:**

Revisit the goals

1 .... 2 ....

3 ....

Outcome for the session:

Goal 1:

Goal 2:

Goal 3:

Actions:

Appendix C

Sample coaching agreements

These are basic templates only and legal advice should be sought if a more complex contract is issued.

AGREEMENT FOR PERSONAL COACHING

Agreement for Personal Coaching

Date:

Coach:

Name

Address

Telephone   Mobile

Email

Coachee:

Name

Address

Telephone   Mobile

Email

Duration of agreement: From   to

Number and length of sessions

Coaching medium (i.e. by telephone or face to face, if so where)

Fee payable monthly in advance … Per session … Total

Confidentiality: Coach undertakes not to disclose any information shared by coachee during sessions to any third party unless explicitly agreed otherwise.

Procedure: When coaching by telephone, coachee will telephone coach.

Cancellation of a session: 24 hours notice or the session is payable.

Disclaimer: Coachee acknowledges that nothing said by coach can be construed as advice or instruction and that coach cannot be held responsible for coachee's decisions or actions.

Signed by:

Coach   **Coachee**

AGREEMENT FOR CORPORATE COACHING

Agreement for Corporate Coaching

Date:

Coach:

Name

Address

Telephone   Mobile

Email

Coachee:

Name

Address

Telephone   Mobile

Email

Sponsor organization:

Name of organization   Contact name

Address

Telephone   Direct line

Duration of agreement: From   to

Number and length of sessions

Coaching medium (i.e. by telephone or face to face, if so where)

Fee payable monthly in advance on receipt of coach's invoice

Per session   Total

Confidentiality: Coach undertakes not to disclose any information shared by coachee during sessions to any third party including organizations unless explicitly agreed otherwise.

Procedure: Coachee will telephone coach for telephone sessions.

Cancellation of a session: 24 hours notice or the session is payable.

Disclaimer: Coachee acknowledges that nothing said by coach can be construed as advice or instruction and that coach cannot be held responsible for coachee's decisions or actions.

Signed by: **Coach**

                      Coachee

                      Organization

Appendix D

Coaching evaluation

Part one: personal outcomes

1. To what extent did you achieve the goals you set at the beginning of the coaching?

    Goal 1: _____ %   Goal 6: _____ %

    Goal 2: _____ %   Goal 7: _____ %

    Goal 3: _____ %   Goal 8: _____ %

    Goal 4: _____ %   Goal 9: _____ %

    Goal 5: _____ %   Goal 10: _____ %

2. Which areas of your life and/or work showed an improvement because of the coaching?
    Please specify how the area improved:

    Individual performance
    ....

    Performance of my team
    ....

    Personal development
    ....

    Career development
    ....

Leadership skills

....

Energy and motivation

....

Work/life balance

....

Improving physical appearance/fitness

....

Home life

....

Finances

....

Creative pursuits

....

Other

....

What financial benefits do you estimate that you or your organization gained from the coaching programme? Please be as specific as possible:

....

....

....

What key insights did you learn about yourself during the coaching?

....

....

....

What is needed to sustain your development?

....

....

....

Part two: coach evaluation

What did you like about what your coach did? For example, insight, depth of questioning, challenging, timekeeping, humour.

....

....

....

What would you like your coach to have done differently?

....

....

....

Part three: organizational benefits

What impact will your coaching have on your organization as a whole?

....

....

....

What are the benefits to your organization of coaching (for example, demonstrating that the organization cares about staff development, improving performance, communication, motivation, staff retention and absentee rates)?

....

....

....

What financial benefits do you estimate the organization gained from the coaching programme? Please be specific, eg 'The monthly review I have now set up gives me an extra six hours a month to research new coachees resulting in an estimated 20% higher billings per year.'

....

....

....

Part four: additional benefits

Please use this space to list any benefits that have not been covered above.

....

....

....

Resources

RECOMMENDED BOOKS

Barrett, R (1998) *Liberating the Corporate Soul: Building a visionary organization,* Butterworth-Heinemann, London

Blanchard, K and Johnson, S (1996) *The One Minute Manager*, HarperCollins, London

Gallwey, T (1974) *The Inner Game of Tennis*, Random House, USA

Goleman, D (1995) *Emotional Intelligence*, Bloomsbury, London

Lawley, J D and Tompkins, P L (2003) *Metaphors in Mind: Transformation through symbolic modelling*, Developing Company Press, London

Passmore, J (ed) (2006) *Excellence in Coaching: An industry guide*, Kogan Page, London

Paul, H, Christensen, J and Lundin, S (2000) *Fish! A remarkable way to boost morale and improve results*, Coronet, London

Risner, N, Gabriel, M and Gabriel, H (2002) *It's a Zoo Around Here! The new rules for better communication*, Forest Oak

Rosinski, P (2003) *Coaching Across Cultures*, Nicholas Brealey, London

Whitmore, J (2002) *Coaching for Performance* (3rd edition), Nicholas Brealey, London

RECOMMENDED WEBSITES

Performance Coach Training: www.performancecoachtraining.com
Carol Wilson: www.carolwilson.co.uk
Performance Consultants International: www.performanceconsultants.com
Grovian Clean techniques: www.cleancoaching.com
www.cleanlanguage.co.uk

Association For Coaching: www.associationforcoaching.com
The Coaching Foundation: www.coachingfoundation.org.uk

REFERENCES AND FURTHER READING

Assagioli, R (1993) *Transpersonal Development: The dimension beyond psychosynthesis*, HarperCollins, London

Assagioli, R (1999) *The Act of Will: A guide to self-actualisation and self-realisation*, The Psychosynthesis & Education Trust

Assagioli, R (2000) *Psychosynthesis: A collection of basic writings*, Synthesis Center

Association for Coaching (2004) Coaching evaluation form, Coaching in organisations, Summary Report: ROI from corporate coaching [Online] http://www.associationforcoaching.com

Bandler, R and Grinder, J (1975) *The Structure of Magic: A book about language and therapy*, Behaviour Books, Palo Alto, Calif

Bandler, R and Grinder, J (1983) *Reframing: Neurolinguistic programming and the transformation of meaning*, Real People Press, Moab, Utah

Barratt, R (1998) *Liberating the Corporate Soul: Building a visionary organization*, Butterworth-Heinemann, Boston

Berne, E (1970) *Games People Play*, Penguin, London

Briggs-Myers, I and McCaulley (1985) *M. H. Manual: A guide to the development and use of the Myers Briggs Type Indicator*, Consulting Psychologists Press

Briggs-Myers, I and Myers, P (1980) *Gifts Differing*, Consulting Psychologists Press

Burrus, K (2006) Coaching the global nomad, *International Journal of Coaching in Organizations*, **4** (4)

Burrus, K and Rosinski, P (2006) From Beijing to Belgium: aggression management, prepared for the workshop 'Leveraging Multiple Perspectives; Practising on a concrete and complex case', ICF European Conference, Brussels, May 2006

Campbell, D (1991) *Manual for the Campbell Leadership Index*, National Computer Systems

Center for Creative Leadership (2000) *Benchmarks Facilitators Manual*

Clutterbuck, D and Sweeney, J (1998) Coaching and mentoring, in *The Gower Handbook of Management*, eds D Lock and N Farrow, Gower, Hants

Cooperrider, D L (2004) Foreword: the birth of global community, in *Birth of Global Community: Appreciative inquiry in action*, Lakeshore, Aurora, OH

Cooperrider, D L (ed) (2004) Introduction, in *Advances in Appreciative Inquiry: Constructive discourse in human organizations*, Vol 1, Elsevier Science, Oxford

Cooperrider, D L (2004) Introduction, in *Constructive Discourse and Human Organization*, Vol 1, Elsevier Science, Oxford

Cooperrider, D L (2004) With our questions we make the world, in *Constructive Discourse and Human Organization* Vol 1, pp 105–25, Elsevier Science, Oxford

de Shazer, S (1988) *Clues: Investigating solutions in brief therapy*, W W Norton, New York

Dilts, R and DeLozier, J (2000) *Encyclopaedia of NLP Vols I & II*, NLP University Press, Scotts Valley, Calif

Dilts, R B, Grinder, J, Bandler, R and DeLozier, J A (1980) *Neuro-Linguistic Programming, Volume I: The Study of the Structure of Subjective Experience*, Meta Publications

Ferrucci, P (1995) *What We May Be*, Thorsons, London

Gallwey, T (1974) *The Inner Game of Tennis*, Random House, USA

Gallwey, T W (2000) *The Inner Game of Work*, Orion Business, London

Goleman, D (1995) *Emotional Intelligence*, Bloomsbury, London

Gray, A (1997) *Modern Differential Geometry of Curves and Surfaces with Mathematics*, CRC Press

Greene, J and Grant, A M (2003) *Solution-Focused Coaching: Managing people in a complex world*, Momentum Press, London

Gross, R D (1999) *Psychology: The science of mind and behaviour*, 2nd edn, Hodder & Stoughton, London

Grove, D and Panzer, B (1989) *Resolving Traumatic Memories: Metaphors and symbols in psychotherapy*, Irvington, New York

Grove, D and Wilson, C (2005) Six degrees to freedom: intuitive problem solving with emergent knowledge, *Resource Magazine*, fifth edition

Grove, D and Wilson, C (2005) Emergent knowledge ΣK^{TM} and clean coaching, *The Model*, edition 2

Hammond, S A (1996) *The Thin Book of Appreciative Inquiry*, Bend, OR

Harris, A and Harris, T (1995) *I'm OK, You're OK*, Arrow, London

Henle, M (1994) *A Combinatorial Introduction to Topology*, Dover

Jarvis, J (2004) *Coaching and Buying Coaching Services: A guide*, Chartered Institute of Personnel Development (CIPD), London

Jay, M (2003) Understanding how to leverage executive coaching, *Organization Development Journal*, **21**(2), pp 6–19

Jeffers, S (2007) *Feel the Fear and Do It Anyway: How to turn your fear and indecision into confidence and action*, 20th anniversary edn, Vermilion, London

Kubler Ross, E (1969) *On Death and Dying*, Scribner, USA

Maslow, A (1954) *Motivation and Personality*, Harper, New York

Maslow, A, *Toward a Psychology of Being*, Paperbackshop-US, Elk Grove Village, Ill

Meichenbaum, D H (1977) *Cognitive-Behaviour Modification*, Plenum Press, New York

Michaelson, G. A (2001) *Sun Tzu: The Art of War for Managers*, Adams

Neenan, M and Dryden, W (2001) *Life Coaching: A cognitive behavioural approach*, Brunner-Routledge, London

Norris, P (ed) Dynamics of visualization and imagery in therapy [Online] www.healthy.net/asp/templates/Article.asp?PageType=Article&Id=392&action=print

O'Connell, B (1998) *Solution-Focused Therapy*, Sage, London

Page, L (2006) Thinking outside our brains, *International Journal of Coaching in Organizations*, **2**

Parsloe, E and Wray, M (2002) *Coaching and Mentoring*, Kogan Page, London

Passmore, J (ed) (2006) Excellence in Coaching: An industry guide, Kogan Page, London

Passmore, J and Pena, A (2005) How to manage trauma, *People Management*, 28 July

Perls, F (1942/1965) *Ego, Hunger and Aggression*, Random House, New York

Perls, F (1969a) *In and Out the Garbage Pail*, Real People, Lafayette, Calif

Perls, F (1969b) *Gestalt Therapy Verbatim*, Real People, Lafayette, Calif

Perls, F, Hefferline, R F and Goodman, P (1951) *Gestalt Therapy*, Julian, New York

Rosinski, P (1998a) Constructive politics: essential for leadership, *Leadership in Action*, **18**(3)

Rosinski, P (1998b) Leading for joy: lessons on leadership from the Judaic tradition, paper for European Forum for Management Development, Forum no 3

Rosinski, P (1999) Coaching across cultures and Coaching from multiple perspectives, Proceedings of International Coaching Conference, Linkage, London

Rosinski, P (2003) *Coaching Across Cultures,* Nicholas Brealey, London

Rosinski, P and Abbott, G (2006) Intercultural coaching, in *Excellence in Coaching: The industry guide*, ed J Passmore, pp. 153–69, Kogan Page, London

Rosinski, P and Abbott, G (2006) Coaching from a cultural perspective, in *Evidence Based Coaching Handbook*, eds D Stober and A Grant, Wiley, Chichester

Stewart, I and Joines, V (2002) *TA Today: A new introduction to transactional analysis*, 2nd edn, Lifespace

Staber, D and Grant, A (eds) (2006) *Evidence Based Coaching Handbook*, Wiley, Chichester

Tompkins, P and Lawley, J (2000) Metaphors in Mind: *Transformation through symbolic modelling*, Developing Company Press [Online] www.cleanlanguage.co.uk

Tompkins, P and Lawley, J (date) *A Strange and Strong Sensation*, video, available from www.cleanlanguage.co.uk

Tulpa, K (2005) Coaching for influence and impact, *Coach the Coach*, **17**

von Senger, H (2006) *The 36 Stratagems for Business*, Cyan, London

Whitmore, D (2000) *Psychosynthesis Counselling in Action*, Sage, London

Whitmore, J (2002) *Coaching For Performance*, 3rd edn, Nicholas Brealey, London

Whitmore, J and Einzig, H (2006) Transpersonal coaching, in *Excellence in Coaching: An industry guide*, ed J Passmore, pp. 119–34, Kogan Page, London

Wilmer, H A (1987) *Practical Jung: Nuts and bolts of Jungian psychotherapy*, Chiron, Wilmette

Wilson, C (2003) Coaching and coach training in the workplace, *Industrial and Commercial Training*, **36**(3), 96–98

Wilson, C (2004) Clarifying: the techniques of summarising, paraphrasing, reiterating and mirroring, *Coach the Coach*

Wilson, C (2005) The effectiveness of coaching in work life balance, *Resource Magazine*, spring, p. 48

Wilson, C (2005) How to develop workplace coaches, *Training Journal*, November

Wilson, C (2005) Tools for corporate coaches, *Coach the Coach*

Wilson, C (2005) Metaphor and symbolic modelling for coaches, *Coach the Coach*

Wilson, C (2006) The history of coaching and the need for accreditation, *AC Bulletin*, August

Wilson, C (2006) *Turning Points: Virgin values, coaching at work*, CIPD, London

Wilson, C (2006) Creating a coaching culture, *Payroll World* conference and magazine

Wilson, C (2006) To whom is your loyalty as a coach/mentor? *Coaching at Work*

Wilson, C and Bresser, F (2006) What is coaching?, in J Passmore (ed) *Excellence in Coaching: An industry guide*, Kogan Page, London

Wilson, C and McMahon, G. (2006) The differences between coaching and its related fields, *Training Journal*

Zohar, D and Marshall, I (2001) *Spiritual Intelligence: The ultimate intelligence*, Bloomsbury, London

Zohar, D and Marshall, I (2004) *Spiritual Capital: Wealth we can live by*, Bloomsbury, London

About the author

Carol Wilson is Honorary Vice President and Head of Accreditation at the Association for Coaching, Managing Director of Performance Coach Training and Culture at Work, and is on the Executive Committee of Sir John Whitmore's Performance Consultants International. She experienced the value of a coaching culture at first hand while working at board level for Richard Branson during the early years of Virgin.

After founding Virgin Music Publishers and elevating it to the position of the third most successful music publishing company in the United Kingdom, Carol became the first woman in the world to found her own chart-topping record label. Called Dindisc, this label today generates over 29,000 pages on Google. Subsequently, Carol held corporate board-level positions at PolyGram, WEA and Pinnacle. While discovering and working with many artists such as Sting, Martha & The Muffins, The Human League and Orchestral Manoeuvres in The Dark, Carol found her greatest satisfaction was in developing staff and artists to reach their full potential.

Carol has since trained or supervised the training of over 400 coaches in the public, corporate and private sectors. She is an international keynote speaker, broadcaster and writer, and was nominated for the Association for Coaching Awards Influence in Coaching and Impact in Coaching. She has contributed many articles to publications including *Training Journal, Coaching at Work* and *Resource Magazine* and a chapter to the Association for Coaching book *Excellence in Coaching: an Industry Guide* (Passmore, 2006). Carol specializes in creating coaching cultures in organizations and training individuals in coaching skills through a worldwide team of coaches and trainers.

In addition to her work in coaching, Carol has partnered David Grove, the founder of Clean Language, in defining his therapeutic Emergent Knowledge techniques into methods which can be used by coaches and other practitioners.

www.carolwilson.co.uk
www.performancecoachtraining.com
www.cleancoaching.com
www.performanceconsultants.com
e-mail info@carolwilson.co.uk

Carol Wilson holds positions in the following organizations:

Performance Coach Training:
co-founder and managing director

In partnership with Sir John Whitmore, PCT designs and delivers coaching programmes to organizations comprising some or all of:

- coaching skills training for managers;
- coaching management and leadership courses for managers;
- training, assessing, supervising/mentoring and accrediting internal coaches;
- performance sales coach training;
- one-to-one external coaching;
- cultural transformation tools for whole system change;
- keynotes, workshops and presentations;
- open courses in coach training leading to Sir John Whitmore's 'Coaching for Performance' accreditation.

All services can be delivered worldwide through our international partners. www.performancecoachtraining.com

Performance Consultants International:
Executive Committee member

Headed by executive chairman Sir John Whitmore, Performance Consultants International provides specialist advisory, coaching, leadership and investment services in selected markets around the world.

www.performanceconsultants.com

Culture at Work: founder

Culture at Work provides courses and materials to Performance Coach Training. The Culture at Work performance coach training course:

- is recognized by the Association for Coaching;
- puts you on the pathway to the University accredited MSc in Coaching and Development delivered in partnership by Performance Consultants Ltd, The Performance Coach and Portsmouth University Business School
- draws from the work of coaching pioneer Sir John Whitmore and Carol Wilson's experience of the leadership techniques of Sir Richard Branson.

Clean Coaching: co-founder with David Grove

Developing and providing training in Clean Language and the Emergent Knowledge work of David Grove.

www.cleancoaching.com

The Association for Coaching: head of accreditation

A non-profit making accrediting body representing the interests of coaches in the United Kingdom and internationally.

www.associationforcoaching.com

Sign up for a free monthly article on

www.performancecoachtraining.com

Index